Films
and the
Second World War

Other Books by
ROGER MANVELL

NON-FICTION:
Film
The Film and the Public
The Living Screen: A Study of Film and Television
New Cinema in Europe
New Cinema in the USA
New Cinema in Britain
This Age of Communication
Shakespeare and the Film

BIOGRAPHY:
Ellen Terry
Sarah Siddons

FICTION:
The Dreamers
The Passion

BIOGRAPHICAL AND OTHER STUDIES
WRITTEN IN COLLABORATION WITH
HEINRICH FRAENKEL
Doctor Goebbels
Hermann Göring
The July Plot
Heinrich Himmler
The Incomparable Crime
The Canaris Conspiracy
Rudolf Hess
Inside Adolf Hitler
The German Cinema
The Hundred Days to Hitler

EDITOR:
The International Encyclopedia of Film

Films
and the
Second World War

by Roger Manvell

South Brunswick and New York: A. S. Barnes and Company

J M Dent & Sons Ltd London

First published 1974
© by Roger Manvell 1974

Library of Congress Cataloging in Publication Data

Manvell, Roger, 1909

   Films and the Second World War.

   Bibliography: p.
   1. World War, 1939–1945, in motion pictures.
I. Title.
D743.23.M36   940.53′0022′2   73-15233
ISBN 0-498-01473-8

A. S. Barnes and Company, Inc.
Cranbury, New Jersey 08512

Published in Great Britain by
J. M. Dent & Sons Ltd
Aldine House • Albemarle St • London W1X 4QY
ISBN 0 460 07856 9 (U.K.)

Printed in the United States of America

Contents

Preface

The purpose of this book is to discuss and illustrate a cross-section of films about the Second World War, both fiction films and factual films—the picture of war and its motivation from the popular viewpoint as it was (and sometimes still is) presented to the public of the principal nations involved, both during and after the actual years of fighting. The few films that anticipated the coming struggle for power are also discussed in a preliminary chapter.

Among the many points of interest are the changes that have taken place in the "image" of the serviceman and civilian variously as hero, patriot, prisoner of war, resistance worker, civilian worker, civil defense member, traitor, coward, psychological case, and not least as an enemy figure. The initial white-versus-black portraiture was soon to give way to a less distinctive, more complex characterization, while in the postwar period, when the former enemies have to live together and even see each other's films, every shade of opinion about the war, its causes, its social, psychological, and political aspects is reflected in the many prominent films that persist in depicting it.

Acknowledgments

I am specially endebted to the editors of *Sight and Sound* and the *Monthly Film Bulletin* (published by the British Film Institute) and of *Documentary News Letter* (published by Film Centre, London, during the war) for permission to quote extensively from these publications, and also to Professor Lewis Jacobs, for making available to me for reference and quotation his invaluable essay "World War II and the American Film" in *Cinema Journal* Winter 1967–68. I am also grateful to Edgar Anstey for contributing a special note on his work for the *March of Time*.

Among the books listed in the Bibliography, I have drawn extensively for information on Joseph L. Anderson and Donald Richie's *The Japanese Film*, Richard Dyer MacCann's *The People's Films*, Paul Rotha's *Documentary Film* (revised edition, 1952, containing Richard Griffith's chapter, "The Use of the Film in the US Armed Services"), and Jay Leyda's *Kino* and *Films Beget Films*.

I am also grateful to Clive Coultass and Anne Fleming of the Imperial War Museum and to John Gillett of the British Film Institute for their constant help and advice, and to the staff of the Information Section of the British Film Institute who answered so many queries during the period of research.

The stills come largely from my own collection, supplemented by additions from the Stills Library of the British Film Institute. I am grateful to all those companies who provided me with stills from their productions.

Films
and the
Second World War

1
Prelude to War

The 1930s were the decade of blind rejection of the possibilities of war by the leading Western democracies, leaving such initiatives to the nations with fascist regimes. In Italy and Japan these regimes had already been established—Mussolini's dictatorship consolidated in the years following the march on Rome in October 1922, while in Japan there occurred a hardening in the autocratic militarist and nationalist outlook that was to dominate the 1930s. In addition, there was the threat represented by the monolithic Stalin regime in the vast territories of the USSR, and the democracies, notably France and Britain, became hesitant and inward-looking—above all anxious to avoid any showdown with the immature but overweening strength of the new fascist states, which they felt represented some kind of "bulwark" against the Soviet Union. The United States, too, gravely shaken by the economic depression following the Wall Street crash, settled for a similar reaction in the form of isolationism.

The 1930s were, therefore, a melancholy period in world history, with the map both in central Europe and Asia constantly reflecting the changes taking place in the balance of power—Italy annexing Abyssinia (Ethiopia) in May 1936, the year in which Hitler marched into the demilitarized Rhineland and established formal relations with Italy and Japan through the foundation of the Rome-Berlin-Tokyo axis. It was the year too for the signing of the anti-Comintern pact between Berlin and Tokyo. The Austrian Anschluss and (following the Munich agreement) the annexation of the Sudetenland came in 1938; Bohemia and Moravia were seized in March 1939. When this was succeeded by the invasion of Poland, the long-delayed retaliation by Britain and France was finally activated. In 1939 Franco won the Civil War in Spain. Meanwhile, Japan had occupied

13

Manchuria in 1931 and reformed it as the vassal state of Manchukuo the following year. Germany and Italy had been the only nations to give recognition to Manchukuo, and semiconcealed military aid to Franco.

It may seem incredible that, with one notable exception, virtually no reflection of these events, which put the whole world in jeopardy, reached the screens of the Western democracies, except in the brief, superficial shots seen contemporaneously in the newsreels. The exception was the American magazine series, *The March of Time*. The reason was not difficult to discover. First, motion picture theaters in the West aim to serve their audiences only with entertainment, and the "escapist" formula was still predominant. This meant that the only wars to be dealt with were those of the past, notably the First World War, exposed, in spite of a certain stylized realism, with pacifist, romantic melancholy in *All Quiet on the Western Front* (Lewis Milestone, 1930), *Westfront 1918* (G. W. Pabst, 1930), and *Tell England* (Anthony Asquith, 1931). The First World War was now "absorbed"; it was falling into the perspective of history, and even those who had fought and suffered in it were mostly prepared to recall it through a misting mirror of memory, so elevating their own minute part in the fifthy, blood-letting holocaust it actually was, or dismissing it altogether as something better forgotten. It had been, after all, a "war to end war."

Though the world was building again the gradually increasing pressures that were to explode in 1939, only the primary aggressor nations were prepared to expand the war ethos in *contemporary* terms. So the threat of war to come found no place in public entertainment, with the exception of the H. G. Wells spectacular, *Things to Come* (1936). Unfortunately, it also found little place in the factual film, obsessed as this was with more domestic, social problems represented by such films as the British *Housing Problems*, the American *The Plow that Broke the Plains*, Holland's *New Earth*, and so forth. In documentary and fiction film alike, the name of Hitler was scarcely mentioned outside Germany before 1939, once again with the honorable exception of *The March of Time*.

Another factor leading to this omission was the nature of film sponsorship. No one producing fiction films during this period, whether in Britain, the United States, or France, cared to affront the new dictators, or putting it more correctly, felt they could afford to do so. The various German embassies would have been quick to denounce any such film, and protests of this kind could only too easily lead to prohibition by government intervention, or by censorship,

with consequent loss of revenue. Whereas it was easy for litera-
ture to examine the contemporary scene, and even on rare occasions the theater, the cinema studiously avoided involvement until war
itself was declared and the opportunity for direct attack was opened
up. There were no "cold war" feature films directed against either
Hitler or Mussolini in the United States, Britain, or France before
1939, though the American film *Blockade* (1938), while naming no
names, was set in Spain and clearly favored the government.

The March of Time during the Period 1935 to 1939

The March of Time (1935–54) was released to theaters internationally once a month; each issue lasted some fifteen minutes, and provided a comment on American and world affairs with an editorial
policy in alignment with that of the sponsoring periodical group,
Time, Life, and *Fortune.* The managing editor was Louis de Rochemont.[1] It made considerable use of archive and newsreel material
in order to provide dramatic, pointed comment on the contemporary
social and political scene, and it did not hesitate to reenact what it
could not obtain by direct film coverage. It covered events in Europe and the Far East, and especially in Nazi Germany, in such depth
as time allowed.

The March of Time dealt with American neutrality in the Italo-
Abyssinian war in its very first issue (Year I, No. 1: October 1935)[2]
and in its second (I, 2: November 1935) with the problems of resettlement by Jewish immigrants in Palestine.[3]

In the eighth issue (I, 8: May 1936), the item *Geneva* concerned
the several threats there had been to the authority of the League of
Nations, most recently in the invasion of Ethiopia. While Hitler was
refortifying the Rhineland, a Peace Ballot was being launched by
the League of Nations Union, and collective action to prevent acts
of aggression was thereby weakened. The British censor removed
considerable material from this item—scenes of Ramsay MacDonald
with Mussolini at Stresa, of British troops en route for Egypt, and of
fleet movements in the Mediterranean, with the suggestion that the
Suez Canal might be closed and economic sanctions imposed on
Mussolini.

In the first issue of the second year (II, 1: June 1936) the history
of the Hapsburg dynasty was surveyed, together with the possibility
of its restoration in Austria, and the effect of this on the maintenance of peace in Europe. A further item on France emphasized first
the traditional power of the peasant (forty-eight percent of the vote,

and holding seventy-two percent of the land) in contrast with his present plight following the economic depression and the rise of Communism in the Popular Front. The commentary stressed that the peasants remained the central, stabilizing factor as government after government rises and falls.

The seventh issue (II, 7: December 1936) had an item in which three students at Princetown, forecasting they would be required to fight in the war the dictators were planning, published a manifesto demanding war bonuses in advance while they were still alive. Forming a Veteran of Future Wars movement, they were joined by students from over two hundred colleges in the United States. Senators in Washington who were war veterans of the past were divided in declaring that if wars had to be paid for in advance they would probably never take place. The whole thing was treated rather "tongue in the cheek."

In the eighth issue (II, 8: January 1937) *The March of Time* dealt with the subject of China. The progress of the country under Chiang Kai-Shek was shown in a favorable light, and the Japanese seizure of Manchuria (now called Manchukuo, and Chiang's native province) and the bombing of Chapei emphasized a problem Chiang has not hitherto been strong enough to resist, except through an economic boycott. The cameras then turned to Shanghai, showing how Chinese refugees from Japanese encroachment had turned the city from an international settlement into a more fully developed Chinese city—a new metropolis in which Chinese-owned industries were rapidly developing. The strange incident of Chiang's kidnapping by Marshall Chang and subsequent unconditional release was also included, and the commentary looked forward to Chiang's military resistance to the Japanese. Later (III, 4: September 1937) *The March of Time* returned to the same subject, showing the problem of the British Embassy endeavoring to a keep a balance of good relations with both Japan and China while they were at war; the British ambassador was in fact seriously injured by Japanese airmen while driving in Shanghai. A historical survey of the various Western settlements in China followed; the British were left now with the task of guarding the 100,000 foreigners in the International Settlement of Shanghai as the war intensified.

The March of Time's coverage of Europe continued (III, 3: August 1937) with an item on Poland, which was shown to be surrounded by potential enemies—the USSR, Germany, and Czechoslovakia. Poland's initial outlet to the sea, the free city of Danzig, which stood under the protection of the League of Nations, was revealed as nationalistically German, with Nazi banners flying, Goebbels making a triumphal entry, and the conduct of anti-Jewish pogroms. The leader of Poland, Pilsudski, and his successor Smigly-Rydz, had developed the seaport of Gdynia as an alternative. Poland, says the commentator, remains a problem area in Europe. A further issue (III, 6: November 1937) entitled *USA—Rehearsal for War*, showed American observation of the Spanish Civil War on both fronts, with a view to studying contemporary strategy.

The last issue of the third year (III, 12: May 1938) was to be one of the most celebrated: the whole sixteen minutes was given up to the single subject: *Inside Nazi Germany*.[4] To understand contemporary reaction to this important film, here is the unsigned review that appeared in the *Monthly Film Bulletin* published by the recently established British Film Institute (1938, p. 128):

March of Time: Inside Nazi Germany (1938).

The film opens with views of Berlin where, it is stated, visitors may be surprised by the general air of prosperity and by the abundance of rich foods served in its restaurants. Nowhere does the visitor see privation or hunger, and Berlin's parks and playgrounds are filled with ostensibly cheerful people showing no apparent signs of dissatisfaction with the Government. Only those behind the scenes, it is claimed, know that this outward cheerfulness is the creation of the Propaganda Minister, Paul Joseph Goebbels. In the most concentrated propaganda campaign the world has ever known he has, in five years, united 65 million people into a nation with one objective—expansion. Today Goebbels thunders more loudly than ever as Germany serves notice that all territories she lost in the world war must eventually be given back to her. To fan the Nazi hatred of Russia, a museum is filled with exhibits demonstrating the horrors of Communism. Goebbels' propaganda machine, the March of Time commentary continues, is also continuing to bear down on the Jews and the Christian churches, for these, almost alone, are still offering resistance to the new order, and the Nazi state tolerates no rival authority over its people. In regimenting German thought all radio programmes, newspapers and letters are subject to censorship, but in millions of little homes there is no longer unemployment and despair. Hitler has given every man able to work a job. The average worker earns about £2 a week and is told by the state what work he must do. Under the new regime, it is stated, he is denied the right to strike, or even ask his employer for a rise. Day and night the great Krupps munitions plant is fed by the self denial of the German people. Germany must import most of the iron ore it is forging into armaments, and to pay for the new raw materials it must cut down shilling for shilling on the imports that might be going to feed its people. German market prices are controlled and kept high to benefit the farmer, who is essential in the Nazi programme to make Germany self sustaining. Although under this pressure Germany now produces 80 per cent of the food it needs, it must expand if the State is ever to become 100 per cent self supporting. The German child, states the March of Time, when scarcely out of the kindergarten must take the place allotted to him in the great Nazi scheme, and from then on think and act as he is told. Views are given of the various youth bodies at work and of the Nazi propaganda bureau in Berlin where the publicity is being prepared which next summer, it is hoped, will draw thousands of tourists to the country. In New York also a former German machine gunner, now a naturalized American, has organised a Nazi movement and claims to have enrolled 200,000 US Germans under the Swastika.

The March of Time returned to the subject of Germany again (IV, 2: July 1938). Again to quote the *Monthly Film Bulletin* (1938, p. 152):

. . . Hitler's return to Austria, after his way had been paved by a German mechanised army of 150,000, thousands of Bavarian police and Austrian Nazi organisers. March of Time shows how Anschluss was the climax of a 14 year old plan, announced in 'Mein Kampf' as a 'necessary condition for the security of the German race'. It shows Hitler as a baby, later as an obscure Austrian ex-corporal who had served in the German army and had been thrown into prison after an unsuccessful Nazi *putsch* in Munich. It mentions how the peace treaties of 1919 paved the way for Hitler, so that by 1933 he had become a power in Europe. It traced his attempts to crush Austrian independence by plotting within the Austrian government and even by the murder of Austria's Chancellor, Dollfuss, and shows the murdered statesman and scenes of his funeral. Under the dictatorship of Kurt von Schuschnigg, Austria resisted Anschluss until the German army marched against her. The sad fate of Austria is here depicted perhaps most poignantly by a shot of a suicide, one of the many which rapidly followed the Nazi conquest. With cleverly chosen, short quotations from 'Mein Kampf', March of Time ends a most dramatic, rather frightening sequence, attempting to show why Germany alone rejoices with Hitler, and why the rest of the world feels that the Austrian union is a prelude to other things.

The next issue (IV, 3: August 1938) turned to Czechoslovakia, surveying the tasks of the National Defense Council in preparing resistance to Hitler. The country was represented as heavily armed, with every man, woman and child prepared to defend her against invasion by Hitler.

The sixth issue (IV, 6: November 1938) gave a survey of Europe and the rest of the world at the time of the Munich crisis. The events leading up to the crisis were recapitulated. The open conflicts in China and Ethiopia were emphasized against the background of the tensions in Europe. Britain's mobilization was interpreted as applying a brake to Hitler's ambitions, because Hitler, according to the *March of Time* commentary, had no intention of involving himself in war with Britain. The British people, we are informed, always resort to prayer in time of crisis; some, however, are shown collecting gas masks, while others congregate on the pavements of Downing Street. The episode ends with Chamberlain's departure for Munich in September, but takes the story no further, though by the time this issue was distributed the following month, the disturbing outcome of these meetings with Hitler was known.

The seventh issue (IV, 7: November 1938) was titled *Inside the Maginot Line,* filmed by special permission of the French War Ministry. France, like Britain, was shown to be rearming at speed following the Munich agreement and Daladier's government by decree and full-scale mobilization. The climax of the film involved coverage of France's all-powerful fortification, the Maginot defenses, the vast bulwarks of steel and concrete and underground bunkers with their pressure systems to expel poison gas, and electrified kitchens providing round-the-clock meals drawing on food stocks designed to sustain 250,000 officers and men for a year's siege. *The March of Time* was privileged to have a defense exercise staged for the cameras, showing the high degree of mechanization to which warfare, Maginot-style, had been raised. The fact that the Maginot Line failed to secure the frontier with Belgium was not queried.

Edgar Anstey, who was British editor for *March of Time* from 1936 to 1939, has the following to say about the political climate of the period, and its influence on the policy and technical approach to the making of the series:

For anyone not fortunate enough to have been concerned with the 'media' in 1936, it is difficult to conjure up the excitement and relief we felt at the sense that at long last there was to be a confrontation between the forces of evil represented by fascism and the new society which had become the passionate concern of journalists, novelists, dramatists and film-makers across the world. After I finished *Enough to Eat?*, a documentary on malnutrition in Britain, Richard de Rochemont asked me to join *March of Time* to direct its British productions. In New York his brother Louis was allying many of his monthly releases with liberal causes, from civil rights for Southern negroes to Roosevelt's financing of public works to reduce unemployment. My first item for M.O.T. dealt with the possible effects of malnutrition on Britain's ability to raise an anti-fascist army, my second with the national debilitation represented by the state of our mining industry at that time.

Like more recent critics, I remember that whoever then wrote about films for the Daily Worker was sceptical and puzzled about the possibility of truly anti-fascist material emanating from a film company associated with Henry Luce and Time Inc. With *Rehearsal for War*—which predicted that what was happening in Spain would shortly be repeated on a wider scale in Europe as a whole—and *Inside Nazi Germany*, which showed how the German war machine was being prepared, it had to be accepted that this particular capitalist publishing house was capable of inner contradictions beyond the comprehension of the Communist party formalists.

In 1937 I went to New York to work with Louis de Rochemont and his team and to experience at first hand the heady excitement of his pioneering form of militant screen journalism. Creatively the richest stage was in editing. The impact of shot upon shot, the precise relationship between the word, indeed the syllable of commentary, and the picture cut which it illuminated or by which it was given an added emotional significance—these were the tools of our trade. Louis was a brilliant editor and in one of many continuous seventy-two hour sessions of work, I remember his scrapping one of the three items of the release and substituting a story about the peril in which Austria then stood, put together entirely from material which he called for from the unit's stock shot library and assembled with his own hands.

I arranged for my old friend Alistair Cooke to speak the commentaries for the English versions of the items for which I was responsible and he was only one of the many figures of the day who became involved in one way or another, from Ernest Hemingway to Fiorel[lo] La Guardia, and from Jan Mazaryk to John Dos Passos. (Jan Mazaryk recorded for me an emotional interview, giving the Czechoslovak view on the Munich agreement). This was after I returned to London to write and direct a story on Anthony Eden's political role in 1938–39. During the course of it I was arrested in Downing Street during one of the many anti-Nazi disturbances following Eden's resignation from Neville Chamberlain's Government. When the film was completed, it was banned from British showing by the British Board of Film Censors (who thought fit to show it unofficially to the Foreign Office) on the ground that it was unfriendly to a friendly power, namely Nazi Germany! Randolph Churchill arranged for me to show it to his father, Winston. Winston said that the film should be seen by everyone in the country, but his days of power and influence were gone and he was powerless to help us. He was ill and depressed, little knowing that the best of his life still lay ahead. My last film for M.O.T. was on the refugees moving across the world to escape persecution in one country or another, and I remember photographing Jewish children arriving at an East Coast port in bewildered ship-loads before moving on to transit camps. I was reminded of Spanish refugees streaming across the border into France a few years before and of the title of that story—'Rehearsal for War'. The prophecy was about to be fulfilled and with the outbreak of war in September 1939, *March of Time* temporarily suspended its British work. As soon as Churchill succeeded Chamberlain, I—in common with my British documentary colleagues, many of us 'premature anti-fascists'—found plenty of work to do.

Spanish Earth

Parallel with *The March of Time*, a group formed in the United States largely by John dos Passos, Ernest Hemingway, Archibald MacLeish, and Lillian Hellman, who acted as sponsors for a film to be made in Spain during the Civil War by Hemingway and the left-wing Dutch director, Joris Ivens. This was *Spanish Earth* (1937). Hemingway spoke and wrote the commentary, and the film was shot by John Ferno and edited by Helen van Dongen, later to be Robert Flaherty's editor for *The Land* and *Louisiana Story*. Music was composed by Marc Blitzstein and Virgil Thomson. It was about the most distinguished team of combined American and Continental European talent as could have been assembled at the time, and the film, the first major blow to be struck on the screen against the menace of dictatorship (apart from *The March of Time*), was also one of the most brilliant documentaries of the 1930s, the period which saw the initial maturity of documentary sound film in Britain and elsewhere.

Spanish Earth used its visuals to link the need for agricultural productivity and irrigation of the parched Spanish earth with the government cause, as distinct from the destruction wrought by the indiscriminate bombing practiced by Franco's reactionary rebel forces. Ferno's camera went into the heat of the conflict; the streets of Madrid are seen mutilated by bombardment; corpses lie rigid in the last gesture of death. A village near Valencia shows the rural areas caught up in war, the struggle of the peasants to survive. The British censor used his scissors to excise virtually all direct reference to Italian and German intervention. Hemingway's part casual, part lyrical commentary has an immediate and personal emotional impact rather than serving to clarify the continuity of the film, and his feeling is backed by an impressionist music score that supplies the atmosphere the sparse amount of natural sound sometimes lacks. This fifty-minute film was ingeniously put together out of excellent material, much of which had to be shot silent though supplemented by sequences or shots with natural sound (the Spanish subtitled). It was backed by Hemingway's commentary (effective because of its lack of any attempt at professional polish in delivery), together with music and occasional choral effects.

Another American filmmaker of importance working during this period was Herbert Kline, whose career began with filming in besieged Madrid. A socially conscious man who had wandered about footloose since his earliest youth, Kline believed that film could do more to expose fascist intransigence than any amount of talk and reportage. He taught himself filmmaking while actually shooting *Heart of Spain* (1937) and *Return to Life* (1937, made with Henri Cartier-Bresson). These films revealed the raw suffering of the Spanish people during the Civil War. Kline stayed in Europe to make *Crisis* (1938) and *Lights out in Europe* (1939), both made with the assistance of the Czech photographer, Alexander Hammid. *Crisis* (with a commentary by Vincent Sheean) recorded the dismemberment of Czechoslovakia after Munich, and was filmed with the actual participation of Henlein's Nazi fifth column in the Sudetenland. *Lights out in Europe* (commentary by James Hilton) offered direct coverage of the Nazi invasion of Poland, which was also the subject of another American film, *Siege* (1939–40), made by Julien Bryan. Kline's personal account of his work in Europe written in

1942 is reprinted in Lewis Jacobs's anthology, *The Documentary Tradition.*

Britain

Britain herself supplemented the portrait of the Spanish Civil War with *Spanish ABC* (1938), directed by Thorold Dickinson and Sidney Cole, an enlightened propaganda film intended to show the efforts of the Spanish republican government to develop sound education even in time of Civil War, establishing thousands of new schools and centers for adult education to combat illiteracy and the previous lack of elementary instruction. Voluntary teachers from the professional classes are shown giving instruction in the factories during workers' rest periods, while some soldiers continue to study even in the front line itself. The rebel armies bring indiscriminate destruction, in which university buildings suffer with the rest. Meanwhile refugee children are cared for in areas as far away as possible from war. The authorities attempt to save works of art from Franco's bombs. Where the insurgent armies overrun a territory, it is stated that they close down the new schools, regarding universal education as harmful.

Much of *Spanish ABC* was photographed under fire in Barcelona and Madrid, by Arthur Graham and Alan Lawson. The whole treatment of the film was quiet and factual, and it was both as art and propaganda to be Britain's principal prewar contribution on film to the resistance against fascism.

An obviously important, but virtually unknown, film on the Spanish Civil War was that compiled from archive material by Luis Buñuel. According to J. F. Aranda, writing in *Films and Filming* (November 1961), Buñuel, following his return to Spain in 1935 after an abortive visit to Hollywood, was given all its official archive material by the Spanish government on the outbreak of the Civil War. Working first in Madrid and then in Paris, Buñuel edited a compilation film of the Civil War—*Madrid 1936* or *Loyal Spain, Take Arms!* This film has been recently re-discovered and should surely be made available for students of history, and of Buñuel's work as a filmmaker.[5]

It is worth remembering here that H. G. Wells's film *Things to Come* (1935), directed by William Cameron Menzies, a specialist in film design, offered in its first part a direct warning of the devastating nature of the war to come. The prewar dialogue between the realist, Cabal, and the over-confident Passworthy, representing the

Things to Come (1935), directed by William Cameron Menzies.

ordinary citizen, emphasized this:

> PASSWORTHY: Well, firstly there. isn't going to be a war, and secondly, war doesn't stop progress. It stimulates progress.
> CABAL *ironically:* Yes war's a *highly* stimulating thing. But you can overdo a stimulant. The next dose may be a fatal one. An overdose.
> PASSWORTHY, *hesitating:* Well, after all, don't we exaggerate about the horrors of war? Aren't we overdoing that song? The last war wasn't as bad as they make out. One didn't worry. Something great seemed to have got hold of you.
> CABAL: Something still greater may get hold of you next time. You're talking through your hat, Passworthy. If we do not end war—war will end us. Everybody says that, millions of people believe it, and nobody does anything.

War does come, suddenly, unannounced, on Christmas Eve, while children are playing at warfare with their toy guns. What happens, in effect, is a remarkable forecast of the German blitzkrieg four years hence on Poland.

During the final days of peace, compilation films began to be hurriedly assembled for release should war actually break out. The more "popular" British attitude to mobilization was to be represented by a half-hour "news documentary" called *Arf a Mo', Hitler* (released October 1939), made on the very eve of war by British Paramount News, directed and commentated by G. T. Cummins. It included coverage from the 1939 Aldershot Tattoo, and cut in shots of the departure of the British Expeditionery Force to France. There were scenes of training for the Royal Marines, and a specially interesting sequence showing undernourished men from the depressed areas of Britain being rehabilitated in preparation for military training. A nice contrast is made between officer cadet drill at Sandhurst, with the sergeant-major addressing his squad as "Gentlemen" while trainees for the other ranks are bawled at in the traditional military style. The film, however, kept its commentary on a relatively restrained and factual note, at least avoiding the worst kind of "jingo" propaganda.

Less effective, and technically maladroit, was Bud Pollard's feature-length *Rule Britannia* (August 1939), which used archive material in a historical survey of the past twenty-five years leading up to the present tensions. Comments by ex-servicemen (German and Italian included) were interspersed between actuality material, while patriotic songs were interspersed with machine-gun fire. A parallel film of greater interest released the same month was a one-hour *Cavalcade of the Navy* (director, Horace Shepherd) made in color and surveying the history of the British Navy by means of a montage of celebrated paintings. By the time all these films were in the theaters, the war had started.

France

The other principal protagonist was, of course, France. But again, no feature film directly opposing the dictators had been made, except for Jean Renoir's feature-length documentary, *La vie est à Nous* (1937). This was a propaganda film made for the French Communist Party, and begins by indicting the Right, the patrician families who, it is claimed, rule France and turn its potential wealth into poverty for the mass of the people, and the French fascists, the Croix du Feu. Hitler is seen speaking, but the sound is the barking of a dog; scenes involving Mussolini are intercut with shots of putrifying corpses and warfare. These contrast with action portraits of the Communist figure-heads—Lenin, Stalin, Dimitrov—together with the Communist leaders in France. Ordinary men (in the persons of a factory worker unjustly dismissed; a bankrupt small farmer; an unemployed intellectual) are seen receiving help from the Party in their difficulties. The film ends on a purely emotional, indeed rather simplistic, note with marching crowds singing the Internationale, but the main sections of the film are strong and authentic in feeling, even when actuality material is mixed with scenes that are reenacted.[6]

The grave political unrest of 1934 and after in France found indirect expression in the themes of many fiction films—"social realism" in the work of Jean Renoir as a filmmaker of the Left (*Toni; Le Crime de Monsieur Lange*) or of Duvivier in *La Belle Equipe*, and the romantic melancholy of Renoir's *La Grande Illusion*, with its pacifist message to German and French alike. Although not intended by Feyder as an advocacy of collaboration, the satiric comedy of *La Kermesse Héroique* in fact turned on the astute form of collaboration the women of a seventeenth-century Flemish village employ to save their frightened menfolk, and their property, from destruction at the hands of the Spanish governor of Flanders, the handsome but ruthless Duc d'Alba. The film raised protests in Flanders on its release, and it was indeed welcomed in Germany by Goebbels, whereas *La Grande Illusion* was, of course, banned.

A predominant theme in French films of the later 1930s was escape into the fatalistic, defeatist poetry that found significant expression in two films made by Marcel Carné, *Quai des Brumes* (1938) and *Le Jour se Lève* (1939), both scripted by Jacques Prévert. In the first, a murderer on the run (played sympathetically by Jean Gabin) and a beautiful girl intent on suicide (Michèle Morgan) fall in love, saving each other momentarily from despair when they meet in the misty setting of the docks of Le Havre. The film ends in the defeat of the hero, whom evil men force to commit a second murder, and the hope raised by love is destroyed as if by an evil destiny. In *Le Jour se Lève* the hero, again Jean Gabin, as another working-class character on the run, ends by killing himself when he is finally besieged in a garret at the top of a tall tenement building; innocence is portrayed by a young flower girl who befriends him; evil by a cruel animal trainer in a derelict circus whose persecuted mistress (Arletty) falls in love with Gabin. The defeat of innocence, beauty, and love lies deep in the film, evident from beginning to end.

Such negative films as these (and others like them, such as Renoir's *Les Bas-Fonds* and *La Bête Humaine*) may seem remote from the war to come, and the tragic collapse of France in 1940, the brave façade of the Maginot Line circumvented and useless. But the self-indulgent melancholy of these exotic films made a virtue out of defeat, representing it as inevitable when faced by pervasive and consuming evil. Without pressing the implications too far, the widespread appreciation of these two films, which appeared at the time to represent the height of French achievement in the cinema, at once encouraged and excused the prevailing mood of defeatism during the period of Munich (September 1938), the final collapse of government defenses in Spain (early 1939), and the months preceding the inevitable, dreaded outbreak of the European war. The Left, vociferating endlessly against Hitler and Mussolini, had the words thrust back down their throats with the announcement of the German-Soviet pact of August 1939.

Two other films reflect more directly the war situation of the 1930s. The first is André Malraux's remarkable *Espoir-Sierra de Teruel* (*Days of Hope*, 1939), a film virtually unseen in France or elsewhere until after the war. It was made in Spain during the last

Days of Hope (1939), directed by André Malraux.

months of the Civil War, and took its action from sections of Malraux's novel, *Days of Hope*. It was made with something of the
roughly styled realism that was later to be associated with the Italian
neo-realist cinema, and it was also much influenced by Russian silent
filmmaking. It was to remain an "outsider" film, little appreciated in
France even when seen later. My own view of it when I first saw it
in 1945 appeared in the *Monthly Film Bulletin* (1945, p. 157):

> André Malraux, a volunteer fighting with the Republican army against
> Franco, made this film. The story is the everyday one of the town
> controlled by the Fascists, of the little group of Republicans, quick-
> thinking, in overalls and plimsols, running down the steps of the narrow
> streets, flattening under fire against the high walls studded with light
> and shadow in the hard sun, of comrades shot to death or wounded,
> but somehow the few of them getting out with arms and dynamite
> to the loyal villagers of Limas, near the Fascist-held bridge and the
> secret airfield which must at all costs be bombed. It is the story of
> an Italian democrat who gave his life for Spain, and a German democrat
> who is carried with a bullet in his stomach down the long craggy
> paths of Limas from the mountain-side where his damaged bomber
> crashed after its successful mission. It is the story of a peasant bemused
> as he looks for the first time at his own countryside from the air until,
> mad with anxiety he should miss it, he points out the secret airfield
> to the bombardier. There are fine sequences such as the great procession
> which forms from all over the district like the mourners in Eisenstein's
> Odessa. The injured and the dead are brought down the mountain
> path and the music of Darius Milhaud rises slowly in a paean of agony
> and lamentation, not without pride and triumph. A coffin bounces
> weirdly on the back of a mule; at the walls of Limas the women wait
> to stare with dark sorrow at the airman whose face is covered with
> bandages and blood. The music rises over the thousands of Spain's
> Republicans gathered to give the salute of the clenched fist to those
> who have given their lives to their cause, and the film ends. It is a
> poet's picture of actuality, harsh and beautiful and intense, an unusual
> picture which the Nazis searched for but did not find as it lay hidden
> in occupied France.

The second film, misunderstood and hated in France when it was
shown in Paris on the eve of war, epitomized certain weaknesses
in French society—Renoir's *La Règle du Jeu*. It opened a few weeks
before the declaration of war and ran for a few days only. Later it
was banned by the French censorship. In it Renoir attempted satire,
using the outwardly mixed moods of burlesque and violence in a
hybrid style far ahead of its time. The result for contemporary audiences was only failure, a cacophony of mood. But it was the one
French film that came nearest to making a political-social comment

on the disrupted state of that branch of French society most liable to collapse before the invader. It is set in a French country mansion, where the host, a marquis, is entertaining a weekend shooting party. The organized destruction of innocent animals by people guilty of every kind of decadence and deceit, finds its reflection in the relationships among the hierarchy in the servants' hall. The film is seen by the left-wing French film historian, the late Georges Sadoul, in the political context of its time:

> The luxurious reception rooms of the castle offered an ideal background for the antics of the jealous gamekeeper, who, firing a revolver in all directions, tries to stop his wife, the parlour-maid, from being pursued by the local poacher. In another part of the house some guests, in the costume of Bavarian peasants, are rehearsing on an improvized stage the famous soldier's song 'En revenant de la Revue', a song which since the early days of Méliès' youth, had been used as the signature tune of the reactionary followers of General Boulanger. The owner of this valuable estate, a renowned collector of mechanical gadgets, is proudly exhibiting his musical instruments to a group of visitors. The lilt of their primitive music spurs on the gamekeeper and the band of domestics in their three-cornered love-chase, while a fight develops between the family and all their guests over the charming hostess; the chase begins, regardless of all obstacles that block its path. The scene gives way to a macabre dance by ghosts and skeletons. This brilliant sequence, following the chase, is an ideal cinematic metaphor, drawing with rare imaginative foresight a parallel to the disturbed and varied emotions of 1939. Renoir was busy shooting these very scenes while Hitler's entry into Prague was being announced over the loudspeakers of the world. This lovely corner of France, the Salogne, with its castles, its forests and marshlands, a country famous for its hunting, whose natural beauty and tempo Renoir had so successfully captured, was but one year later to see the last sad battles of the French troops in the terrible year, 1940. Historically speaking, *La Règle du Jeu* was both in style and in theme absolutely the film of the moment.[7]

The United States: Up to the Period of Pearl Harbor, December 1941

The United States declared war on Germany on 11 December 1941, five days after the Japanese assault on Pearl Harbor. This was some 2¼ years after the British and French entry into the war. Hitler had meanwhile partitioned Poland with Russia, which had invaded from the West (following the secret agreement of August 1939), invaded Denmark, Norway, Holland, Belgium, France, Luxembourg, Yugoslavia, and Greece, as well as established his control over the oilfields of Romania. His armies had reached the outskirts of Moscow in October 1941, after the blitzkrieg launched on the Soviet Union the previous June. He had also penetrated the Ukraine. On 8 December Britain joined with the United States in declaring war on Japan. The European war had become a world war.

The gradual alignment of the United States under Roosevelt with Britain under Churchill (who became Prime Minister in succession to Chamberlain on 10 May 1940, simultaneously with Hitler's assault on Holland and Belgium) had become increasingly obvious during the years preceding the open declaration of war, and this was reflected in the production of feature films that took the situation in Europe as their subject. In April 1941 Roosevelt had proclaimed a state of national emergency following Hitler's moves in Europe, and introduced the Selective Service Act. Increasingly, therefore, anti-Nazi feeling grew in American films once war had broken out in Europe, in spite of the fact that Germany was represented diplomatically in the United States until December 1941, and the German embassy was always ready to protest.[8]

A few bold spirits even anticipated the outbreak of war in Europe. Directors had to adjust the techniques of screen entertainment to a conflict that was becoming increasingly real, though still happily very remote from Hollywood. Press correspondents based in Europe, the documentaries (in particular, *The March of Time*) began to bring home to American filmmakers and their audiences the dire predicament of the Europeans. This was reinforced by the presence of many refugees from Hitler who were to be absorbed into the industry. In 1938 Walter Wanger produced *Blockade* (William Dieterle; script, John Howard Lawson; with Madeleine Carroll, Henry Fonda); ostensibly a melodrama of espionage, this film was set in a blockaded port in Spain during the Civil War. Though no direct identification was made with either side, the film revealed a strong bias toward the government cause; it ended with an open plea from the hero, a progressive peasant farmer (Henry Fonda): "Where is the conscience of the world that it allows the killing and maiming of civilians to go on?" Warners, who had become the producers of many social films with some conscience during the 1930s (such as *I am a Fugitive from a Chain Gang, They Won't Forget, Black Legion, Massacre, Heroes For Sale*) allowed Lloyd Bacon to make *Espionage Agent* and Anatole Litvak to make *Confessions of a Nazi Spy*, both released in 1939 and made before the outbreak of war in Europe. Both films would be acceptable to audiences on the level of spy melodramas, but both were to be given at least a powerful veneer of actuality in their handling. *Espionage Agent*, described in a review by Ernest Lindgren written at the time as a "topical thriller," concerned the predicament of an American consular representative (Joel McCrea) who innocently marries an actress (Brenda Marshall) who has sold herself when in financial difficulties to the German Secret Service as a spy. He only learns of her situation after their marriage; he resigns from the diplomatic service and returns with his wife to Europe in order to expose, for the benefit of Americans, the ramifications of Nazi espionage that penetrates the United States. The problem was to combine a serious approach to such events as the Spanish Civil War and the Munich crisis with the paramount object of creating also exciting entertainment. The propaganda value of the film—for in 1939 it was propaganda—was largely dissipated.

An anomalous short feature-length film of more interest for its subject than its realization also appeared in 1939. It featured a young American journalist, Isobel Steele, in a reenactment of what she alleged were her experiences in Nazi Germany during 1934. In the process of scripting an account of recent events in Germany, she is arrested, subjected to severe interrogation, and imprisoned first in the Alexanderplatz prison, and later in the Moabit. The American Consul proves powerless to help her, but she is released suddenly and deported after her mother's intervention with the authorities in the United States. The film, using commentary over newsreel and other record material, exposes Nazi injustice and persecution of the Jews, though the scenes of imprisonment and interrogation by the Gestapo are reenacted without undue exaggeration. Apart from Isobel Steele herself, neither the players nor the director are named and the film achieved limited distribution in Britain as a result of its topicality. Celebrated as one of the first American anti-Nazi films was *Confessions of a Nazi Spy* (Spring 1939), with a distinguished cast including Edward G. Robinson, Franz Lederer, George Sanders, and Paul Lukas. This dealt with Nazi activity in the United States through the branches of the German-American Bund, which was spread throughout the states and battened on the racial loyalties of men and women of German stock, as well as extremists of the American Right who encouraged fascism in the United States.[9] Seen again today, it appears crude and melodramatic, but the impact of this film on American opinion is described by the eminent film historian, Lewis Jacobs:

> What made *Confessions of a Nazi Spy* so disturbing was its timing. American nerves were taut, and feeling was running high over Hitler's ruthless aggression in Europe. The FBI had arrested a number of Nazi agents operating in the United States. Fritz Kuhn, head of the

Confessions of a Nazi Spy (1939), directed by Anatole Litvak, with Edward G. Robinson and Francis Lederer.

American Bund, threatened a $5,000,000 libel suit against the producers of the film. 'We are loyal Americans,' he claimed, 'organized to uphold the Constitution of the United States.' The German Consulate called the picture part of an American conspiracy. Many South American countries favourable to fascism immediately banned the movie. Its producers, the Warner Brothers, were said to have received murder threats for making it. The film's depiction of Nazi groups draping together the American flag and the swastika and saluting them with 'Heil Hitler' at a time when the Third Reich's contempt for democracy was common knowledge came as a shocking provocation to that public which abhorred totalitarianism.[10]

During the pre-American-German war period further feature films were made with anti-Nazi subjects. These were:

1940 *Escape* (Mervyn LeRoy, with Norma Shearer, Robert Taylor, the

former German star Conrad Veidt, the Dutch-born Philip Dorn,
and Nazimova).
Foreign Correspondent (Alfred Hitchcock, with Joel McCrea,
Laraine Day, Herbert Marshall, George Sanders).
Four Sons (Archie Mayo, with Don Ameche, Eugénie Leontovich,
Mary Beth Hughes).
The Mortal Storm (Frank Borzage, with Margaret Sullavan,
James Stewart, Robert Young, Frank Morgan); based on Phyllis
Bottome's celebrated novel.
The Great Dictator (Charles Chaplin, with himself, Jack Oakie,
Paulette Goddard).
The Man I Married (Irving Pichel, with Francis Lederer, Joan
Bennett, Lloyd Nolan).

1941   *Man Hunt* (Fritz Lang, with Walter Pidgeon, Joan Bennett,
George Sanders).
Underground (Vincent Sherman, with Jeffrey Lynn, Philip Dorn,
the Norwegian Kaaren Verne, Mona Maris).
World Premiere (Ted Tetzlaff, with Fritz Feld, and the German
character actor Sig Rumann).
So Ends Our Night (John Cromwell, with Fredric March, Erich
von Stroheim).[11]

Some of these films were seriously intended dramas that had
Nazi Germany as a setting for action that could not help leaning in
the direction of the thriller, the danger which always threatened those
who were at once horrified and fascinated by the violence in Germany and wanted to project it in the form of the novel, play, or
film. The problem was to avoid actors presenting this in terms of
stereotyped screen melodrama, however restrained the script and
dialogue provided by writers who wanted to avoid Hollywood clichés
because the subject dealt with sufferings that were to a varying extent real to themselves and to at least certain members of the audience—the Jewish and other refugees in Britain and the United States.
The Mortal Storm was adapted from a best-seller,[12] and in the process
turned a documentary novel, conceived in restrained and serious terms,
into a filmland melodrama with an almost complete absence of German atmosphere and background in the studio reconstruction. The
story concerned a German middle-class family in a small university
town in Southern Germany broken apart at the time of Hitler's seizure of power. The father (Frank Morgan), a Jewish professor, is sent
to a concentration camp; his stepsons and his daughter Freya's fiancé
(Robert Young) become ardent young Nazis; his wife, his son, and
Freya—drawn now to a young farmer of independent views (James
Stewart)—eventually manage to escape to Austria, but Freya who has
been detained and questioned by the Gestapo, is mortally wounded

Man Hunt (1941), directed by Fritz Lang, with Walter Pidgeon.

at the frontier. The cast faithfully enact the situation; the concentration camp scenes reveal (without too much emphasis) the suffering of the prisoners, and the Gestapo agents are correctly brutal. James Stewart lends his open American sincerity and energy to the part of the young farmer; only Maria Ouspenskaya as the professor's wife seems to belong to the reality the film seeks to portray. But the film as a whole has little or nothing of the urgency and actuality of the novel. *Four Sons,* with a similar theme of the disintegration of a family under political pressures in Czechoslovakia, was similarly unreal.

Division in relationships is also at the root of a film of German resistance to Hitler, *Underground,* which was more violent in its projection of the Gestapo's methods with their prisoners. (The contemporary reviewers in both the British Film Institute's *Sight and Sound* and the *Monthly Film Bulletin* use the same word in describing the Gestapo scenes—"overwhelming.") The story concerns the gradual involvement of a young soldier invalided out of the German army in his brother's illegal radio activities, largely through his love for a girl also involved in the underground movement; the plot has complex ramifications of spying and betrayal, and the Gestapo figure largely in it.

In *Escape* Robert Taylor plays Mark Preysing, an American of German origin who returns to Hitler's Germany to trace his mother, Emmy Ritter; through the friend of an American-born German countess (Norma Shearer), General Kurt von Kalb (Conrad Veidt), he discovers she is confined in a concentration camp—in so many Hollywood films the most obvious arcane symbol of the ultimate threat that Nazi Germany held over its victims, together with the Gestapo interrogation scene with its gangster overtones. The film resorts to the wilder shores of fancy when Mark induces the concentration camp doctor to inject his mother, of whom the doctor is a secret admirer, with a coma-inducing drug, so that the "body" can be smuggled out of the camp, and the elderly actress (once recovered) spirited out of the country disguised as a young woman. The film is remarkable only for the return to the screen of the silent film star, Nazimova, as the largely comatose actress. Another film of a return to Germany that leads to the breakup of a family as a result of political tension was Irving Pichel's *The Man I Married. So Ends Our Night*, a further political melodrama, dealt with the fate of Jewish refugees fleeing from Berlin to Prague, with Fredric March as an anti-Nazi German Officer who finally commits suicide when he falls into the hands of the Gestapo.

Hitchcock's brilliant thriller, *Foreign Correspondent*, was set in Europe just prior to the outbreak of war. Hitchcock had been urged by the British authorities not to return to wartime Britain, but stay in Hollywood (to which he had moved under contract at the age of forty in the summer of 1939) in order to do what he could to counteract American isolationism. After directing *Rebecca* for David O. Selznick, he made *Foreign Correspondent* for Walter Wanger early in 1940; it was released in August 1940 and received exceptional reviews. Its release coincided with the collapse of Western Europe and the blitz raids on London, and it was deliberately scripted (by Charles Bennett, Joan Harrison, James Hilton, and Robert Benchley, as well as Hitchcock himself) to shake the United States into awareness of what must threaten her if she turned her back on Europe. The plot is complex because it contains a succession of "blinds" familiar in Hitchcock's espionage stories. Briefly, it concerns a naïve American journalist (Joel McCrea) deliberately exposed by his employer to the dangers of the European scene. He becomes Hitchcock's typical honest innocent involved in bitter and educative experience when he falls in love with the beautiful daughter of a Nazi master spy (Herbert Marshall) whose disguise is that of the head of an international peace organization. The chain of exciting climaxes includes the celebrated sequence of assassination by a supposed press photographer of a Dutch diplomat, holder of a secret treaty the Nazis want to steal. The journalist gradually loses his innocence as he becomes more deeply involved in exposing the spy ring, and several spectacular attempts on his life are made in Holland, Britain, and finally during the flight on the Clipper back to the States, when the plane is shot down into the sea. But the story is his to give the American press, and the film ends with his impassioned plea over the radio from London as the bombs fall that America arm herself against the coming world struggle against fascism.

Hitchcock claimed in his interviews with Truffaut that Joel McCrea was too easy-going for his taste; he had wanted Gary Cooper, who had earlier made the mistake of turning the part down on the ground that the film was a mere thriller. Cooper could have brought a greater seriousness, even profundity, to the changeover from innocence to experience in the journalist. Actuality material shot by Osmond Borrodaile in both London and Amsterdam was included in the film, which often had great dramatic plausibility, as in the assassination sequence on the steps and the subsequent chase of the killer through the closely packed tramcars in the crowded rain-soaked streeets.[13] Nevertheless, Hitchcock claimed to Truffaut, "the picture was pure fantasy and, as you know, in my fantasies, plausibility is not allowed to rear its ugly head." But what mattered most in this film was its impact on the public imagination. Goebbels, who had a sardonic taste for films made by the opposition, is said greatly to have enjoyed the print he obtained—probably, according to Hitchcock, through Switzerland.

Another exceptional film, made by the exiled Austrian director, Fritz Lang, was *Man Hunt*, realized from a wholly independent script by Dudley Nichols and based on the novel *Rogue Male* by Geoffrey Household. The plot turns on the manhunt of Thorndike (Walter Pidgeon), a British big-game hunter and crack shot, who at the beginning of the film is in a position to shoot Hitler at Berchtesgaden, with a telescopic sighted rifle, but lowers his weapon at the crucial moment, since the rifle is not loaded. He then inserts a bullet—and at that very moment is caught by the Gestapo who burst in on him. So he has deliberately missed the chance to shoot the world's most dangerous man.[14] Pidgeon, interrogated by the Gestapo officer (George Sanders) himself escapes being killed and reaches Britain, only to be hunted down by Nazi agents, his only friend a street-girl played by Joan Bennett. Once again, a thriller becomes a vehicle for significant propaganda.

This leaves the totally different approach to propaganda of comedy. Ted Tetzlaff's *World Premiere* would appear not to have been shown in Britain; it has been described recently, by Charles Higham and Joel Greenberg, as "a comic masterpiece," with the German comedians Fritz Feld and Sig Rumann forming a team equal to that of Laurel and Hardy. They play two Nazi agents sent to Hollywood to sabotage the film industry. Feld is small, with a toothbrush moustache, Rumann vast and clumsy. But the comedy that went round the world was Chaplin's *The Great Dictator* (released October 1940), the production with which he finally settled his long vendetta against the sound film, and produced one that was accused by some of talking too much.

Chaplin had been planning his farcical satire against Hitler for long prior to the war, and began his script in January 1939.[15] Production preliminaries began before the war but were temporarily abandoned, and then resumed when he became convinced that ridicule was as good a weapon against Hitler as serious propaganda. Production proper began on 9 September and ran until March 1940; editing and other technical processes lasted until the autumn. The cost had been some two million dollars.

Chaplin retained his traditional physical appearance but stepped almost entirely out of his previous screen character to impersonate a little Jewish barber suffering from prolonged amnesia following a crash-landing during the First World War, and wholly out of character to play the second part, the barber's double, the dictator of Tomania, Adenoid Hynkel. The actual plot, as in many of Chaplin's feature films, is sometimes labored in conception—he has never been a skilful story-contriver—though his later films are more like fables than realistic stories.[16] Chaplin's brilliance lies in the development of situation, in comic invention, in performance: the scene of Hynkel's speech to the sons and daughters of the Double Cross, the beautiful ballet danced to Wagner with the giant globe, the shaving of a customer (Chester Conklin) to Brahms's Hungarian Dance, the arrival of Hynkel's fellow dictator, Benzino Napaloni, and the comic business with the carpet and the train. What upset critics was the six-minute outburst made by the Jewish barber in the person of Hynkel to the troops invading the neighboring country of Austerlich. This becomes an emotional and intensely personal plea by Chaplin for world peace and humanity. "They had had their laughs, and it was fun," he has said. "Now I wanted them to listen. . . . I did this picture for the Jews of the world. . . . I wanted to see the return of decency and kindness."[17]

During the making of the film Chaplin was warned by both the British and American censorship that an anti-Hitler picture would inevitably be banned. However, he was determined to go ahead. Significantly, he adds in his autobiography: "Had I known of the actual horrors of the German concentration camps, I could not have made *The Great Dictator;* I could not have made fun of the homicidal insanity of the Nazis. However, I was determined to ridicule their mystic bilge about pureblooded race." Chaplin also received threatening letters from (presumably) Nazi sympathizers. Harry Hopkins, Roosevelt's chief adviser, attended the evening press show in New York with Chaplin, and told him it was "a very worthwhile thing to do." He was dubious of its success, and the reviews were mixed, the critics objecting to the speech as sentimental and out of character; some even went so far as to think it communistic in implication. It was, in fact, almost naïvely humanitarian, expressed in the simplest, most open terms; it was Chaplin speaking fom his heart to the world—"We want to live by each other's happiness—not by each other's misery. . . . The way of life can be free and beautiful, but we have lost the way. Greed has poisoned men's souls. . . . More than cleverness, we need kindness and gentleness. . . . Soldiers! Don't give yourselves to these brutes—who despise you—enslave you. . . . Let us fight for a new world—a decent world which will give men a chance to work—that will give youth a future and old age a security.[18]" Chaplin was to recite the speech later over the air from the Hall of the Daughters of the American Revolution in Washington, but was rendered so nervous by the hostile coughing in the audience that he had to hold up the broadcast and call for water. Nevertheless, in spite of pronounced hostility in certain quarters of both the press and the public, the film was a box-office success in the United States and Europe. But it met with hostility in the Argentine, as the American president told Chaplin when he went to the White House.

So the first anti-Nazi gestures on the Western screen were made in peacetime America. Other, stronger gestures had been made in the Soviet Union, except for the awkward period of strategic peace between August 1939 and the initial invasion of Russia by Hitler's armies on 22 June 1941.

The Soviet Union, Up to June 1941

The Soviet Union's relationship with Germany during the period of gathering tension between them, 1933–39, was temporarily modified by the cynical and opportunistic agreement reached between Stalin and Hitler in August 1939, the Soviet-German pact, with its secret clauses for the carve-up of Poland and the mutual understanding concerning spheres of influence in the territories lying between their frontiers to the south. The motives of both Stalin and Hitler were to gain time; each paid lip service to the "understanding," accepting its usefulness. Neither believed the "peace" they had bought on each other's terms could be more than temporary.

The "cold war" of 1933–39 was for a while stayed. Russian filmmakers, more intent, like Russia herself, on internal developments in their vast country than on issuing a direct challenge to Germany, made few anti-German films until, with the fall of Austria and Czechoslovakia in 1938–39, and Hitler's violent threats to Poland, German forces drew ever closer to Russia's western frontiers. The small number of Russian feature films directly challenging Hitler belong substantially to this period. The more nationalistic Russian films concentrated on reinterpretation of the great "heroes" of the past— Vladimir Petrov's impressive but wholly idealized portrait in *Peter the Great*, showing Peter as a "peoples' Tsar" in his two-part film (1937 and 1939) based on Alexei Tolstoy's novel, V. I. Pudovkin's *Suvurov*, a study of the aged general who opposed Napoleon's forces in the Alps, and Igor Savchenko's *Bogdan Hmelnitzki*, set in the seventeenth century and concerning a Cossack leader who successfully opposed the Poles in the Ukraine, and united the Ukraine with Russia. These films, coupled with those featuring the achievements of Lenin and Stalin—*Lenin in October, Lenin in 1918* (1939) and the actor-impersonated figure of Stalin (by a fellow-Georgian, Michael Gelovani) in Chiaureli's *Great Dawn* (1938) —offered the Soviet Union and those across her frontiers free to see them the new consolidated nationalism that the Union represented. Needless to say, the Germans did not see these films, even between 1939 and 1941, the period of the "entente."

Of these historical films the only one to offer a direct challenge to the Germans was Sergei Eisenstein's *Alexander Nevsky* (1938). Prince Alexander, leader of the people of Novgorod, defeated the invading Teutonic Knights on the ice-covered lake Peipus in the thirteenth century. The film was conceived on a legendary epic scale; the characterization was simplified to the heroic, and the film, when not spectacularly beautiful in its combination of highly pictorial, stylized visuals and magnificent music by Sergei Prokofiev, became at times as light-hearted as a schoolboy's historical adventure story. Its characteristic spirit was the vigor of a youthful nation during the period of its birth, and the challenge that its newfound unity offered to all those threatening it.[19] The great, stylized figure of Alexander, played by Nicolai Cherkasov, closed the film with these words spoken twice direct from the screen to the audience: "Whosoever comes against us by the sword shall perish by the sword. Such is the law of the Russian land, and such it will always be."

The principal anti-Nazi films appeared in the height of the tensions of 1938–39. These were *Professor Mamlock* (1938; directors Adolf Minkin and Herbert Rappoport), adapted from a play by Friedrich Wolff, *Swamp-Soldiers* (1938, Alexander Macheret), and *The Oppenheims* (Grigori Roshal, 1939), adapted from a novel by the Jewish writer, Lion Feuchtwanger, about the persecution of a Jewish family in Germany, originally published in 1933. *Swamp-Soldiers* dealt with life in the German concentration camps: it was made without too great caricature of the Nazis, for whose portraiture a special hard, close-shot lens was used. According to Catherine de la Roche, in her account of the film, the prisoners are shown pri-

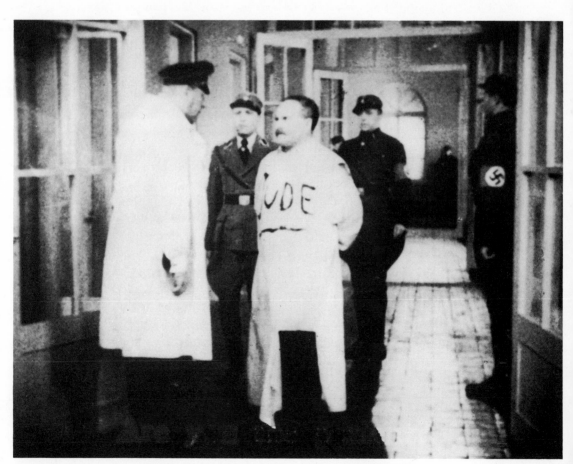

Professor Mamlock (1938), directed by A. Minkin.

marily as united through being members of a persecuted group, while the Nazis are seen as isolated figures remote from the human beings in their power.

Of these films *Professor Mamlock* was the most significant, and was shown soon after its completion in the United States, and in Britain early in 1939, some six months before the war, introduced by the London Film Society. It concerned the persecution of a distinguished Jewish surgeon by the Nazis after the seizure of power in 1933. Uninvolved in politics, he is humiliated solely because of his race, paraded through the streets, forced to attempt suicide, and finally shot when he offers open resistance. His son escapes to join a resistance group. The film, treated as straight, realistic narrative, was skillfully made, achieving a rare degree of propaganda effect because of its restraint and powerful dramatic impact. The distinction is brought out between the central core of armed Nazi supporters, the mass of the people driven through fear to support them, those directly suffering persecution, and those who, with supreme courage, plan resistance from inside Germany. The film included the character of a woman doctor who is at first sympathetic to the Nazis but who through experience becomes their opponent. The authenticity of the German atmosphere and background was undoubtedly due to one of the directors, Herbert Rappoport, having been an assistant to the Austrian director, G. W. Pabst, and seeking asylum from Nazism in Russia.[20]

There followed next the unhappy phase in which filmmakers had to endure a total change of policy. By secret pact with Germany, the Red Army moved into Eastern and South-Eastern Poland, along with what was termed "Western Ukraine" and "Western Byelorussia." These territories and their peoples became subsequently the subject of a number of Russian films, notably the Ukrainian director Alexander Dovzhenko and his wife Yulia Solntseva's *Liberation* (1940), a study of conditions in the new Soviet-occupied zones using special news coverage; others were Solntseva's *Bukovina-Ukrainian Earth* (1941) and Abram Room's story film, *Wind from the East* (1940–41).

Six weeks after Germany's invasion of Poland came Russia's protest to Finland about the strengthening of the Mannerheim Line and the threat it represented to Leningrad; this was followed by invasion on 30 November 1939. This invasion blackened the image of Stalin and made him appear little different from Hitler as an aggressor against his smaller neighbors, which included the Baltic states of Estonia, Latvia, and Lithuania, absorbed in June 1940.

The first films dealing with the Finnish war were Victor Eisimont's studio production *Front Line Girl-Friends* (or *The Girl from Leningrad,* early 1941) and Yevgeni Schneider's *In the Rear of the Enemy* (also early 1941), in which the Finnish forces are shown as officered by Germans, and the Russians as efficient and good-humored fighting in arctic conditions. Meanwhile, Esther Schub (maker of *Spain,* see note 20) had a year before made the front-line newsreel compilation film, *Mannerheim Line* (April 1940), on the winter campaign. Other films using newsreel coverage were *To the Danube* (August 1940) and *Estonian Earth* (1941). According to Jay Leyda, decorations and Stalin prizes were given during 1940–41 to the film workers whose firsthand records had been the basis of these propaganda documentaries and newsreels.

Anti-Polish feeling lay behind the historical film *Bogdan Khrnelnitsky* (1941), made in Kiev by V. Savchenko, celebrating the alliance in 1648 of the Russian and Ukrainian people against the Poles; it was conceived on a grand scale under the influence of Dovzhenko, then head of the studios at Kiev.[21]

Italy

As Germany's partner in the establishment of fascism in Europe, Italy made her own contribution to the film expressing fascist policy. The regime favored the cinema, Mussolini's son Vittorio being especially interested in filmmaking; Italy's celebrated Cine Citta Studios, at the time considered the largest in Europe, were established in 1937 together with the Istituto Luce, for short films and documentaries, and the film training school, the Centro Sperimentale. The Venice Film Festival had also been founded in 1932, and was to become for some years a center where German and Italian propaganda spectaculars were displayed alongside films from the democracies.

The undoubted flair of the Italians for filmmaking, demonstrated from early in the century, was to some extent dimmed during the period of Mussolini's full-scale control of Italy during the 1930s and early 1940s, and it is sad to see certain honored names in Italian film history, from Alexander Blasetti to Roberto Rossellini himself, making films in support of the regime and of the war in Africa and Europe. Blasetti, whose great film of the Risorgimento, *1860* (1934) has been widely regarded as one of the best films to be made during the fascist era in Italy, also made *La Vecchia Guardia* (*The Old Guards,* 1934); this celebrated the march on Rome. Bardèche and Brasillach, film historians who had a penchant for the fascist film, described *The Old Guards* as restrained, and then continued, giving a contemporary reaction:

> The concluding scenes show the men of the village leaving to join the militia on the march to Rome. We see only the profiles and the helmets of these men as they climb into the trucks. The headlights give out a small, pale beam in the rising dawn. Nothing is heard but the slow throb of the engines, interrupted now and then by the distant crowing of a cock. This chilly and silent departure is singularly impressive, with the long, pale road stretching out under the grey of a hesitant dawn—no songs, no triumph, no glory—only some trucks on the way to the city, and the leader's name printed in big type like an advertisement for patent medicine. We can still look forward with considerable hope, this film suggests, to Italy's providing us with its own epic of modern life and endeavour.

With the rise of Italian interest in Africa, colonial subjects began to appear, *Lo Squadrone Bianco* (*The White Squadron*, 1936, Au-

Lo Squadrone Bianco (1936), directed by Augusto Genina.

gusto Genina), *Sentinelle di Bronzo* (*Sentinels of Bronze*, 1937, Romolo Marcellini), and *Sotto Croce del Sud* (*Under the Southern Cross*, 1938; Guido Brignone). Of all these films, *The White Squadron* is possibly the best; set largely in the Libyan desert, it shows how heroes are made by absenting themselves from the problems of love in order to follow the true and honorable path of warfare, to fight and die for one's country. Technically impeccable, it was the kind of mindless heroism not unknown in British films of colonial warfare, in which the loyal "natives" are led by honorable Whites against those who rebel. A film set back in classical times, *Scipio Africanus* (Carmine Gallone, 1937) reinforced Italy's primal right to a place in the African sun, with an equally grandiose pictorial conception.

When the Abyssinian campaign had to be justified, Mario Camerini made *Il Grande Appelo* (*The Great Challenge*, 1936), and vast footage shot by the special unit covering the war under Luciano de Feo was edited to make the propaganda film *Il Cammino degli Eroi* (*The Path of the Heroes*, 1937), a short feature-documentary of some seventy minutes.[22] The preparations for the campaign in Italy are followed by the hazardous transportation of the troops and their supplies and the dropping of food and even animals by parachute; the war itself is seen being fought on land and from the air, leading up to the entry of the Italians into the capital, and the scenes of rejoicing in Rome while Mussolini orates. The contrast lies in the poorly equipped Abyssinians trying to resist the mechanized might of Italy.

In 1938, Vittorio Mussolini himself acted as supervisor of a film of some interest, *Luciano Serra, Pilota* (Goffredo Alessandrini), with a screenplay in which the youthful Roberto Rossellini shared a credit. Its subject was an inborn passion for flying, which a son can inherit from his father; the father in this case sacrifices his life to save his son during the Abyssinian war, and it appears that Rossellini may well have reshot some of the film.[23]

The Spanish Civil War—in which Italy's intervention was nominally unacknowledged though generally well enough known—was featured in Genina's *The Seige of Alcazar* (1940), remarkable, according to Vernon Jarratt, for the comparative fairness of its portrayal of the Spanish government forces. The director, naturally, favors Franco, who by the time the film was being made had seized power in Spain.

Japan: Up to the Period of Pearl Harbor, December 1941

Japanese filmmaking developed into big business with the coming of sound and the full establishment of the rival, monolithic companies. The Japanese taste for nationalistic subjects was expressed in the large output of historical and period films, many dealing with the warlike samurai, the mercenary warriors whose deadly swordplay was as legendary as the gunplay of America's Western heroes. The traditional member of the samurai was governed by the strict military code of bushido, which demanded, among much else, that a warrior disembowel himself if his honor were lost. One of the leading directors of period films, a man of marked liberal tendencies, Sadao Yamanaka, was called to the army and, serving in China in the ranks, was killed in 1938. His films had tended to show, realistically and humanely, how the samurai, faced with poverty and unemployment, sank to humble circumstances. Directors of note in Japan, such as Kenji Mizoguchi, Yasujiro Shimazu, Heinosuke Gosho, and Yasujiro Ozu, avoided the more militant subjects favored by the authorities during the Chinese War by concentrating on period dramas, and contemporary subjects that developed into some of the most personal films of the period, especially in the case of Ozu. Although anything savoring of social realism was liable to strict censorship, especially if it exposed poverty or corruption in Japanese life, Joseph L. Anderson and Donald Richie have pointed out in their history of the Japanese film that certain directors were able to a modest extent to counter the hardening atmosphere of militarism that came with the escalation of the war against China in 1936–37.

These films, which amounted to a form of exposure of social evils in contemporary Japan, had to be achieved through the established genres of domestic drama, such as Mizoguchi's films, *Osaka Elegy* (1936), the realistic story of a girl telephone operator whose life is ruined through her need for more money than she can earn, and *Sisters of the Gion* (1936), which exposed the evils to which women could become subject through the geisha system. Many films, especially those of Mizoguchi, revealed the hardships of women betrayed by men; others, such as *Theatre of Life* (1936) made by Tomo Uchida, a former assistant to Mizoguchi, exposed the excessive worship of money and material success in Japanese life.[24]

1937 was the year of intensification of the undeclared war upon China, leading to the occupation of Pekin and Tientsin, and the

Japanese industry had to face the need to make contemporary war films, in which the filmmakers were totally inexperienced. Between 1939 and the attack on Pearl Harbor (7 December 1941), which precipitated both the Japanese and American entry into what now became a world war against fascism, a number of war films appeared. The first of importance, Tomotaka Tasaka's *Five Scouts* (1938), revealed a careful, tentative approach, almost lacking in war fever. With quiet realism it shows a company of Japanese soldiers in North China; five scouts sent out on reconnaissance face a terrifying attack from an unseen enemy whom they can only attempt to resist before making their way back to their unit with the news that sends the company out to attack. The men themselves appear more concerned with memories of home than with any urge to fight, and the emphasis of the film is more humanist than militant. The film really belonged to the new social realism the more advanced directors were endeavoring to achieve against the grain of the times. Since there was never any question in the minds of the Japanese that, if required to fight, they would do so, there was no need to use

Shanhai Rikusentai (A Naval Brigade of Shanghai) (1939), directed by Hisatora Kumagai.

the film to incite a war mood. The war was accepted as a simple duty to emperor and fatherland. In the same year Tasaka also made *Mud and Soldiers,* showing a scattered, indeterminate battlefront, emphasizing the endless nature of warfare. This film was shot on location in China, whereas the first film was studio-made. During this period the director Akira Iwasaki, whose political sympathies were with the Left, made a film after the fall of Shanghai to the Japanese in 1937. Although *Shanghai* was produced with the co-operation of the Japanese army, its exposure of army methods infuriated the military authorities. The "victory" was shown as anything but glorious, and achieved only at great cost in Japanese lives. The treatment of Chinese civilians was shown to be cruel.

In 1940 another humanistic war film, Kimisaburo Yoshimura's *The Story of Tank Commander Nishizumi,* set again in China, showed the commandant helping Chinese civilians and living on friendly personal terms with his men. However, such films, though popular with the public, were not to the taste of the authorities. The model became increasingly that of wartime Nazi Germany, with its severe control

Tsuchi to Heitai (Mud and Soldiers), (1939), directed by Tomotaka Tasaka.

Gonin No Sekkohei (Five Scouts) (1939), directed by Tomotaka Tasaka.

Gonin No Sekkohei (Five Scouts) (1939), directed by Tomotaka Tasaka.

Nishizumi Senshacho Den (The Story of Tank Commander Nishizumi) (1940), directed by Kimisaburo Yoshimura.

over the industry.[25] An Office of Public Information was set up in 1940, with the positive task of initiating propaganda.

The new genre of war films, before Pearl Harbor, is illustrated by the work of Yutaka Abe—*Flaming Sky* (1940), produced by Toho, showed planes in action; Eiichi Koishi made *Soaring Passion* (1941) about a farm boy who succeeds in becoming a pilot, filmed on location. Také Sado produced a more sentimental film, *Chocolate and Soldiers* (1941), about a villager who became a soldier in China and sends home chocolate wrappers for his son's collection. The father dies on a suicide mission, but when the son wins a prize with the collection he becomes the object of interest to his father's army company, and they decide to sponsor the child's education. This was meant to appeal to civilian audiences in Japan, just as Takeo Murato's *Prayer to Mother Earth* (1941), a film about nurses on the front in China, was meant to appeal to women. Another film addressed to the home audience was Tasaka's *Airplane Drone* (1939), in which a village prepares to welcome the mayor's son, who is a pilot due to fly over his native area in his plane. The film was in aid of a campaign to encourage the public to contribute to buying aircraft. Minoru Shibuya's *Cherry Country* (1941) was really addressed to women, and their need to sacrifice their private happiness or desires in time of war. Shiro Toyoda's *A Record of My Love* (1941) encouraged working women to marry and support disabled soldiers, thus saving the public money which would otherwise be needed to support the men who had done their duty by their country.

Between the period when the war opened up in 1942 and the final acceptance of defeat after the atom-bombing of Hiroshima and Nagasaki (August 1945), the Japanese were (as we shall see) to develop war subjects that represented some of the most efficient filmmaking of the war years.

Germany 1933–39

Germany during the 1920s had developed the largest film production industry in Western Europe. By the 1930s, however, the general economy was less secure following the withdrawal of substantial American investment and the political upheaval represented by the growing threat of the Nazi Party, which, battening on Germany's economic misfortunes and the high level of unemployment, increased their vote from 810,000 in 1928, with 12 seats in the Reichstag, to 13,745,000 in 1932, with 230 seats, or 37 percent of the House. Hitler was appointed chancellor in January 1933, and (following the dramatic Reichstag fire in February, Nazi allegations of danger of a Communist *coup d'état* and the consequent arrest of many of the Communist deputies in the Reichstag) pushed the Enabling Act through in March, which gave him the absolute power with which he was to rule Germany until his final defeat in 1945.

The Ministry of Propaganda and Public Enlightenment under Dr. Joseph Goebbels was established in March 1933. The film industry was already largely in right-wing, nationalistic hands, since Alfred Hugenberg, chairman of the German National Party, an ally of the

National Socialists, had bought up the principal production complex, UFA, in 1927; UFA embraced not only a considerable wing of feature production, but had control over a cross-section of German cinemas. In addition, UFA was responsible for some four-fifths of German newsreel production. When Goebbels came to power, he found a partially integrated industry at his disposal. The Party propaganda machinery had for some years made use of film records of the Party "struggle" for power at sponsored screenings all over the country.[26] Now the full resources of the nation's production of feature and factual films alike had come under his control.

Goebbels never allowed this situation to go to his head. For example, he did not want to nationalize the industry at this early stage, and he certainly did not want to empty the cinemas by demanding that every German film should henceforth become a work of propaganda. Rather what he wanted to see was a nationwide use of the cinema for popular entertainment into which he could from time to time infiltrate a state-sponsored prestige film with a strong political message. Propaganda of the "hard sell" kind was to be mainly confined to short films and newsreels, all the more effective because they were screened in well-filled theaters primarily devoted to mass entertainment.

Control of the industry was ensured in a number of ways—at the top, through increasing economic control of the raw materials of the film industry and its flow of capital, and by the establishment of strict control not only of subject matter through censorship (regularized by the Reich Film Law of February 1934), but of distribution and exhibition at home and abroad. At studio level, control was exercised by bringing all workers in the industry, artistic and technical alike, into line through the establishment during 1933 of a Reichsfilmkammer, or State Film Chamber, which controlled everyone participating in film production, including investigation into their racial origin. All Jews were automatically banned, and they were precluded, though other state chambers for the arts, from working in the fine arts, music, the theatre, authorship, press, or broadcasting. All workers had to become members of the only recognized trade union—the Deutsche Arbeitsfront; all previous unions were abolished. Goebbels even controlled film criticism; while politically "undesirable" films (such as Pabst's pre-Hitler pacifist film, Westfront 1918 or his attack on nationalism, Kameradschaft, or films in which Jews had played some part, such as Lang's M, with Peter Lorre) were banned outright, politically "desirable" films were expected to be praised in the press for their patriotism.

S. A. Mann Brandt (1933), directed by Franz Seitz.

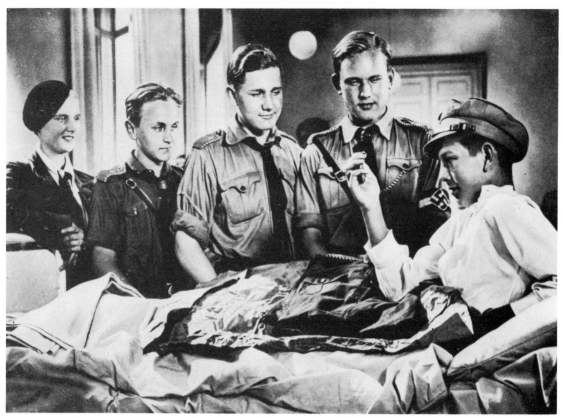

Hitlerjunge Quex (1933), directed by Hans Steinhoff.

The German film industry lost much of its hard-won international strength of the 1920s and early 1930s. The films remained technically polished, as in the entertainment films of Willi Forst and Reinhold Schünzel. But comparatively few of the German films of 1933–45 are memorable; paradoxically, those that are most memorable are among the ones specializing in political subjects and, in effect, state sponsored.

The system of state sponsorship began early; nationalistic and Party prestige films were evident from the start—for example, *Hans Westmar* (Franz Wenzler, 1933), which represented the Nazi street brawler and pimp, Horst Wessel, as a martyr killed by the Communists, and *S. A. Mann Brandt* (Franz Seitz, 1933), the story of a young Nazi also killed by the opposition. *Hitlerjunge Quex* (Hans Steinhoff, 1933) featured another murdered Nazi youth. Other films stressed German nationalism as distinct from Nazism—for example, *Der Herrscher* (Carl Froelich, 1937) with its strong emphasis on leadership in industry, and *Togger* (Jürgen von Alten, 1937), which attacked attempts by foreign powers to acquire controls in German industry. The favorite national figure of Frederick the Great appeared in several films, such as *Fridericus* (Johannes Mayer, 1936), in which the emperor, after opposing the Austrians, the French, and the Russians, returns to found the German Reich of his time, a forecast, it is implied, of Hitler a century and a half later. Films, too, harked back constantly to the First World War—from the film made before Hitler's accession, *Morgenrot* (Gustav Ucicky, 1933) to *Ein Mann will nach Deutschland* (Paul Wegener, 1934), *Patrioten* and *Pour le Mérite* (Karl Ritter, 1937 and 1938). Even the right-wing fighters, the notorious Frei-korps—the anti-Communist "defence" forces of the immediate postwar period—were celebrated in *Um das Menschenrecht* (Hans Zoberlein, 1934).

Among the earlier Nazi documentaries, *The Eternal Forest* (Hans Springer, 1936) was lyrical and "idealistic," representing the German racial stock as imperishable, an "eternal forest'" constantly renewing its youth and reaching its climax in the youthful Third Reich of Hitler. No film expressed this more forcibly than the production specially commissioned and titled by Hitler himself—Leni Riefenstahl's *Triumph of the Will* (1934–35), an emotional hymn of praise to Hitler with its setting the vast Party Rally at Nuremberg staged in Septem-

Triumph of the Will (1934-35), directed by Leni Riefenstahl.

Triumph of the Will (1934-35), directed by Leni Riefenstahl.

Triumph of the Will (1934-35), directed by Leni Riefenstahl.

Triumph of the Will (1934–35), directed by Leni Riefenstahl.

Triumph of the Will (1934–35), directed by Leni Riefenstahl.

ber 1934. In this militarism is already expressed through the mass parades of workers using spades as if they were rifles. The figures of Hitler and his associates, such as Himmler and Hess, isolated as they march through the massed ranks of their followers in the great stadium at Nuremberg, forecast the might which in a bare six years was to be opposed to the democracies of Europe. *Triumph of the Will* was made for showing at home and abroad, and it was presented at the 1935 Venice Film Festival. Another Nazi documentary, *Für Uns* (*For Us*, 1937) was in effect a film commemorating the "martyrs" of the Party, with a climax carefully staged for the cameras when the roll call of the dead men is called and those present cry collectively, "Present!" The Nazis, as the historian Siegfried Kracauer points out, had an allergy where death was concerned, and preferred to neglect it unless it represented the fate of their enemies.

In August 1939, at the time of the signing of the German-Soviet pact, Germany had to withdraw from circulation the anti-Soviet film, *Friesennot* (Peter Hagen, 1935). This film was kept in the vaults unseen until the invasion of Russia in June 1941, when it was redistributed under the title *Dorf in Roten Sturm* (*Village in the Red Attack*).

2

The War: I. Single Combat—The British Commonwealth versus Germany, 1939-41

The war opened up suddenly in Europe. Hitler's armies invaded Poland on 1 September 1939; Britain and France declared war on Germany on 3 September. By October Polish territory was being divided up in accordance with the secret treaty between Germany and the USSR; in November, as we have seen, the USSR invaded Finland. In December, the Battle of the River Plate ended with the scuttling of the German battleship, *Graf Spee*, off Montevideo, but in British home waters the German U-boats began to take their toll of the merchant ships, which were essential to the supply of the island. Meanwhile, President Roosevelt had amended the American Neutrality Act to enable Britain and France to buy arms in the United States.

April 1940 ended the apparent stalemate that had characterized the period of the so-called phoney war during which the combatants were preparing for the struggle to come. Germany suddenly invaded Denmark and Norway. Russia meanwhile had concluded a peace treaty with Finland. On 7 May Churchill took over from Chamberlain the leadership of Britain, three days after Hitler had successfully invaded Holland, Belgium, and Luxembourg. The British Expeditionary Force was evacuated from Dunkirk 29 May to 3 June, and on 10 June Italy declared war on France and Britain.[1] On 14 June the Germans entered Paris, and on 15 June the United States formally refused the French appeal for help. On 22 June France capitulated; meanwhile Russia quietly occupied the Baltic States, and later in the month crossed the frontier of Romania. Romania placed herself under German protection, and as a consequence Germany seized the Roman-ian oilfields later in the year. In August the British concluded agreements with the exiled Polish, French, and Czechoslovak governments, resident now in Britain.

During the summer of 1940 intensive German air raids began over Britain; Britain retaliated with the first night raids over Germany. The loss of British merchant shipping continued, but in the air the RAF began to impose heavy losses on German aircraft, while in North Africa the British scored their first victories against the Italians. The following March, in 1941, the British invaded Italian-occupied Abyssinia, but Germany began her drive south through Yugoslavia and her counteroffensive in North Africa. In May, the British were forced to evacuate Greece and Crete, but were, however, victorious in Abyssinia, and also sank the German battleship *Bismarck* west of Brest.

On 22 June 1941 Germany invaded Russia; the Russians abandoned occupied Poland, the Baltic States, and the territory of Romania they had invaded. On 12 July an Anglo-Russian pact of mutual assistance was signed. On 27 July the German armies penetrated the Ukraine, and by September reached the outskirts of Leningrad, advancing also in October toward Moscow from Smolensk. Only in October did the Russians manage to check the German advance short of Moscow, and launch a winter counteroffensive.

The British also mounted counteroffensives in the North African desert. Meanwhile, the Japanese had landed troops in Indo-China in July, preparatory to making their major territorial offensive early in 1942. Hong Kong was forced to surrender to the Japanese on Christmas Day. The Japanese air attack on Pearl Harbor had come on 7 December; Britain and the United States were at last able to acknowledge their full alliance against fascism when they jointly declared war on Japan the following day; on 11 December, the United States declared war on Germany and Italy. Hitler was preoccupied with the checks on his Russian front, but paused to acknowledge in public his state of war with the United States in a speech that same day.

Wartime Cinema in Great Britain

The war started for Britain with closed cinemas and live theaters, the streets darkened and the lights shaded. Extreme violence was anticipated from the skies, delivered with full force by the Luftwaffe. The image in peoples' minds was like that of the vast, black bombers that had brought wholesale destruction on the screen in *Things to Come*. But no German bombers appeared, and the places of entertainment soon reopened. In 1939 almost half the population went to the movie theaters each week, and it was recognized by the authorities that national morale depended strongly on this entrenched form of leisure-time occupation. BBC television, which had been transmitting regular programs since 1936 to the few who owned television receivers, closed down permanently on the outbreak of war. Patronage of the cinemas was to grow, not lessen, attendance rising from some twenty million a week to some thirty million by 1945. Entertainments Tax was increased to assist the war economy. To save dollar expenditure, the government restricted the annual import of American films to 400, instead of the prewar 550 to 600. Nevertheless, the legal quota for British films was dropped to fifteen percent, since home production itself sank to between fifty and sixty features a year, about half the level of 1938. Studios were requisitioned for war needs; studio staff and technicians were called up. In 1939 twenty-two studios with sixty-five sound stages had been in operation; by 1942 there were only nine studios active with thirty sound stages.

The round dozen feature films directly concerned in one way or another with war which Britain released between September 1939 and December 1941—when United States entry into the war with both Japan and Germany so greatly widened and intensified the conflict— were typical of the uncertainty with which filmmakers and the general public alike faced the war during its first phase. Until a new war establishes its actual nature (its timing and geographical location, the strategy and techniques to be adopted, the initial death rate among the armed services and civilian population, its impact on the economic and domestic life of a country, and so forth), it tends to be forecast in the popular imagination in terms of any previous war that occurred in the more immediate past. This meant for the British the First World War of some twenty years before; memories of this recalled prolonged, arduous, widespread trench warfare, horrifically costly in casualties but fought, apart from a few air raids with minimal damage, on territory outside Britain. The popular "image" of war, therefore, was daily casualty lists, a mounting toll of death that affected almost every family in the land, of women involved more fully than ever before both on the fighting fronts and in industry at home, and of privations in food because of U-boat activity against the shipping bringing in supplies. The long period of "stalemate" from September 1939 to the fall of France some nine months later, which left Britain and the Commonwealth (which seemed rather far distant) alarmingly on their own in opposition to an enemy so spectacularly successful, was quite unexpected. Apart from the unsuccessful intrusion of the British Expeditionary Force and the extraordinary outcome of Dunkirk (an "impossible" rescue operation of a kind dear to the heart of the British),

the people at home did not experience war directly until the brutal
air raids of the summer and winter of 1940–41. Then the previous
mood of dogged complacency, waiting on the inevitable event, gave
way to a mixture of alarm and rage. A mounting lust to hit back
dispelled the earlier boredom, and found immediate expression in the
magnificent resistance in the air, which became known as the Battle
of Britain.

The island began to feel like a fortress, with Churchill as commandant. At the same time the original, utterly unrealistic tendency to
regard Hitler as an absurdity, symbolized in Tommy Handley's song
identifying him with Charlie Chaplin, or dismissing the German army
as easy to defeat once Britain "got going" ("We'll hang out our wash-
ing on the Siegfried Line/ If the Siegfried Line's still there"), was
replaced in mid-1940 by a far grimmer sense of actuality. The romantic British faith in spirited amateurism (the Home guard; the brave
and brilliant action of the "little ships" at Dunkirk) gave way to the
kind of real professionalism that made the young fighter-pilots of the
RAF the golden boys of 1940–41. Britain became increasingly pro-
ficient on all fronts—the home front, the industrial front, the fighting
fronts—after the summer of 1940. One Dunkirk was enough—and so
was one fire-stricken London, Coventry, Bristol, Plymouth. The shock
of the fire raids brought home to the British public the meaning of
the German innovation of *blitzkrieg* from the air. War was being
fought this time as much—sometimes more—on the civilian home
front, than in any conveniently far-off trenches.

The films of this difficult period of adjustment, of gradual realization of what war with Hitler was really to mean to the British
people as a whole, reflect the general unpreparedness of anti-Nazi
propaganda. Once again, it was in general a case of well-meaning
amateurism giving place to a professionalism gradually acquired under
stress. The first wartime propaganda feature film was to be rushed
onto the screen, representing at least a feat of production by Alexander Korda and his colleaques. With Michael Powell, Brian Desmond
Hurst, and Adrian Brunel working as co-directors, *The Lion Has
Wings* reached the screens by November 1939. Its cost was some
£30,000, raised (according to Korda's biographer, Paul Tabori) on
Korda's life insurance policy. The story was by Ian Dalrymple. It was
shot in twelve days, and finished in five weeks; every player, star, and
bit performer alike, received an advance payment of £5 only. When
the film proved internationally successful, the senior players received
more adequate fees. The film came to be sponsored by the newly
established and very "amateur" and gentlemanly Ministry of Infor-

mation, and was shown widely abroad, especially in the United States.

On the simpler level, the film made the obvious points—contrasting the peaceful pursuits of the British people with the favorite image (so soon to become a standardized cliché) of the marching jackboots of the Nazi robot ranks. Hitler, flanked by uniformed guards and mouthing aggression, was contrasted with the quiet-looking English king, moving freely among his subjects, but ill-judged comic effects were introduced cutting in Hitler with the bleating of sheep or with bookmakers shouting their odds. Then comes war; Chamberlain's speech formally declaring that Britain is at war with Germany was cut in with scenes from "a typical English home." The isolated incident of the RAF's raid on the Kiel Canal had to be reconstructed, but authentic material was available to insert recording the return of the raiders from Germany. The actors included Ralph Richardson, Merle Oberon, Miles Malleson, Bernard Miles, and Flora Robson, mostly in small, typical parts—such as husband and wife, youthful RAF pilot and his girl—while the film was held together by a narration spoken on a quiet note by the well-known voice of the newsreel and documentary commentator, E. V. H. Emmett. An inserted extract from Korda's earlier historical production, *Fire over England,* struck a false note, but the gravest error was the inclusion of a long section about England's air defenses, with special emphasis on barrage balloons. The film was received without much enthusiasm in Britain, but was seen widely abroad. A copy was pirated for the Germans in Lisbon, and was rumored to have made Hitler very angry and to have excited derision at Britain's air defenses.

The British, in fact, were determined not to be stampeded into indulging in the kind of violent propaganda associated with Nazi Germany; they were determined, initially at least, to remain cultured and gentlemanly in the face of an enemy whom at heart they despised as uncouth—not in fact a gentleman at all. Propaganda before Churchill (and even after) was noticeably uncertain in policy, receiving little guidance from any central source. The feature film industry, apart from government wartime restrictions, was virtually left to create what propaganda stories it liked.

The result could have been forecast. Free at last to use the Nazis as melodramatic villains, the espionage subjects began to appear, stories conceived wholly as thrillers though with the Nazis specified now as the enemy. The first was Walter Summers's *Traitor Spy* (1939); Ted Healey (Bruce Cabot) works in an "anti-submarine" factory, but is in the pay of the Germans; he is detected by a British secret service agent disguised as a reporter, and finally trapped with his distressed wife in a house on the Waterloo Road, where they are suitably burnt to death. An action picture, with an elaborate plot, it was concerned to create thrills rather than make any real significance out of the betrayal of security matters to the enemy. On a different level was *Contraband* (April 1940), an intelligent thriller resulting from the combined talents of Michael Powell and Emeric Pressburger, the Hungarian writer whom Korda had brought to England. It was made very quickly and was the second film by Powell to star the German actor, Conrad Veidt. The story concerned the captain of a neutral ship who tries to avoid alike British Contraband Control and the German submarine menace. Forced to enter a British port for inspection, he becomes involved in a pursuit in blacked-out London (filmed, according to Powell, for the first time in a dramatic film), during which German Intelligence work in Britain is exposed.

Carol Reed's *Gestapo* (1940), starring Margaret Lockwood and Rex Harrison, was another thriller. Bennett of the English Secret Service (Rex Harrison) is responsible for getting the Czech inventor, Dr. Bomasch to Britain, along with his "secret invention" concerned with the manufacture of munitions. Bomasch's daughter Anna is used by the Nazis as a decoy to trap her father, and the action turns on the refugees' final escape to Switzerland, helped by Bennett and two cricket enthusiasts—the inevitable English upper-class comics (Basil Radford and Naunton Wayne). Marcel Varnel's *Neutral Port* (1940), with Will Fyffe, Leslie Banks, and Yvonne Arnaud, turned on the comic devices of a Scottish skipper (Will Fyffe) subjecting the enemy U-boats to a kind of personal vendetta because they have sunk his ship off the neutral port of "Esperanto"; he has constantly to return to port in a rowing boat after his by no means unsuccessful encounter. It is best to say that *Neutral Port* bears no relation to actuality whatsoever; it exists as a vehicle for the pawky humor of its star. Similarly, Sergei Nolbandov's *Ships with Wings*, with a background of the Fleet Air Arm and the aircraft carrier *Ark Royal*, failed to combine actuality with an elaborately romantic drama of a young flier (John Clements) dismissed the Service prewar, and subsequently involved in the German attack on Greece, where he undertakes a suicide mission because of a lost love. What was best about this film was Roy Kellino's photographic coverage of the *Ark Royal*.

Leslie Howard's *Pimpernel Smith* (1941) also turned on the personality of its director-star, who had already played the romantic period figure of the Pimpernel. In this film he is a contemporary Cambridge professor whose quick intelligence is concealed beneath the cover of absent-mindedness, and whose preoccupation is to contrive escape for distinguished refugees. Again the plot is utterly unreal, with the bulky character actor, Francis Sullivan, playing the head of the German Secret Service; the aim is still thriller-entertainment, and the propaganda is so facile that it would have been better if the Nazis had been omitted altogether, leaving the film to the skillful charm of Leslie Howard, who was two years later (in 1943) to die when the civilian plane in which he was flying was shot down by the Luftwaffe.

These films were at the lighter end of the propaganda spectrum. Other films developed at once a more romantic, but more emotionally involved attitude to the threat of Nazi victory. The first was *Pastor Hall*, (1940), John and Roy Boulting's adaptation of Ernst Toller's play, based on the experiences of Pastor Niemöller in the hands of the Nazis. Wilfrid Lawson plays a village pastor who, having denounced the regime, is sent in 1934 to a concentration camp from which his escape is contrived with the help of an SS guard who was once in his congregation. His daughter's idea is that he should flee to the United States. However he refuses, preaches once more against the regime, and so directly brings about his death. What he says in his church attempted to confront audiences with the true meaning of Nazism; indeed *Pastor Hall* was the first true and serious statement about the deprivation of the freedom of the German people by Hitler to be made in a British feature film.

Freedom Radio (Anthony Asquith, 1941), with Clive Brook and Diana Wynyard, concerns resistance in Nazi Germany on the level of two generations—that of Dr. Karl Roder, a distinguished Viennese specialist, who is anti-Nazi though his wife is a supporter of the Party, and that of the young radio mechanic, Hans, who is involved in constructing a transmitter for the German resistance on the eve of the invasion of Poland. The plot becomes complex, but not incredible; although Karl's life is forfeit, Hans survives to continue broadcasting. The propaganda value here lay particularly in the relationship of husband and wife, and the latter's disillusion with the ideology she had initially thought to be right. It also showed something of the special degree of courage necessary to resist the regime inside Germany, and implied that the German resistance was ultimately fighting on the same side as the British, even though this had virtually ceased to be recognized in Britain after the invasion of France. However, with a strong script and story involving no less than nine writers (including Louis Golding, Bridget Boland, Anatole de Grunwald, and Jeffrey Dell), *Freedom Radio* emerged as a relatively conventional film, Clive Brook remaining very English as a Viennese doctor fighting for

Pastor Hall (1940), directed by John Boulting, with Wilfrid Lawson, and Bernard Miles.

freedom, and Diana Wynyard smoothly genteel as a Nazi hostess.[2]

In *Dangerous Moonlight* (Brian Desmond Hurst, 1941), the romantic drama of war involved a Polish flier (Anton Walbrook) who is in civilian life a pianist and who escapes from Poland and finally

Dangerous Moonlight (1941), directed by Brian Desmond Hurst.

reaches the United States via Romania. In the States he plays in concerts for Polish relief work and renews his acquaintance with an American girl (Sally Gray), a journalist who had been working in Poland. The two fall in love and marry, but he cannnot be deterred from joining the Free Polish squadron in England. He crashes during the Battle of Britain, losing alike his nerve and his musical talent, but he is restored through the love of his wife. The original story was sketched out by the writer-director, Terence Young, after hearing a concerto over the radio while on duty in an army camp in 1940. The film's emotive force as propaganda was deepened by the constant resort to music, the rich bravura combination of art and warfare playing on the audience's dual response to the heroism and the culture of Poland. Richard Addinsell's celebrated "Warsaw Concerto" was composed specially for the film in the style of Rachmaninoff; it was a nine-minute pastiche composition that became immediately famous, a commercial record being rushed out from a discarded "take" recorded in the studios by Louis Kentner and the London Symphony Orchestra conducted by Muir Mathieson. A factor of importance that made this film popular was the special emotional relationship the British felt to the Poles. The British rush to arms on Hitler's invasion of Poland somehow redeemed the national honor that had seemed compromised when Chamberlain had sacrificed the Czechs at Munich. The presence of Polish men in uniform in Britain was a constant reminder that the British had at last "done right by" an oppressed people.

The most serious attempt to come to terms with the Nazi mentality, and contrast this with the democratic standpoint, was Michael Powell's and Emeric Pressburger's *49th Parallel* (1941; called *The Invaders* in the United States). This elaborate film, shot largely in Canada, was financed by the British Ministry of Information, drawing on a Treasury grant of £500,000 for propaganda feature films. It was in every respect a "prestige" production, with a fine music score by Ralph Vaughan Williams, his first for film. It was brilliantly photographed by Freddie Young, and cut by David Lean. Its stars were Eric Portman, Leslie Howard, Raymond Massey, Laurence Olivier, and Anton Walbrook.

Kenneth Clark had been put in charge of the newly established Films Division of the Ministry of Information by the Minister, Sir A. Duff Cooper, and Michael Powell (quoted in Kevin Gough-Yates's study of him) tells how, through a mutual friend, John Sutro, the idea of making an officially sponsored film was put to him by Clark:

49th Parallel (1941), produced and directed by Michael Powell and Emeric Pressburger with Leslie Howard, and Eric Portman.

We went to dinner with John, and Kenneth said, 'Would you do a film for us—we'll give you *carte blanche* on minesweeping?' I said, 'No, I don't want to do a film on minesweeping—that's sort of First World War stuff, I want to make a film about Canada. I have been reading an article in the 'Sunday Express' and it is quite obvious that Canada being next to the USA, they will help to bring the USA in'. Simple as that and Kenneth Clark said, 'It sounds rather a good idea.' Somehow Clark managed to get a grant out of the Government for about £3 or £4,000 to go to Canada and find out . . .

The film was an outstanding success, though it would have been more effective still if it could have appeared earlier, in the darker days of 1940 and early 1941. Although it cost the greater part of the Ministry's total grant of £500,000, Powell claims it grossed some £2,000,000 in the United States. He and Preminger worked for a small percentage in lieu of fee.

The story concerned the odyssey of the six survivors of a German submarine crew when their craft is sunk by the Royal Canadian Air Force in the Gulf of St. Lawrence. The film consisted of successive, interlocked episodes as the Germans, led by their commandant (Eric Portman), pass from one place to another, their numbers lessening as they progress. On one occasion, for example, they meet a Hutterite community of German refugees from Nazism; when one of the invaders transfers his allegiance from Hitler to the community he is shot by the others. Finally, the last two meet an English intellectual (Leslie Howard), an expert on Indian affairs, whose life's work they destroy, thereby turning the pacifist intellectual into a vengeful man of action. The final survivor faces a Canadian soldier (Raymond Massey) on a train bound for the undefended frontier, the 49th parallel, between Canada and the neutral United States and he is finally captured.

The film, widely praised for its effectiveness, nevertheless met with some interesting opposition, which is summarized in the very favorable review appearing in *Documentary News Letter* (*DNL*), the journal published by Film Centre during the War:

Granted, however, that the film has strong entertainment value, there still remains the consideration of its value as propaganda. Views on this appear to differ. On the negative side it has been claimed (a) that we have been so conditioned by Hollywood to being on the side of the hunted rather than the hunters that there is bound to be some sympathy with the pursued Nazis; (b) that it's a pretty poor show if six Germans can be at large for so long in a hostile country; and (c) that an episode such as that in which an Englishman is presented as a dilettante is just playing into German hands, and that the toughness of the pay-off doesn't redress the negative effect.

On the whole these accusations will probably turn out to be more academic than real. The film throughout shows signs of the most careful scripting from the propaganda point of view, and each episode may be said to be conceived as a positive answer to questions arising from insinuations regarding the democratic standpoint. . . . And if Eric Portman's brilliant performance as the Nazi commander gains a certain warmth at times, it is only in terms of that blind and fanatical loyalty which has so far been one of Hitler's major secrets of success. It is a loyalty which this film, step by step, reveals as a false faith. It just doesn't make the grade in the long run. [DNL, Nov. 1941]

The film did not make the fatal mistake of caricaturing the enemy, after the style of the old Russian "typage" of the capitalist and tsarist villains. Rather it showed the unswerving loyalty Hitler inspired along with the nature of the cold-blooded violence this loyalty engendered. No one should complain that Eric Portman created a star performance as the Nazi commandant, and in fact dominated the film —the same problem was to arise later in the case of Hitchcock's *Lifeboat*. The complex character of the intellectual, played by Leslie Howard, subtly showed the half-cynical unpreparedness of those who found themselves opposed to Hitler, while at the same time allowing him the strength to attack the Nazis once his anger at their wanton vandalism was roused. *DNL* had an interesting contemporary comment:

Leslie Howard's portrayal of the dilettante is bound to cause a certain amount of heartburn over here. But there is a good deal of justification for this particular sequence as far as opinion in the New World is concerned. Whether we like it or not, a picture of the Englishman as soft and decadent has grown up over the past ten years, especially in the USA, and it is probably good propaganda to take the bull by the horns and put him on the screen. Here the trick is to give your audience a picture of someone whom they wrongly think is representative, and to turn the tables on them by revealing him as unexpectedly tough. Whatever opinion over here may be, it's a likely bet that Howard's knock-out of the Nazi will be a good propaganda stroke in the USA.

"It is", says *DNL*, "one of the best made films ever produced in this country."

Three lesser films than *49th Parallel* attempted to introduce a greater degree of documentary realism into the war feature film. *For Freedom* (April 1940), directed by Maurice Elvey and Castleton Knight, with Will Fyffe, dealt with an isolated British naval victory during the early phase of the war, and included for climax a reconstruction of the Battle of the River Plate, with a commentary by Vice-Admiral

Harper. Men of the *Exeter* and *Ajax,* as well as captains of British merchant ships and Altmark prisoners appeared in this film, with its strong mixture of actors and servicemen in their real-life capacities. The frame-story is original—a newsreel producer (Will Fyffe) is planning to make a *March of Time*-styled film about the shadow over Europe, but events catch up on him when Hitler marches into Czechoslovakia; later his son (who had for a while after Munich prevailed on his father to abandon the film) is fortunate enough to be in Latin America at the time war is declared, and so is able to cover the *Graf Spee* incident. The film, made by Gainsborough with the cooperation of the Admiralty, had magnificent coverage of the Navy at sea, but the reconstructions of the naval battles with models were indifferent. What is specially interesting about the earlier part of the film is the astringent nature of the commentary by Fyffe and E. V. H. Emmett during the prewar vacillation at the time of Munich. *DNL,* generally praising the film, notes its timeliness since it was released during the depressing period when Scandinavia was being overrun by Germany.

This England (David MacDonald, February 1941) was a propaganda film of some eighty minutes with Emlyn Williams, John Clements, and Constance Cummings. Once again the American woman journalist comes to England to get her story, which in this case is a pageant of British history seen from the point of view of a village which in the past has had to face invasion or its threat—in Norman times, at the period of the Armada, and in the time of Napoleon; the same characters (and actors) span the centuries in an oversimplified propaganda statement.

Far more effective, since it initiated a new policy at Michael Balcon's Ealing Studios, was *Convoy* (Penn Tennyson, June 1940) with Clive Brook and John Clements. This was the first attempt at a documentary-styled war film, in which the balance was weighted fully on the factual side rather than emphasizing the artificial romantic threads that had disintegrated many previous war films, such as Balcon's own *Ships with Wings. Convoy* is concerned with the delaying action fought by the commander of a British cruiser against a German pocket battleship in order to give the ships of the convoy for which he is responsible a chance to escape destruction. *Convoy* was the most realistically constructed film of action at sea so far produced in Britain; it was once again Roy Kellino who, with Penn Tennyson, went on real convoys to obtain first hand coverage.

It is revealing to discuss something of the problems through which the official attitude to propaganda was passing in Britain—the first country to have to face these problems among the democracies

Convoy (1940), directed by Penn Tennyson, with Clive Brook.

at war with Hitler, though these also included the countries of the Commonwealth, notably Canada and Australia.

The British Ministry of Information had been preplanned and established from the first days of war, initially to guide and where necessary control and censor the media of communication (press; radio; film) for the purpose of security and the maintenance of public morale. Both the press and the BBC, as professional purveyors of information, were from the first resentful of the "amateurs" who rushed to their new, wartime desks at the Ministry and assumed an uneasy authority over what might or might not be said in print or over the air or released on the screen. There had been many preliminary discussions, dating back as far as 1935, about the exact functions a wartime Ministry of Information should fulfil. Many personalities had been envisaged for the crucial post of director-general of the Ministry, including Sir Stephen Tallents, who was specially knowledgeable about public relations in general and film in particular, and Sir John (later Lord) Reith, director-general until 1938 of the BBC. The struggles concerning censorship became paramount, the services preferring to conduct their own in preference to having censorship coordinated for them by a Ministry predominantly under civilian, civil service control. The final planning of the new Ministry was placed under Sir Samuel Hoare in June 1939, but the various directors-general designate, their deputies, and heads of departments were too often preoccupied during 1939 with other duties, as well as being for the most part ill-suited by temperament and knowledge to the tasks before them.

The Ministry, the M. O. I., based in the University of London's tall building, the Senate House, came formally into existence two days after the outbreak of war. It was not until January 1940 that Sir John Reith was invited to become Minister of Information at a time when, according to himself, the Ministry was "in notorious disrepute, the object of fierce, running criticism in Parliament and the press"; he was to take over from the first Minister, Lord Macmillan, who, as Reith put it, had "no experience of the tortuous ways of propaganda . . . too much of a gentleman." Reith, to say the least, was an unwilling victim of pressure, taking over a ministry with "no terms of reference and no authority." Reith found that, quite unlike Goebbels's highly controlled ministry in Nazi Germany, his was full of contradictions. Essential news and censorship services were subject to other ministries (such as the Foreign Office), while a virtually impossible balance of responsibilities existed as between the autonomous British press and radio (BBC) and those divisions within the Ministry that tried to maintain continuous liaison with them.

Reith attempted, in a document published later in his biography, *Into the Wind*, to summarize his views on propaganda policy in Britain as they were in January 1940. He wanted above all else to coordinate the scattered responsibilities into a single, combined administration. It was Reith who appointed Sir Kenneth Clark initially to take charge of the MOI's Films Division, though this specific task was soon to be delegated to Jack Beddington, while Clark took over supervision of all creative work initiated by the MOI. But when Winston Churchill became prime minister in May 1940, he displaced Reith as minister and appointed Sir A. Duff Cooper (later Viscount Norwich) in his place.

Duff Cooper was fifty, and ambitious, and he does not hesitate to emphasize in his autobiography, *Old Men Forget*, how unhappy he was with the task before him. He conferred about propaganda policy on 2 June with his opposite number in Paris, the French minister of information, Luc-Oliver Frossard. "An atmospere of unreality hung over our proceedings," he wrote. "We felt like a party of the condemned playing at cards while awaiting the summons to the battlefield." Nothing could have been more different than the atmosphere in Goebbels's streamlined and aggressive Ministry, where every voice was a coordinated part of a single, calculated whole. Duff Cooper's summation of the false atmosphere in the British Ministry is notable:

> A monster had been created, so large, so voluminous, so amorphous, that no single man could cope with it. . . . Ex-ambassadors and retired Indian Civil Servants abounded, the brightest ornaments of the Bar were employed on minor duties, distinguished men of letters held their pens at the monster's service.
>   . . . The presence of so many able, undisciplined men in one Ministry was bound to lead to a great deal of internal friction, and we were at the same time subjected to a continual bombardment of criticism from without.

Duff Cooper came under virulent fire himself largely because the press gathered increasing censorship was likely, while the Ministry had a network of "carefully selected" people all over the country continually testing out morale—"Cooper's snoopers" as they came to be called. Duff Cooper came finally to the conclusion that

> there is no place in the British scheme of government for a Ministry of Information. [Publicity has assumed in our days an increased importance owing to the rapidity and diverse methods of communication. We have not yet learnt how to deal with it, but let us hope that the lessons of the last war have been taken to heart. All foreign propaganda should be under the direct control of the Foreign Office. A small branch should exist to deal with it in peacetime, capable of swift and wide expansion on the outbreak of war]. . . . When I appealed for support to the Prime Minister I seldom got it. He was not interested in the subject. He knew that propaganda was not going to win the war. Looking back, I think he was right, but I could not think so at the time.

Duff Cooper was finally relieved of office at his own request, and Brendan Bracken, a friend and confidant of the prime minister, became minister from mid-1941 to the end of the war. He fulfilled the office as well as anyone could considering there was so much continual divergence between the services and other ministries in the matter of both propaganda and censorship policy.

This story of vacillation and controversy is worth outlining and contrasting with the conduct of Germany's propaganda service, which was dependent absolutely on the calculation of one man who in his turn was in close personal contact with the head of state. In Germany the minister of information issued his instructions, and that was that;

Goebbels's Ministry conducted a highly organized sales campaign for Nazi Germany at war. In Britain, the minister had unhappily to become the focal point for every kind of criticism both internally, within government circles and the service departments, and externally, from the press and the public. It is worth noting that both Reith and Duff Cooper emphasize the seeming lack of interest on the part of both Chamberlain and Churchill in the nature and administration of propaganda, in such marked contrast to the British attitude to propaganda during the First World War, when Northcliffe's organization at Crewe House was in constant touch with the Cabinet, and was believed by many to have assisted substantially in breaking German morale in 1918.

However, as everyone knows, Churchill as a personal performer on public occasions knew as well as Hitler how to weld the nation together through the emotive forces of the spoken word. But in spite of the experience gained during the First World War,[3] the British had to relearn slowly and sometimes harshly, by trial and error, the need for and nature of propaganda and wartime public relations. A hard-pressed public is quickly resentful of the "official" point of view, and rumors started carelessly or maliciously flow uncontrolled through multifarious channels of tongues. "Propaganda" itself can easily sound a dirty word in democratically organized countries, and British propaganda largely took the form of "information"—telling the public as much of the truth about the war situation as security permitted, explaining the need for this or that regulation or restriction, and boosting morale when there was fear that undue or dangerous forms of "malaise" were setting in. It was frequently necessary, for example, to release films drawing on the wealth of patriotic emotion that, in spite of divergencies, bound people together in a common warmth of feeling when things were going badly or when bombs were falling on virtually defenseless civilians.

Documentary News Letter, launched three months after the outbreak of war, and published by Film Centre, became the voice of the documentary filmmakers of Britain.[4] This small, but highly professional group of specialists had been learning their craft in Britain throughout the 1930s under the inspiring leadership of John Grierson, who was now working overseas setting up the National Film Board of Canada.[5] The movement, in spite of many brilliant members, now lacked a focal point, and the journal, especially through its hard-hitting editorials and reviews of documentary and feature films, became a platform for the expression of common feeling. *DNL* claimed that the skills of the filmmakers were being neglected or wasted by this official organization made up so largely of the "amateurs" who, they thought, only served to fill the tortuous corridors of the MOI Senate House.

Article after article in *DNL* complains of the lack of a forthright film policy in Britain. I make no apology for quoting at some length from these often finely written pieces conceived in the heart of the bad years of major defeat in Europe:

> Our policy of national publicity by film is yet to be determined, and in drafting it we begin with the advantage of a clean slate. But a policy must be written and it must be a policy which provides for the screen examination of social issues, whether controversial or not. For these can never be official secrets. If we continue to starve our cinema audiences at home or abroad of information on principles so vital that we are willing to go to war for them, it must be at the cost of throwing those principles open to world-wide doubt. . . . Can it be argued that to admit that our democracy is no lightning cure for every wartime ill would deprive the neutral countries of all faith in us and all hope of our victory? If so, the American film tradition of self-criticism should already have laid democracy low before a totalitarian blow could be struck. . . . Controversy is the lifeblood of democracy and America, by her self-criticism, has demonstrated a vitality which springs from the roots of the people. By her freedom of speech, the essential symbol of democracy, America has demonstrated a full-blooded vigour which has done much to give her the reputation of the world's greatest democracy. [March 1940]

> In the present situation, the world will pay less heed to the might of our war machine than to such evidence as there may be of the spirit of our people. [May 1940]

> . . . a nation fighting desperately to defend the present, lacks the inspiration which springs from a vision of the future. Now, more than ever, it is necessary to repair past errors and fortify national morale with an articulation of democratic citizenship as a constructive force which can mould the future. [July 1940]

> The [Films] Division has in its possession plans which cover every field of propaganda effort, from long-term prestige films right down to the day by day recording of the war. But through slowness and inefficiency it is stultifying even its own half-hearted efforts to meet the varied needs of propaganda and morale. . . . The answer, we are afraid, is too familiar. Plans are either 'under consideration'; or a few films have been put into production in a scattered and speculative manner—a few films which bureaucratic delays and inefficiency will hold-up for so long that they will have lost most of their point by the time they reach the screen. [July 1940]

In August 1940 the important decision to release a weekly five-minute film to all cinemas (information; propaganda; inspiration) was announced. The theater proprietors agreed to cooperate by screening these in every program. *DNL* meanwhile continued its campaign:

> The Germans had known all along that in the coming war, propaganda was to be as important as guns. Had we developed an equally clear propaganda conception of the democratic freedom for which we are fighting, it is not a wild statement to say that an imaginative Ministry of Information, working closely with the War Department could have done much to save the day in France. But the bravery and strategy of our troops and airmen and the men in the little boats were not matched by an equal bravery of outlook, and an equal moral strategy on the part of the Ministry. . . . It was the Ministry's job to give the Government a lead on the vital matter of public information. If the Treasury held up money, it was the Ministry's job to fight for it. The function of a lively Ministry of Information can never be to accept orders and to carry out other people's ideas or, because other people have no ideas at all, to do nothing. [September 1940]

> The defeat of the Ministry of Information in its recent struggle for increased powers was appropriately announced in the House of Commons by Sir John Anderson, the choice of whom as Government spokesman would appear to have been a definite indication that neither the War Cabinet nor the Prime Minister have any real belief in the importance of propaganda, or, for that matter, the informational services. Briefly stated, the policy of the Government is retention of the Foreign Office stranglehold, refusal to grant greater responsibility as regards news to the MOI, and in general the maintenance of the *status quo*—that is, chaotic and unco-ordinated conditions due to the fact that the MOI is debarred from any authoritative say in the expression of national policy. Practically the entire press (including 'The Times') has greeted the Government's decision with something near execration; and this attitude correctly expresses the general feeling of the public. [July 1941]

In October 1940, *DNL* discussed the nontheatrical plans announced by the MOI Films Division—to put seventy-six sixteen-millimeter projectors on the road in the charge of full-time projectionists based in the various regions into which Britain was divided for civil defense purposes, and where the MOI maintained its regional offices. Film programs were to be made up of existant, independently produced information films from British, Commonwealth, and Allied sources, selections from films already commissioned by the MOI (such as the best of the five-minute releases), and further films specially commissioned for this service (including domestic, agricultural, and civil defense propaganda and instruction). It was estimated that the audiences reached by these means, outside the cinemas and on their home ground in town, village, factory, and institution, could amount to one million.[6]

All the films involved were gathered into the newly established Central Film Library and were available for public borrowing—one hundred were listed in the Library's first catalogue issued in May 1941. The Ministry encouraged this open public use by providing a limited number of projectors for such institutions as public libraries.

In a *DNL* survey in June 1941, the position is clearly recognized that films are now fully established in the broad field of the British Commonwealth at war—in Canada (under Grierson), in India (under Alexander Shaw), in Australia and New Zealand. Nevertheless, with the war in its twenty-first month, there was still an uneasy feeling about the central propaganda content of the films, now that their screening was on so extensive a scale, especially in the vital area of the United States (with its fifteen thousand movie theaters) during that nation's final months of peace. Correspondence between like-minded filmmakers on both sides of the Atlantic led to the point quoted from an American correspondent—"the films are grand but we are not so sure about the message they carry."

> The documentary movement is bound to feel that it was early in the field against fascism, and that it can bring to bear upon the present issues a mature and sophisticated eye. It is hard to forget that our present European war against fascism began in Spain, and that we are still in the throes of proving that it was not also lost there. Yet Spanish fascism was (and is) tolerantly regarded by many people who remain in high places in this country, and whose anti-fascism is presumably of very recent and unusual vintage.
>
> Is it then surprising if documentary film-makers occasionally detect a nervousness in some quarters to face the implications of a fully matured anti-fascist policy? . . . Films of democracy on the social offensive are missing. . . . Because of the absence of any new social vision from our screens, documentary propagandists feel they are being given no opportunity to combat Nazi propaganda for a New Order with propaganda for social progress by democratic methods. [June 1941]

The discussion of "war aims" inevitably met with one reply only from the Cabinet—the only war aim that mattered now was to win the war. To discuss anything further would be both dangerous and politically divisive. This was to become a long-standing source of contention between the broadly Left and the broadly Right in the vocal areas of the nation. *DNL* went on:

> . . . our propaganda campaigns must be based on a forward-looking conception which is prepared here and now for the permanent jettisoning of all the brakes on progress, represented by 'bitter greybeards', the mentally stunted reactionaries, and the bloodless bureaucrats who

live of their own freewill, in a Hades of paper, tape and rusting type-writers.

Further stock-taking took place with the appointment of Brendan Bracken: *DNL* urged him to "make the MOI into a department with the power in its own, instead of other hands."

The transworld alliance represented by the entry of Russia into the war, and the increasing alignment of the United States with the British Commonwealth against Hitler appeared as a great new oppor-tunity to the writers of *DNL*:

> Today, Britain and her Empire, Russia, China, and the USA are firmly ranged as an anti-fascist bloc. Division is at last sharply defined. Churchill confers with Roosevelt. A three-power conference is held in Moscow. The International set-up when peace shall have been won has now taken on a more definite shape. All this makes it at last possible for a reconsideration of propaganda on a wider and more powerful basis. It is no longer sensible for each national government to operate its propaganda machine—be it good or bad—from a purely individual standpoint. The path lies open for a joint and unified effort, and at the end of that path is a post-war prospect which we must at all costs try, as best we may, to focus now. . . .
>
> True propaganda should be firstly concerned with the dissemination of knowledge, and thereby linked with education; secondly its aim should be persuasion and not imposition; thirdly it should be regarded as a science which is largely useless unless it can operate over the surface of the whole globe, and unless it can use those media with the widest and most immediate coverage, such as radio, film and printing. There is only one other requisite—that it must be operated by experts, and in the interests of humanity at large. [September 1941]

Such was the position at the time of Pearl Harbor and the American entry into the war.

But what films had been produced that could be held in any way to be outstanding during this long-drawn-out propaganda struggle? The GPO Film Unit, formerly under Grierson but led now by Alberto Cavalcanti, the celebrated Brazilian who had come from France to as-sist Grierson in 1934, stepped off with a twenty-three minute study of Britain in September 1939—*The First Days*,[7] a quiet factual record of what preparedness for war in London meant in simple human terms, such as the first air-raid warning, the first use by the public of the air-raid shelters, the evacuation of old people and children from danger areas, the temporary closure of theaters and cinemas, the continuing life of hospitals, the black-out, and so forth, ending with London stand-ing alert in the sunlight on the second day of war, ready for the "blitz" that did not on this occasion come. It was an impressionist, slice-of-life film, its interest centering in the often very subtle human details it had managed to catch—a record film the propaganda value of which lay in its restrained, almost meditative value—people retaining their personal identity in the face of an unknown violence to come. But it was an isolated exercise, shot in September and released in November.

There was a long gap before the next film of note, *Squadron 992* (Harry Watt, April 1940). This was produced by the GPO Film Unit before its adoption by the Ministry under the name of the Crown Film Unit (April 1940).[8] The film played twenty-five minutes, and featured a unit of the Balloon Barrage from training to action, when they were posted to guard the Forth Bridge in Scotland after the notorious German raid early in the war, which is brilliantly reconstructed in the film. Harry Watt, director of *North Sea*, knew his men and encouraged them to record their experiences with an authentic, personal, laconically humorous touch. The photography by Jonah Jones and the music by Walter Leigh secured the full artistry of this film.

But, like *The First Days*, it epitomized the mood of a brief moment in the continuum of war, and needed to be shown to saturation as soon as ever possible. What is valuable at one moment in this intimate style of filmmaking can be, if not disastrous, at least unhappily inappropriate the next. *Squadron 992* belonged to the "waiting war"; its subject was, of course, essentially defensive, and in concentrating on the humanity of the people involved Watt drew the best there was to be drawn out of the situation. But the film remained still substantially unseen when Hitler's European campaigns were succeeding so precipitately, and balloons, however useful in practice against dive bombers or low-flying aircraft, were the wrong image to oppose to Hitler's sudden blitzkrieg on France. The film, ready by early April, had still not been publicly released by early June, while in September it had reached the United States, where (according to a DNL correspondent) it was felt to be too long and "too late," its reconstruction of the Forth Bridge raid too "slight" and lacking anything of the urgency of the newsreels showing convoys being shelled in the English Channel. So it was recut to a single reel to "get some pace into it."

By now, however, with the war a year old, the films were beginning to flow—*Men of the Lightship* (David MacDonald, 1940), another GPO Film Unit production, told the story of an air attack on an unarmed lightship, and served to generate anger. But however well made, the film still represented a "defensive" attitude. It did not suggest that the British might one day win the war, but rather that they were

Men of the Lightship (1940), directed by David MacDonald.

brave and calm-minded sufferers on land and sea awaiting a fate
dictated by Hitler. After all, the British had declared war on Hitler,
and were not the victims of his unannounced aggression. However in
the defensive vein some good work appeared—J. B. Priestley's finely
spoken *Britain at Bay* (September 1940) proclaimed the spirit of Britain after the fall of France in doggedly emotional terms; *Health in
War* (Pat Jackson, 1940) revealed the plans to maintain the health
services. *Behind the Guns* (Montgomery Tully, 1940), on the other
hand, gave an impressionistic account of round-the-clock labor in the
war industries, the furnaces and foundries, the munitions works and
shipyards; it was propaganda of the unanalytical, hammer-blow class,
a crescendo of image and music. But the film that won all the heartfelt praise at home and abroad was one released in versions—the one-
reel *London Can Take It* and the five-minute *Britain Can Take It*
(Harry Watt and Humphrey Jennings, 1940), the projection of the
Battle of Britain and London under bombing with a droning but sin-
cerely emotional commentary by the American correspondent, Quentin
Reynolds of *Collier's Weekly*.[9] It brought tears to the eyes of the Brit-

Wartime newsreel, period of the Blitz (1940).

Wartime newsreel, period of the Blitz (1940).

London Can Take It (1940), directed by Harry Watt and Humphrey Jennings.

London under bombing (1940).

ish and Americans alike, although the very title reflected the old defensive attitude. As some said at the time, "Why the hell can't Britain dish it out!" But the wonderful authenticity of this American talking (seemingly) while the bombs came down on a London lit up by fire was first-rate and immediate propaganda, mostly for the United States.

Some of the five-minute films were purely domestic and instructional, on salvage, for example, or careless talk. Some were "inspirational," such as Humphrey Jennings's *Words for Battle* (1941), with its quotations from English poetry and prose spoken (somewhat reverentially) by Laurence Olivier while emotive scenes of British life and landscape counterpointed the words of Shakespeare, Milton, Browning, Blake, and others, not forgetting Churchill himself. Such films "softened up" audiences, but there was a tougher propaganda attitude in *Dover Front Line*, with a pugnacious pay-off by the mayor speaking from under a forbidding bowler hat.

By now the Crown Film Unit had been established under the imaginative leadership of Ian Dalrymple, who became producer in August 1940, and was to be responsible for many of Crown's finest productions until 1943, when he became an associate producer with Alexander Korda on the latter's return to Britain from the United States. One of the outstanding films of 1941 was *Merchant Seamen* (J. B. Holmes). This twenty-five minute film began with the torpedoing of a merchantman on its way to join a convoy. The shipwrecked men are picked up, and one of them, a youngster, decides to take a gunnery course before joining a new ship. On a second convoy he is responsible for sinking a U-boat. However, it was not so much the war action, excitingly done though this was, that mattered, but the humanely dramatized handling of the men involved, their life at sea and on land. Humphrey Jennings made the one-reel *Heart of Britain* (U.S. title, *This is England*, 1941) for Crown, another poetic survey of Britain at war, this time centered in the Midlands and the North of England, including the Halle Orchestra playing Beethoven and the Leeds Choral Society singing "The Messiah." However, it was Harry Watt once again who stole public attention with the short feature, *Target for Tonight* (August 1941), the story of a deliberately routine raid over Germany, one of the chain of similar raids the RAF conducted nightly as the public heard on the radio the next morning—"Aircraft of the Bomber Command last night attacked industrial objectives at Freihausen. Fires were started and heavy high explosive bombs were seen to burst on the Target." As the anonymous, in this case RAF, reviewer put it in the *DNL* review:

Everything is in order, though first there is the Wellington in the air to remind the audience of the essential in a mass of detail. The photographers annotate the target, the Air Staff decide when, how, and with what strength it is to be attacked, a mild civilian looks at the weather, an energetic Station Commander extracts information from his intelligence officers, the crews casually accept the instructions of the experts, the mechanics get the aircraft ready, the crews put on their flying kit, and the night begins. And so do the moments of emotion in the film.

The camera is used as a most flexible instrument, recording every mood so well that one hardly feels the need of speech. The pilot's face lit by the flash of an anti-aircraft shell, the long procession of cloud-scapes which so skilfully suggest the long voyage to Germany, the anxious silhouettes of station and squadron commanders waiting in the mist for a late bomber to return—these require no commentary to drive their meaning home. But elsewhere speech is almost as illuminating and there is something almost uncanny in Mr Watt's art of turning everyone into a master of highly realistic acting. He does it, of course, by recording single sentences at a time.

This film hit the note needed; this was Britain "dishing it out" not in terms of crude newsreel coverage or pedestrian documentary, but in terms of understanding the kind of men who had to make these dangerous missions as a nightly exercise in their dark Wellingtons.

Target for Tonight (1941), directed by Harry Watt.

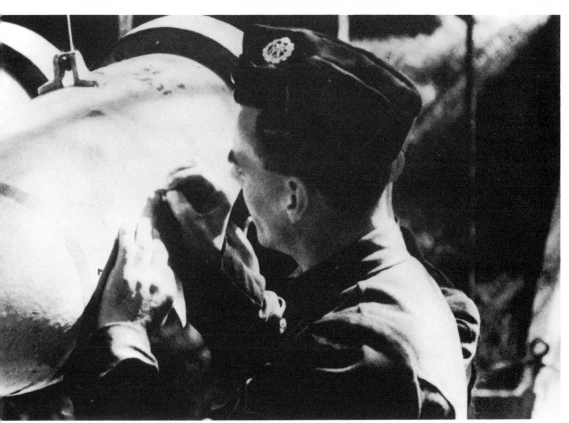

Target for Tonight (1941), directed by Harry Watt.

Merchant Seamen (1941), directed by J. B. Holmes.

Target for Tonight was to become one of the most celebrated documentaries of the war, partly through the sheer timeliness of its release. It was widely shown in the United States, Canada, and South America.

The March of Time, September 1939–December 1941

The main series of issues during this two-and-a-quarter-year period were devoted to North America. *The March of Time* (still, until 1943, in the charge of Louis de Rochemont) concentrated on aligning American opinion with the British and the Commonwealth at war. Very early in 1940 *Canada at War* (V, 12: April 1940) appeared. It epitomized Canada's contribution to the war effort, acting as a vast supply base for the sea convoys to Britain and as a training center for tens of thousands of pilots and crews for the RAF and the Royal Canadian Air Force. Canada's population at this period was only eleven million, but Americans in particular could judge from this film what Canada had set out to do in advance of what they themselves might one day have to undertake on a vastly greater scale. Even John Grierson appeared momentarily, in the words of *DNL*, "censoring a screen battleship." By this time he was in charge of the Film Board.

The March of Time then turned through 1940–41 to a succession of issues that dealt with United States preparations for what was known at this stage as her "defense." *America's Youth* (VI, 3: July 1940) concerned the twenty-one million young people whose future was threatened by war. Though dealing primarily with their normal social life—college education (mostly coed) and training for well-paid careers for the privileged minority; no college education and a much harder life for the majority—the film also faced the effects of the depression on youth—unemployment (as high as one-fourth of American youth), frustration, lowered health, a twenty-two-percent increase in the city crime rate committed by youth, culminating in the significance of the war in Europe and the decline of the Atlantic as a strong protective barrier between the two continents. Hundreds of Americans were already enlisting in Canada; thousands were enlisting in the United States armed forces, with far more applicants than the services could absorb. The film cited case histories from the records of the American Youth Commission. Succeeding issues in 1940 dealt with the expansion of the American navy (VI, 4: August 1940), with the increase of its air arm to ten thousand planes, and the all-important extensions to be made to the Panama Canal, with its strategic link to the British, French, and Dutch colonies in the Caribbean. This latter issue, *Gateways to Panama* (VI, 5: September 1940), foresaw possible German exploitation of weaknesses in the Caribbean island chain, notably in French Guiana, site of Devil's Island penal colony. The security of the islands rested now, after the fall of France and Holland, it was claimed, with the American navy.

During the period of peace left to the United States (from September 1939 to Pearl Harbor in December 1941), *The March of Time* released over twenty issues with subjects relevant to the war or the prewar situation in the Pacific, Australia, and China; in Europe; and in North and South America, the bias in quantity naturally favoring the home area. In addition, in 1940, a feature-length film, *The Ramparts We Watch*, gave a historical survey of America since 1914, seen from the point of view of a single, typical community in Connecticut, New England.[10] Louis de Rochemont took the Nazi bull by the horns and incorporated sections of *Baptism of Fire*, the film celebrating the German victory in Poland, into this *March of Time* survey, but with a new, anti-Nazi commentary. The German Embassy, which had been trying to arrange for the distribution of the original in the United States without success, threatened *The March of Time* with a lawsuit.

The four issues dealing with the Pacific, Australia, and China began with *Crisis in the Pacific* (V, 10: February 1940). It dealt first of all with Hong Kong surrounded by the armies of Japan. The tone of the film is critical of America's role in this situation, having supplied Japan with raw materials; perhaps, it is suggested, the United States can put a brake on Japanese aggression, especially since she has an important foothold in the Pacific on the small island of Guam, which, as part of the United States rearmament program, was being rapidly strengthened as a base for the United States fleet.

The March of Time did not refer to the Pacific area again for over a year, when in May 1941 an issue was devoted to *Australia at War* (VI, 3: June 1941). This survey of Australia's virtually self-contained war effort by her seven million population was related to the total strategic pattern in the South Pacific, alongside the Dutch East Indies, Singapore, Hong Kong, and not least the islands of Hawaii, where the United States Navy was assembled (with its main base at Pearl Harbor) acting as a watchdog to Japan. Meanwhile, in the roster of subjects China reappeared in *China Fights Back* (VII, 3: August 1941); the commentary argued that China in her long-term resistance to Japan had borne longer than anyone the heat of the battle that free men everywhere should be fighting. The issue reviewed the manpower of Japan and her potentiality for continuing the struggle. It also surveyed as it had done in 1936 and 1937 the domestic achievements of Chiang Kai-shek for the new China, and how the Japanese had demolished much that had been built—houses, hospitals, schools, and so forth. The Chinese had withdrawn to the interior of their vast country, carrying all they could salvage on their backs, in some cases whole factories transported in this way in minute sections. There were shots of the Burma Road supply route under attack, and the film did not hesitate to show the dead amid the ruins caused by the bombs.

The European scene was covered initially early in 1940 by an eighteen-minute issue on *The Republic of Finland* (V, 11: March 1940), which was made in the general atmosphere of sympathy felt for the small, twenty-one-year-old state in its struggle with the invader, a battle that seemed so utterly unequal. The history of Finland—from the twelfth to the nineteenth century it had been a province of Sweden, and from 1809 to 1917 a dependent of Czarist Russia—and the sturdy construction of its modern economy were outlined. Stalin's demands in 1939 for territorial concessions had led to war, and it was stated that Americans of Finnish origin were doing much to help their beleaguered kinsmen. In spite of Finland's victories, her survival appeared increasingly to depend on such outside support.

Britain's RAF (VI, 5: October 1940) followed, and the tone of the *DNL* review is interesting for its reflection of the mood of the period, both British and American:

> It is not really a satisfactory job. It opens with an air battle over Dover, including some sensational shots of barrage balloons being shot down and the AA shells bursting round the machines, and then goes on to a review of the Fighter, Bomber and Coastal Commands, passing en route a meeting of the Air Council and the Canadian training scheme. . . . As the hypnotising voice of the commentator booms on, we suddenly find that we have passed from one Command to the next without noticing it. . . . It is high time they learned that you can't establish facts and figures over shots of youths filing through doorways and such like fill-ups; March of Time ought to be above such laziness and sloppy scripting. But where they get down to showing an actual job being done, as in the work of Coastal Command, the film comes alive, though the emphasis on the Lockheed Hudsons being American seems overstrained. Perhaps American war jitters and their feeling of helpless frustration precludes them from balanced comment on the war. Otherwise they could never have committed the dreadful bloomer of finishing the film with trainees singing, in no very enthusiastic fashion, that mournful dirge 'There'll always be an England'.

On Foreign Newfronts (VI, 6: November 1940) came in the same period. It showed the most dramatic news stories of the year as reported by United States press and cameramen—the defense of Westerplatte fortress at Danzig against the Germans; the Russian entry into

Eastern Poland; the "quiet confidence" of the French army before the invasion, followed by the evacuation at Dunkirk and the fall of France; Roosevelt's condemnation of Italy when she entered the war; coverage of the Battle of Britain and the stand Britain put up as the sole remaining opponent of Hitler in Europe. This was followed virtually a year later by *Men of Norway* (VII, 6: November 1941), which showed how free Norwegians were helping to supply Britain by carrying more than half of the gasoline and oil coming into the island, while in Canada others were training to be pilots. Meanwhile, in Norway, resistance to the occupation forces was making the life of Germans stationed there hazardous following the valiant sixty-two-day battle against invasion.

Peace—by Adolf Hitler (VII, 4: September 1941) was a film directed against isolationists in the United States during the last months preceding American entry into the war. The technique adopted was to show Hitler's broken promises as offered, one by one, to neutral countries, and then abandoned—the last being the Russo-German peace pact broken the previous June. The implication was that ultimately the United States would be faced by the threat of a Europe under Hitler's dictatorship. The DNL has a valuable comment to make on the fall-off in technical adroitness in recent issues of *The March of Time*:

The approach is dry and academic and without that delayed dramatic punch which can come from clever understatement. This fault has lately been noticeable in many *March of Time* items. One has the impression that less care than formerly is taken with the commentary and that, as a result, the dramatic overtones and emphases which were once a characteristic, particularly of the international items, are now missing. There are few examples these days of the old *March of Time* trick of giving a line of commentary an unexpected twist by a particularly brilliant choice of image. One remembers, also, the opposite process of giving new significance to a familiar image by some *mot juste* in commentary. The item on Austria of a few years ago was particularly strong in such examples of *March of Time* virtuosity in relating picture to the spoken word. You may remember that it ended with a megalomaniac extract from 'Mein Kampf' viciously attacking France and asserting Germany's determination to dominate the world, and that this was illustrated with quiet scenes of French peasants working amongst German war graves of 1914–18. It is very much to be hoped that *March of Time*, which still leads the field in pictorial journalism, is not going to slip back into commonplace, run-of-the-week, picture-commentary stuff. There obviously must be a danger of staleness after so many years of the same kind of production, and perhaps all that is needed is a reminder of the original *March of Time* discovery that the greatest dramatic power does not come exclusively from picture or from commentary but from the imaginative skill with which the two are related. [October 1941]

In 1941, *The March of Time*'s policy was obviously to concentrate even further on preparing the American public for entry into war with Germany. The very titles show this—*America Prepares* (VI, 10: February 1941), covering war industries and the training of a "citizen army"; *Labour and Defence—USA* (VI, 11: April 1941), a survey of labor disputes during the First World War and after, and the need to avoid anything of this kind which might sabotage current war production; and *America Speaks Her Mind* (VI, 10: March 1941). The latter surveyed the war scene in Europe and the general effect it had had on the United States. The picture consisted primarily of German-shot material including emotive scenes of the occupation of France. Finally, Britain's dependence on increased American help was emphasized, while at the same time some German material was incorporated to show damage inflicted by the RAF. This film was plainly pro-British, anti-Nazi propaganda, and was reinforced by *Crisis in the Atlantic—1941* (VII, 1: June 1941), in which the story of the Atlantic convoys was told, emphasizing the importance of the new American bases in Greenland to the defense of the United States and to the further protection of British merchantmen at sea. *G-Men Combat Saboteurs* (VII, 2: July 1941) showed FBI action against espionage in American defense industries, while *Sailors with Wings* (VII, 7: December 1941) returned once again to the Atlantic and showed the part United States naval aviation and aircraft carriers were playing in the protection of the convoys.

In the 1941 Spring issue of *Sight and Sound*, Louis de Rochemont as managing editor of *The March of Time* had launched a scathing attack on the ineffectual nature of British film propaganda, contrasting it unfavorably with that coming from Germany. It was intended as the tough, uncompromising advice of a good friend:

> With one lone exception, that of the Crown Film Unit short commented by Quentin Reynolds and sold here as *London Can Take It*, no British-made message-film has had any lasting impact on the American public.
>
> The favourable position of British propaganda here is attributable to the fact that America, psychologically, is *in* the war, and audience-attitudes are strongly bent towards Britain. Then, too, the British blockade of the Continent, though imperfect, has managed to reduce the supply of Axis propaganda films to a mere trickle. But in spite of the fact that audiences do not want to see German films, and in spite of their scarcity, those which have come through have been

remembered. *Feldzug in Polen* and the later *Blitzkrieg im Westen* were most effective as released by the Germans through their specialised cinemas in the German quarters of several of our large cities. . . .

Since Britain has in a great degree won its own battle for audience-consciousness by the daily newspaper and radio reports of how bravely its people are resisting Hitler in their homes and at their work, the task of the films themselves is not to convert but to reassure and explain. The American public is already solid on the justice of the essential British case; to-day it needs to be made constantly aware of the fact that in accepting Britain as a symbol of right it has made no mistake. . . .

British films, news reel or other, have laid far too much emphasis on the slap-happy character of British resistance. . . .

We Americans are an excessively violent people, and when we get confused and irritated we are likely to sock somebody in the jaw. We don't much care who it is. The nearest person, mostly. This is a definite *katharis* for us, and we feel better after it. And we like to see others acting in the way that we consider normal. The films which have come from England have given Americans little emotional support in this respect. We have seen all types and conditions of men and men smiling amid inconceivable ruins. We have seen them do "thumbs up". We have heard them sing. And we feel, more and more, that if we were in the same boat we would not feel that way about it at all. And since we are beginning to climb into the boat with you, we wish you would act a little more the way we would.

Americans, after as much war as there has been, are somewhat suspicious that "business as usual" underlies the British way of war even now. The Germans, in their films, have carefully kept away from us any indication that life is pursuing its even tenor in Germany, though we suspect that since Germany has been living on a war footing for many more years than Britain there is relatively little external change. The German propaganda films have definitely kept up the illusion of a continuous forward march, created the image of something rolling which will be difficult to stop. British films have given the all-over impression of the Empire as an immovable object, and however sound and true this may be, it just isn't good drama or good cinema.

Therefore, America needs now films from Britain which will show the nation on the offensive, both on the war fronts and the home front. . . . Such films full of progress and action would be infinitely convincing to us that Britain was ready, once the war was won, to do more than merely restore the *status quo ante*.

First you must win the war, we agree. We want you to win it. We want to help. But if we are to judge by the films you send us, we feel entitled to say "Wipe that silly grin off your face and get in there and punch!" As a matter of fact, we know that you are in there punching, but it isn't through your films that we learn it, except in an occasional glimpse of a set, stern face in the third row from the lens. If your ordinary people are too shy and embarrassed in front of the camera, you may have to use actors. But if the idea should permeate all your directors and cameramen and documentarians that the period for slap-happiness for export has gone by, I think they would soon begin to turn out the real stuff for us in America, and for you too.

So far, the most effective British propaganda has come from the American cutting-rooms and studios. This is easier for us because we can talk about England in that curious way we like to think about her. We can say the things which your own reserve forbids you to say. We can be as corny as we please about it, corny in the good old American way which has made Hollywood the capital of the mass emotions of the world. . . .

England, according to good and reliable friends of mine, is putting on the greatest show on earth, full of thrills and drama and emotion, better than anything Hollywood will ever imagine. We feel we should be getting more of this in our cinema, where we Americans go for our emotional purges.

Germany, 1939–1941

For Germany the period of the war that saw the greatest measure of success was 1939–41. The fact that the United States declared war on Germany on 11 December 1941 (five days after Pearl Harbor) almost passed as a formality. Hitler's attention was fixed on Russia and the consolidation of the deep inroads he had made into Soviet territory, frustrated only by the failure to overrun Leningrad and Moscow before Russian resistance and the hard Russian winter froze his armies to a standstill.

The propaganda films the Germans made during this period of their ascendency in Europe reflected the mood of elation and triumph. The feature-length documentaries, *Baptism of Fire* (*Feuertaufe*, Hans Bertram; April 1940) and *Victory in the West* (*Sieg im Westen;* January 1941) represented national self-congratulation on the grand scale, their corresponding parallels later to be the films made by the Allies following the counterinvasion in Europe—notably *The True Glory* (Garson Kanin and Carol Reed, 1945). The German army, navy, and air force alike had their celebratory documentaries—such as *Front im Himmel* (1940), which concerned the air-raid defenses in Germany and the bombing of Britain.

The essential factor in the German documentaries was their frontline actuality—if Nazi statistics may in this instance be trusted, twenty-three camera war correspondents lost their lives between September 1939 and April 1940. Whatever tricks of propaganda emphasis might be played through editing or commentary, the visual material on the screen was strikingly authentic, and thrust the viewer into the jaws of violent warfare. Goebbels set the highest store by the German newsreel service, and lengthened the newsreels, which frequently extended up to forty minutes, and gave up-to-the-minute coverage of the fighting fronts. The prints were increased in number and delivered by the speediest means to every cinema, with high priority over the feature film. In this way, the newsreels became in their way the center of the program, the *raison d'être,* as it were, of a wartime visit to the cinema, supported by the entertainment that followed them. Every effort was made to ensure that the maximum number possible in the population saw the feature-documentaries, such as *Baptism of Fire,* which were often compilation films of the highspots of past newsreels relating to a given campaign, supplemented by specially shot material.[11] These victory prestige films were shown to invited audiences of diplomats in such vulnerable capitals as Bucharest, Oslo, Belgrade, Ankara, Sofia, and elsewhere. The German public, too, pressed into listening to the radio war reports and reaching the daily press coverage of victories east and west, became saturated, as if through some giant, highly coordinated advertising campaign, with the messages of victory and goaded into the supreme efforts and sacrifices needed to secure Hitler's expanding aggression.

In his analysis of Nazi wartime propaganda techniques in film, Siegfried Kracauer in *From Caligari to Hitler* points out how the onset and outcome of a blitzkrieg campaign was usually compressed into a single crescendo of continuity, eliminating any reference to the realities of resistance or the moments of set-back that the enemy might have mustered. The German development of blitzkrieg thus appears like some kind of irresistible magic, of which the ministers are the screaming, dive-bombing Stukas, plunging down from the sky like avenging thunderbolts. Maps were used with stabbing arrows showing the overwhelming advances of the invading armies. Nazi territory was shown gleaming white, while enemy territory was symbolically black, the powers of light opposed to those of darkness. Nazi newsreels were not informative, they were impressionist, emotive, all-conquering—a blitz in themselves of sound and image. The enemy always appeared to be humiliated to the point of absurdity, or at least utter, frozen inactivity—he was a mere gaping observer of the all-conquering armies which rolled swiftly and unopposed along his roads, his streets, or crept hideously on caterpillar tracks over his fields. Meanwhile music, bombastic, Wagnerian, hymnlike or merely gay and tuneful, mocked the civilian and soldier alike who failed to stem this onslaught by the Führer.

These films say, or imply, only what policy dictates they should say, or imply.[12] Their emphasis is on the invincible might of the German armed services; there is little or no reference to the National Socialist Party or the regime as such. Only the armed services, Hitler, their leader, and the swastika emblem prevail. Hitler, too, passes through apotheosis—at first ever-present, the leader among his generals, he becomes more and more remote visually as time and the war evolve. Only his name rings clear on the sound track, his visible presence on the screen attentuated, limited to the occasional "war leader" shot, bending over maps, attended by a silent, ministering general staff. Actual information about planning or organization is minimal, deliberately left on the impressionist level. The films are weighed down with scenes of warfare, men in action, the spearhead of actual, penetrative fighting; advance follows advance follows advance. Such scenes are supplemented by shots of the "soldiers behind the scenes," the handsome young protagonists in Hitler's drama, idealistic and upward-looking with the sky reflected in their eyes. These are the men of the "new order," the dynamic German "revolution." They are, under Hitler, men of destiny. The German penchant for myth, for the irrational, always predominates. As Kracauer has pointed out, there is virtually a complete absence of death and even of wounds in any severe form in these films, as if myth must not be soiled by such alien realities.

At the same time the enemy is denigrated—the Poles are shown as degenerate, torturing German victims (*Baptism of Fire*), the French as flippant, the British as absurd—representative of "powers" that for centuries have surrounded Germany and malevolently conspired to crush her. This picture enhances the myth—the phoenix rise of the youthful nation against ancient, demonic powers that encircled her, the conspirators of Versailles. The challenging voice at the end of *Baptism of Fire* mocks Chamberlain and the British as the airborne cameras peer down on the ruined shell of Warsaw:

> What have you to say now, Mr. Chamberlain? Here you will find conclusive evidence of the catastrophe you brought about in the Polish capital. Do you not fear the curse of a betrayed people? Here you have the results of your unprincipled war politics. All this is your work, yours is the guilt, and you will have to answer for it one day at the last judgment. And remember one thing: this is what happens when the German Luftwaffe strikes. They will also know how to strike at the guiltiest of the guilty.

After a short speech by Göring praising the Luftwaffe for its "feats which will go down to posterity," the film ends with a rousing Luftwaffe song:

> Thus our youngest weapon has been baptized and tempered in the

Baptism of Fire (1940), directed by Hans Bertram.

flames. Now the winged host reaches out to the sea; we are ready
for battle. Forward against the British Lion, for the 1st decisive blow.
We sit here in judgment, an Empire is crumbling—to this end, German
soldiers are fighting. . . .
Do you hear the password? Forward at the enemy! Do you hear the
password? Forward at the enemy! Onward! Onward! Bombs on
England! Bombs, bombs, bombs on England!

The structure of such campaign films as *Baptism of Fire* is essentially dramatic, even epic, dependent on emotional drive from climax,
to climax, pausing now and then for "rests" with peaceful, even idyllic,
"by-play."

Fiction films commending the spirit of the Luftwaffe were made
parallel to the feature documentaries. For example, *Stukas* (Karl Ritter, 1941) had for its background the conquest of Western Europe,
the debacle of Dunkirk, the moral collapse of France, the defeat of
the British Expeditionary Force. Ritter's other military films of 1941
were *Over Everyone in the World* (*Über Alles in der Welt*) on the
fate of Germans outside Germany when war was declared, and *Cadets*
(*Kadetten*), a period film with anti-Russian undertones, originally
made in 1939.

In the category of nationalist films *Bismarck* (Wolfgang Lieben-

Stukas (1941), directed by Karl Ritter.

einer, 1940) stands out. In the Nazi national mythology, Bismarck ranks alongside Frederick the Great as the outstanding unifier of the disintegrated German people, divided as they were into forty separate states. Bismarck is seen as the autocrat who unites them, escaping assassination at the hands of an English Jew (Cohen), defeating Austria, and then aligning her with Germany against France, and bringing about the proclamation of Wilhelm I of Prussia as the new German Emperor. In contrast, on the contemporary domestic front, a subtly developed film, *Ich Klage An* (Wolfgang Liebeneiner, 1941) dealt with the case for euthanasia advanced here on humanitarian grounds parallel with Hitler's secret campaign to rid the state of mental defectives confined in institutions. *Ich Klage An* was a Staatsauftragsfilm, a film made with financial support from the State.

The direct attack on Britain began early with *Aufruhr in Damaskus* (Gustav Ucicky, 1939), set in the period of Lawrence of Arabia's campaigns in Jordan, but dealing with the relief of Germans under siege in the area, and their safe return to Germany. This was followed by *Karl Peters* (Herbert Selpin, 1941), in which Peters, a German, stands for the policy of extending German colonial possessions in Africa; in fact something of an adventurer, Peters is represented as a

Ohm Krüger (1941), directed by Hans Steinhoff.

patriotic hero anxious only to acquire Zanzibar for Germany, and opposed not only by the British but by the Jews, who combine in a plot to have him murdered. *My Life for Ireland* (*Mein Leben für Irland;* Max W. Kimmich, 1941) exposes the British as oppressors in Ireland before the establishment of the Irish Free State.[13]

By far the best and most celebrated of the anti-British films was *Uncle Krüger* (*Ohm Krüger;* Hans Steinhoff, 1941), in which Emil Jannings starred as the great Boer hero, whom the Germans traditionally favored in his resistance to the British in the period leading up to the Boer War. The British are portrayed as anxious to seize possession of the gold fields of the Transvaal, tricking the Boer leader when he visits London and is presented to the queen. The arch conspirators are Rhodes, Austen Chamberlain ("Providence has called on England to educate small and backward nations"), and the queen herself, who is portrayed as a cunning old harridan addicted to whisky. Among the lesser villains are the Prince of Wales, obese and lecherous, and Winston Churchill, portrayed as the overfed commandant of a concentration camp for Boer women, who are kept in a condition of starvation. In contrast, Krüger has all the mystique of the great national leader—"With England one cannot come to an understanding"; "We had only one aim, peace and liberty"; "One must be a dreamer to become a ruler." Kitchener, the British war leader, is portrayed as a sadist—"No more humanity. We must be without mercy. We must set up concentration camps." Krüger's son, educated in Oxford, is at first pro-British, but changes completely when a drunken British sergeant assaults his young wife. He becomes the martyr for the Boer cause, hanged by the British on a hill that looks like Golgotha. "I die for the Fatherland," he cries. The film opens and closes with Krüger, old and blind, confined in a European sanatorium. He reflects on the defeat of the Boers. "We were a small people," he says. "But great and powerful nations will arise to reduce the British to pulp."

German anti-Polish films appeared during 1941, notably *Heimkehr* (Gustav Ucicky). This alleged that the Poles had committed atrocities against the Germans in Lodz. But by far the most virulent propaganda films were those expressing anti-Semitic feeling, of which Veit Harlan's period film *Jüd Suss* (1940) and *Die Rothschilds* (Erich Waschruck, 1940) are the best known among the fiction films. But *The Eternal Jew* (*Der Ewige Jude;* Franz Hippler, 1940)[14] is by far the most vicious and obscene propaganda film released by the Nazi regime. This film used shots of poverty-stricken Polish Jews driven into degradation in the ghettoes of Poland to demonstrate to German audiences the dire necessity of driving such people out of the "Aryan" civilization, which they were alleged only to contaminate. With these sequences as the basis of the case against international Jewry, the director, using bogus historical references and statistics, attacks the presence of the Jews in civilized society everywhere, and their assumed pernicious influence on the culture and economy of all countries. The climax of the film is the promulgation of the Nuremberg Race Laws aiming to eliminate the Jews from Germany, and later all occupied territories.

An anonymous contributor ("a leading figure in the international field of commercial public relations") wrote in DNL in August 1941 on the high place propaganda occupied in Germany's total war policy:

> One has only to look at the tremendous achievements of the Germans —involving infinitesimal losses, until the present Russian campaign—to realize the part played by propaganda in the German war machine. Practically the whole of Europe has been conquered with losses smaller than those in one major battle in the last war.

What clearly emerges is that practically all German military moves may be said to have been timed, if not dictated, by propaganda considerations, no less, and probably often more so, than by military ones.

The Russian campaign, whatever other reasons lie behind it, has undoubted propaganda motives in the reactions hoped for in the USA, and in Spain; on the Vichy Government and on the hesitating Japanese Government.

Propaganda is used by the Germans to prepare and facilitate the way for military action. Conversely, the propaganda effects of military action are all carefully calculated. The German military tactics themselves have their calculated propaganda effects—intensive violence designed to create panic—deliberate action on the civilian population as demonstrated in Belgium and France to hamper defence, etc.

He contrasted this with the weak position of the British propaganda minister, concluding:

Briefly, the Propaganda Minister cannot fulfil his functions unless he is intimately concerned with the shaping of our grand strategy. No man can make a greater contribution to the shaping of this strategy if we accept, as accept we must, that this is a war of ideas and ideals—in other words, of human emotions and reactions.

3

The War: II. The Middle Phase—The War until Hitler's Defeat at Stalingrad, January 1943

The year 1942 was one in which Hitler's advances, after vast and extensive victories, were finally brought to a halt. With his empire to the West and North unimpaired, his reverses began in other of his chosen fields—North Africa and Russia. With the Battle of Britain effectively won against the Luftwaffe, the United Kingdom was relieved of the concentrated bombing of her cities so that Hitler might turn his full attention upon Russia.

In North Africa Auchinleck's successes in the first battle of El Alamein halted Rommel's advance toward Egypt in June–July, while in October–November Montgomery's great offensive began the final drive that was to lead to the defeat of the Axis armies. This was followed in November by the Anglo-American occupation of French North Africa. In Russia, however, the picture was at first very different. The Russian front had obviously become the heartland of the European war; by December 1941 the German North, Center, and South army groups had penetrated to the gates of Leningrad, to the western approaches of Moscow and, in the South, much farther eastward still, as far as the Crimea and Rostov-on-Don. Russian prisoners of war were counted in millions.

These advances were only stayed by the momentous victory of Stalingrad in an engagement that began in the final weeks of 1942.

Britain

1942 was to be one of the richest periods for the war film in Britain. It was the year in which human considerations began to overcome the jingoistic nationalism with which most countries blinkered themselves at the beginning of a war. Similarly, the "war story" with a patriotic slant began to give place to the "war documentary," which derived the action and to a greater extent the characterization from real events and real people. Not that the studio-styled war stories and melodramas ceased altogether; they continued, for example, in *This Was Paris* (John Harlow), *Secret Mission, Unpublished Story,* and *The Day Will Dawn* (Harold French), *Flying Fortress* (Walter Forde), *Squadron-Leader X* (Lance Comfort), *Tomorrow We Live* (George King), and, sadly, in Anthony Asquith's cliché-ridden story of the underground press in occupied Belgium, *Uncensored.* A lighter approach to the war situation appeared in the comedy *The Goose Steps Out* (Basil Dearden and Will Hay, with Will Hay and Charles Hawtry), a "spy extravaganza." Of Harold French's numerous films of the period, *The Day Will Dawn,* set in occupied Norway, came closest to a sense of actuality with sound performances by Hugh Williams, Deborah Kerr, and Finlay Currie. Films of this kind were in general condemned as bad propaganda by *DNL* "because they present the war in absurdly romantic terms and their entertainment value is impaired by the conflict in the mind of the audience between the hard facts of real war and its glamorous embellishments on the screen."[1]

After the relative disaster of the overdramatized *Ships with Wings,* it was Michael Balcon's considered policy at Ealing from 1941 to make his war films reflect the qualities that prewar British documentary had pioneered. "I naturally turned," he writes in his autobiography, *Michael Balcon Presents,* "to the documentary school of filmmakers." Cavalcanti and later Harry Watt joined Ealing Studios from the ranks of the Crown Film Unit. He adds, "We learned to snatch our stories from the headlines and they had the ring of truth."[2] With their productions starting in 1941, the studios released four films during 1942, the feature-documentary *The Big Blockade,* and the features *The Foreman Went to France, Next of Kin,* and *Went the Day Well?*

The first two were directed by Charles Frend, "a man with his roots firmly planted in the soil of this country," as Balcon has put it. After working during the 1930s as cutter and editor, he became a staff editor at Ealing, where he stayed from 1941 to the mid-1950s. *The Big Blockade* was his first assignment as a director; running an hour only, it had a cast as varied as Leslie Banks, Will Hay, John Mills, Robert

Morley, and Bernard Miles, and was described at the time as a "propaganda documentary in dramatic form." It was made with the help of the Ministry of Economic Warfare, the War Office, the Royal Navy, and the RAF. The subject was the important one of the economic blockade of Germany and Nazi-occupied Europe, and it was presented within the framework of a commentary spoken by Frank Owen, editor of the London *Evening Standard* before war service, who opened the film by making the point, "Fighting is one side of war. There is another side—that is, stopping the enemy from fighting." The machinery of the blockade was explained and the enacted episodes included a prewar conversation between a German businessman and a British economist, a wartime discussion between a group of collaborationists revealing how Hitler drained the economy of the occupied territories, a visit by a Russian to Nazi Germany (suffering from air raids), and (for comedy) an argument between a skipper (Bernard Miles) and his mate (Will Hay) on the navicert system. *DNL* condemned the film as a "'soursweet hotch-potch, a curious compound of academics and box-office tricks, which failed to be either informative or entertaining.'"[3]

This film had Cavalcanti as its associate producer, and Ealing was also responsible for making under Cavalcanti's supervision a number of shorts for the MOI. Cavalcanti was also associate producer of Frend's first great success, *The Foreman Went to France*, with Clifford Evans, Constance Cummins, Gordon Jackson, and the comedian Tommy Trinder. Derived by the Ealing staff screenwriter Angus Macphail from a true story initially written by J. B. Priestley, the film recounted an unusual example of individual initiative set back in the period of the fall of France when the foreman of an aircraft works in Birmingham asked if he might go to France in an attempt to retrieve an important piece of war machinery recently delivered there. The foreman (Clifford Evans) arrives in France, and with the help of two British soldiers and an American girl get the machinery back to England in an army lorry. They are confronted by every kind of difficulty, not the least being the refugees who block the roads. The film belonged to the "heartening" branch of propaganda because of its emphasis on the courage and, above all, the humanity of this closely knit group who, while sharing the common purpose of getting the machinery back to Britain, share also in the sufferings of the French people. There could scarcely be a better answer to *Baptism of Fire*, and it initiated the Ealing "style," the production of relatively low-budget war films derived from actual wartime incidents, reconstructed and dramatized. It also brought to the screen in a creditable way that

The Foreman Went to France (1942), directed by Charles Frend.

still rare phenomenon, a British workingman who was a serious and not a comic character. British films were still closely orientated to a strictly middle-class outlook.

Ealing's collaboration with the service departments led directly to one of the more important productions of the war years, Thorold Dickinson's *Next of Kin* (with Jack Hawkins, Mervyn Johns, Stephen Murray, Nova Pilbeam). This film about security in the forces was initiated by General Hawkesworth, director of Military Training, at a period when the Army Kinematograph Service had not been established. The services of Thorold Dickinson, who was in uniform, were offered to Ealing; he would be granted leave of absence to direct the film for the War Office on a £20,000 budget if Ealing would adopt the subject, together with Sir Basil Bartlett to assist with the script and act as military liaison officer. On Balcon's advice, the subject was extended to encourage a greater sense of security among civilians as well—"careless talk costs lives" was the universal slogan—and on the strength of this Ealing invested an additional £50,000 in the project against an agreement that the money (plus a small percentage) would be recoverable should the film make a distribution profit. Otherwise, profits would go to the Crown. In the end, the government made enough money out of the film, Balcon asserts, to pay for the establishment of their own Army Film Unit. This was a measure of the public response to an outstandingly exciting and well-made film.[4]

Next of Kin used an invented but typical incident—a commando raid to be made on the French coast—as the occasion for two special German agents to put two and two together from information dropped into their laps by careless talk. Although one of the agents is caught, the other (Mervyn Johns) continues his work with the greatest skill, even obtaining the map detailing the location of the raid, which takes place and even achieves its objective, but at exceptionally high cost in men and materials, because the Germans were alerted in advance. Many of those taking part were regular service officers and men, successfully blending with actors such as Mervyn Johns and David Hutcheson, who plays the security officer desperately trying to stem the flow of talk which bit by bit gives away the nature of the raid. Credit was due to Thorold Dickinson for creating the atmosphere of actuality and suspense that drove home, again in human terms, the propaganda message of the film. At the end, the spy remains in action, traveling by train in the course of duty like any soldier. The film had to carry authenticity since its initial audiences were the very servicemen whose lives (including scenes of war action in the raid) were being portrayed on the screen. Such films could only be made with the closest collaboration and understanding between the service authorities and the film industry, and this was to grow during the remaining years of the war.

Ealing's fourth film of the year, *Went the Day Well?*, directed by Cavalcanti himself, with Leslie Banks, Basil Sydney, Frank Lawton, and Elizabeth Allan, explored a similar subject in a wholly different way in a story originated by Graham Greene, who up to the war had been film critic for both *The Listener* and *The Spectator* as well as a novelist and screenwriter (the script of *The Green Cockatoo*, 1938, and the original story for *Twenty-One Days*, 1940). *Went the Day Well?* is especially interesting for its social undertones. A sleepy English village remote from war suddenly finds itself visited by an unannounced contingent of Royal Engineers. They are, in fact, a German commando detachment, and they are received by the village squire, who is a collaborator. The village becomes for a while German occupied territory, isolated and helpless until eventually, at some cost in human life, the alarm is given and the village relieved by the British army and the regional Home Guard. The film was unfortunately uneven both in its script development and certain aspects of characterization, and did not meet the mood of the time. What is interesting is its note of disillusion, its broad suggestion that certain elements in the upper class, the social "elite," could become a breeding ground for collaboration should Germany win the war. But the film lacked the necessary actuality to make its unexpectedness credible, its touch of "disenchantment" real. But it was commendable of Ealing to have attempted it, and it is not without interest that the film owed to Cavalcanti a certain un-English quality, a foreign, Latin emphasis on the ruthlessness of violence .

Other British studios were adopting the 'new realism' which matched the quietly determined mood of the middle years of the war. As I wrote myself only five years later, with the period still fresh in my mind:

Popular behaviour in this new war showed little desire for heroics or national self-display. Public speeches were for the most part toned down to expressions of solidarity and determination. When eventually the real war subjects began to be produced as distinct from the melodramas such as *Neutral Port*, this quiet sense of national feeling, this reticence and wry humour became part of the tradition which was to guide the conception of the remarkable films of 1942–45. The influence of this style of war film spread to Hollywood, where a few, though by no means all, of their films revealed a calm confidence rather than a flamboyant gesture (for example *Guadalcanal Diary* and *The Story of G.I. Joe*). The British people went about the war as a difficult task to be worked off as efficiently as possible and actions of unusual endurance or exceptional bravery were carried out as part of a routine. This desire for understatement developed as a regular attitude in the Services, and was faithfully put in the films by screenwriters, directors and actors only too conscious of the emotional implications and the wider national significance of the stories they were representing. . . . Everyone knew something of war through the common experience of sons and daughters, husbands and lovers. Almost everyone knew the sound of bombing and the vivid state of tension before the crash of explosion. The film producers were dealing with a psychologically aware audience. . . . These stories of war dwelt on personal issues of comradeship, bravery, fear, tension, endurance, skill, boredom and hard work. The actors and actresses had to learn to combine the natural charm expected of screen personalities with great fidelity to the service people they were portraying. The personal always had to be merged into the general: the story into the common mass of experience.[5]

It was this spirit that determined the nature of such midwar British films, released in 1942, as *One of Our Aircraft Is Missing* (Michael

Powell, with Godfrey Tearle, Eric Portman, Hugh Williams), and *The First of the Few* (Leslie Howard, starring himself and David Niven). The first reconstructed in as authentic a manner as possible the actual escape story of a British bomber crew forced to bale out over Holland following a raid on Stuttgart. It started brilliantly with interior shots of an empty aircraft flying on, abandoned by its crew and out of control, crashing finally into a pylon. It showed how, passing from contact, airmen in this situation could be spirited out of an enemy-occupied country. Eric Portman, who had played the Nazi commander in *49th Parallel*, this time headed the crew of the British bomber. The Dutch backgrounds, and the impression of life in the occupied Netherlands, was carefully presented with the help of the Royal Netherlands government in exile. Any extraneous love interest—the bane still of too many war films—was excluded, and so was music in order that the subject should not appear sentimentally or romantically "decorated." Nevertheless, it still had something of the studio touch.

The First of the Few told the story of R. J. Mitchell (Leslie How-

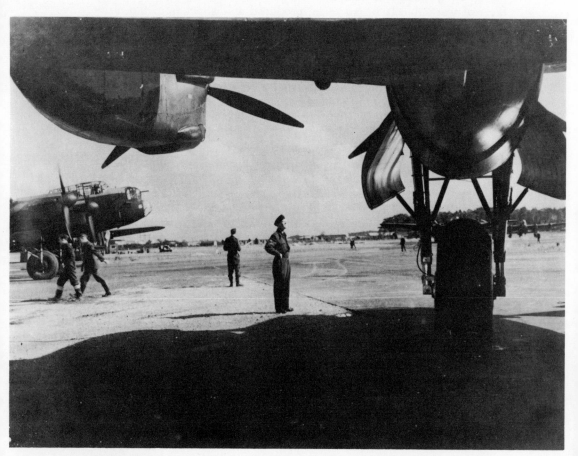

One of Our Aircraft Is Missing (1942), produced and directed by Michael Powell and Emeric Pressburger.

ard), the designer of the Spitfire, the plane that had saved Britain during the crucial air battles in 1940. Mitchell's dream of designing a streamlined, birdlike aircraft is shown to have dated back to the 1920s, and his many test pilots are combined in the film in the single figure of Wing-Commander Crisp (David Niven). When Mitchell, on holiday in prewar Nazi Germany, realizes that Germany is aiming for ultimate supremacy in the air, he returns home to fight for the opportunity to design a fighter of unparalleled performance. Faced with the burden of an incurable disease, he literally sacrifices his life through overwork in order to give Britain an outstanding aircraft, the Spitfire. This reticent and moving film biography aimed at achieving a quiet but cumulative emotional effect, and the music was carefully scored by William Walton. Leslie Howard's portrayal of Michell became, of course, a sensitive reenactment by a well-known star in a manner very familiar to the public—Mitchell was Howard rather than Howard, Mitchell. But this was inevitable unless an unknown actor had been chosen to fullfil the role. The *DNL* reviewer complained that the exact nature of the political opposition to Mitchell in the 1930s, which hardened his task and shortened his life, was not made sufficiently clear.

A film that looked at the war exclusively from the civilian angle was Maurice Elvey's *Salute John Citizen*, with Edward Rigby, Stanley Holloway, George Robey, and Jimmy Hanley. Edward Rigby was the British citizen whose sons go to war, finally leaving the old man and his wife to see in the New Year with their baby grandson. The emphasis again was on the actuality of war as experienced by a British family in a British home, sentimentally patriotic but not mawkish.

Two films of 1942 proved of exceptional interest—*Thunder Rock* (Roy Boulting, with Michael Redgrave, Barbara Mullen, James Mason, Lilli Palmer), based on Robert Ardrey's play attacking American isolationsim, and *In Which We Serve* (Noël Coward and David Lean, with Noël Coward, John Mills, Celia Johnson, Kay Walsh, Bernard Miles). *Thunder Rock* was the first, and indeed only, film of the period to adopt an allegorical approach to the war and the struggle for social progress, through the figure of a press reporter, Charleston (Michael Redgrave), who retires in despair to live in a lighthouse when his warnings about Europe go unheeded. In the end he finds himself driven back to face his problems in the open through the influence of the dream characters of European emigrants in the past who had been wrecked on the lighthouse rock and who become his ghostly companions during his period of withdrawal.

In Which We Serve remains one of the most remarkable British films of the war, closely identified with the personality of Noël Coward. It established David Lean, after some ten years as a film editor, in his career as a director, since he worked as Noël Coward's associate. The director of photography was Ronald Neame, later to beome a distinctive producer and director in his own right. The cast included many future stars, then virtually unknown on the screen, including John Mills, Richard Attenborough, and Celia Johnson. Its aim was frankly emotional—to link together in a common cause captain, officers, and crew on a destroyer which is sunk in the battle of Crete. The home ties of the men singled out as "characters" were stressed. It corresponded exactly to the emotions of the time; it was an immediate success in Britain and abroad, and its propaganda value was incalculable. It was chosen by the United States National Board of Review of Motion Pictures as the outstanding film of 1942. If this in so many respects admirable film had an Achilles heel, it was the incorrigibly middle-class way in which it bound all classes together in the common cause entirely through the uniformed figure of the Captain, played with distinction by Coward. It drew on the almost obligatory understatement which was to become, for the British, a characteristic of national vanity. The code of understatement was essentially an invention of the middle class and the public school; *In Which We Serve* did not escape criticism on this count, and also because it became too closely bound up with the particular personality of Coward as an archetypal middle- or upper-class Englishman not always easily understood or appreciated by the working classes of Britain or by North Americans across the Atlantic. But, given these points, the sincerity of the film was patent; at this stage in the war, when adversity was uppermost, the British responded to the united "family" image Coward created with a dramatic touch that had its own "genius," a genius other films, however skilled and sincere, lacked. *In Which We Serve* had national stature.

In an interesting comment printed in *DNL* (No 1, 1944), V. I. Pudovkin, the celebrated Russian director, said of the film, which he saw in Russia:

> It's a splendid job, overwhelming in its complete and well-thought out frankness. One of my comrades called it profoundly national, and I fully agree with him. The picture is English through and through. You can see the face of the real England in it. The scene in which the Captain, taking leave, shakes the hand of a whole file of his compatriots, and each conducts himself as though he were like no one but himself, and yet at the same time all are like each other, will remain long in my memory.

In Which We Serve (1942), directed by Noel Coward and David Lean.

In Which We Serve (1942), directed by Noel Coward and David Lean, with John Mills and Kay Walsh.

Meanwhile, the longer documentary films, encouraged by the success of *Target for Tonight* began to look beyond adversity for the first signs of victory. The Crown Film Unit's *Wavell's 30,000* (John Monck; 1942, forty-eight minutes) was the first of the feature or short-feature campaign films, and, using authentic on-the-spot material, showed Wavell's advance into Libya in order to secure Egypt, and his rout of the Italian fascist forces; Crown's *Coastal Command* (J. B. Holmes, 1942), ran seventy-three minutes, and, with music by Vaughan Williams and photography by Jonah Jones, revealed the elaborate machinery of air defense of the convoys at sea. The audience is led to identify with the dangers of the crew of a Sunderland Flying Boat called *T for Tommy*. Ealing Studios contributed *Find, Fix and Strike* (Compton Bennett, 1942) on the training of the Fleet Air Arm, while Crown's *Ferry Pilot* (Pat Jackson, 1941) had dealt with the work of the Air Transport Auxiliary. A quite unique production of 1942 was *Our Film*, which told the story of the formation of a Joint Production Committee of workers and management; it was made and financed by the workers and technicians of Denham Film Studios.

Humphrey Jennings, the painter and poet who became a director initially during the 1930s, directed for Crown his first distinctive and personal impressionist film, *Listen to Britain* (1942). This is still the finest evocation of wartime Britain assembled in image and sound in a bare twenty minutes; every carefully chosen image is left to speak for itself with no intrusive comment—"the music of a people at war," as Jennings himself put it. Track and image carried the rush and roar of Spitfires, the thunder of tanks, the clangour of furnace and factory, the marching music of soldiers, the sentimental songs of Flanagan and Allen (performed in factory canteens), the rhythm of the wartime dance halls, as well as the playing of Dame Myra Hess with the RAF Orchestra performing at a lunch time concert in the National Gallery.

During the year, John Grierson, writing from Canada, set out what he felt were the current propaganda needs, the thinking and the policy that British and Commonwealth propaganda should be expressing. His views were printed in *DNL* (January 1942); here are some statements from this highly significant essay:

> The penalty of realism is that it is about reality and has to bother for ever not about being 'beautiful' but about being right.
> [About the British documentary movement of the 1930s]: We were reformers open and avowed: concerned—to use the old jargon—with 'bringing alive the new materials of citizenship', 'crystallising sentiments' and creating those 'new loyalties from which a progressive civic will might derive'. Take that away and I'd be hard put to it to say what

Coastal Command (1942), directed by J. B. Holmes.

Coastal Command (1942), directed by J. B. Holmes.

Listen to Britain (1942), directed by Humphrey Jennings.

Coastal Command (1942), directed by J. B. Holmes.

Fireguard (1942), directed by Geoffrey Bell.

Control Room (1942), directed by Geoffrey Bell.

Nightshift (1942), directed by J. D. Chambers.

Control Room (1942), directed by Geoffrey Bell.

I have been working for these past fifteen years. What, of course, made documentary successful as a movement was that in a decade of spiritual weariness it reached out, almost alone among the media, toward the future.

The materials of citizenship today are different and the perspectives wider and more difficult; but we have, as ever, the duty of exploring them and of waking the heart and will in regard to them. (Documentary is at once a critique of propaganda and a practice of it.)

No war aims, I am told, becomes 'no policy' for documentary. Yet those who insist on 'no policy' are correctly reflecting a phase which dares not go right and dares not go left and has no easy solution to offer except first winning the war. It would be wise to see the 'no policy' business for what it is, a present political necessity for governments which, for many reasons—some schizophrenic, some more realistically involving allies—may not speak their minds; and explore what can be done nonetheless and in spite of it.

The important shapes are obviously those directly related to the national and international management of industrial, economic and human forces. They are important in winning the war without. They also represent, on a longer term view, a new way of thought which may be the deepest need of our generation. In so far as documentary is primarily concerned with attitudes of mind, this aspect of the matter is worth a great deal of attention.

The *DNL* editorials had been expressing similar thoughts, complaining of the absence of any long-term social objectives behind the day-to-day decisions of those who chose the subjects for current filmmaking. The question of the second front was being widely debated, and morale in Britain was not at its highest, with the German conquests in Russia and Japanese conquests in the Far East. As an editorial put it at the close of 1942:

> The peoples of the world, including those under Axis domination, are not merely fighting this war to beat Germany, Italy and Japan. They are fighting it because by beating Germany, Italy and Japan they will at the same time be laying the foundations for a new life for the common people of the world. Even if the world to them is limited by their own street or their own town, their attitude of mind is none the less positive and practical in universal terms.[7]

The United States: War in Europe and Asia

The United States declared war on Germany on 11 December 1941, five days after Pearl Harbor, and four days after the United States and Britain had declared war on Japan. At the same time Hitler acceded to a request from Japan to declare war on the United States. As in

Britain, there was an initial general scepticism in the USA about the sponsorship of propaganda, a scepticism shared by the President himself. The official emphasis, most people felt, should be on news, rather than persuasion.

On 18 December Lowell Mellett, a newspaper man without specific knowledge of film affairs, was appointed by the United States president to handle all matters connected with motion pictures so that they could "usefully serve the National Defence effort." An organization already existed in Hollywood that brought the film colony together—the Motion Picture Committee Co-operative for National Defense, founded after Dunkirk; this was conveniently transformed by Mellett into the War Activities Committee, embracing the whole industry, including producers, distributors, exhibitors, and the filmmakers' union. Lewis Jacobs quotes the six aims put before the industry by government for their guidance now that war had actually been declared:

> Keeping in mind the aim of combining purpose with entertainment, six basic categories and themes were suggested by the government to serve as a guide for Hollywood's contribution to the all-out struggle: (1) The Issues of the War: what we are fighting for, the American way of life; (2) The Nature of the Enemy: his ideology, his objectives, his methods; (3) The United Nations: our allies in arms; (4) The Production Front: supplying the materials for victory; (5) The Home Front: civilian responsibility; the Fighting Forces: our armed services, our allies and our associates. In treating these subjects, film-makers were advised that freedom of the screen, like freedom of the press would be respected.[8]

The studios were invited to create morale "vitamins." How little Hollywood at this stage understood the realities of war is reflected in the rash of overmelodramatized stories that followed this official signal—*All through the Night, Salute to Courage, Dangerously We Live, The Lady Has Plans,* or *Captain of the Clouds* (which at least showed something of training in the Royal Canadian Air Force). Others were *Berlin Correspondent, A Yank in Libya, Sabotage Squad, Danger in the Pacific, Submarine Alert, Journey into Fear.* The home front was represented initially by *Wings for the Eagle, Girl Trouble, Swing Shift, Blondie for Victory.* As the war grew sterner in 1942, the action pictures began to flow: *Atlantic Convoy, Flying Tigers, War Dogs, Thunderbirds, Suicide Squadron.*

Among these films the first efforts to sift truth and actuality from fiction began to emerge in *This Above All* (Anatole Litvak, with Tyrone Power and Joan Fontaine), *Mrs. Miniver* (William Wyler, with Greer Garson, Walter Pidgeon, Teresa Wright), *Wake Island* (John

Farrow, with Brian Donlevy, Robert Preston, William Bendix, Mac-
Donald Carey), *Desperate Journey* (Raoul Walsh, with Errol Flynn,
Ronald Reagan), and *Journey for Margaret* (W. S. Van Dyke II, with
Robert Young, Laraine Day, and Margaret O'Brien).

Mrs. Miniver, for all the edgy criticism of it in Britain from those
who enjoyed picking the obvious holes, was a sincere attempt by
Hollywood to pay tribute to Britain, and its effect in the United States
was vital. As Lewis Jacobs put it, writing as an American critic, it was
"One of the most articulate pictures of the day. Without talking or
preaching about upper class snobbery, heroism, British tradition, or
patriotism, it quietly dramatized these qualities through the humor
and pathos of a middle-class family in war-time England. . . . Mrs.
Miniver's family became the audience's family. . . . It articulated the
meaning of a 'people's war' most forcefully and through the most
potent kind of propaganda." Eric Knight's contemporary reaction was,
however, somewhat different—"Just saw *Mrs. Miniver.* It stinks. It's tremendous. It's hogwash. It makes people cheer. . . . Oh God, these
Hollywood men with their funny ideas of what this war's about. . . .

Mrs. Miniver (1942), directed by William Wyler, starring Greer Garson.

Nothing makes me surer of democracy than its ability to remain clear and shining despite Hollywood version and perversion."

What did *Mrs. Miniver* set out to do? It showed a "typical," but nonetheless wealthy, middle-class family with a riverside house and sea-going pleasure boat, and their involvement in war—their son, an Oxford undergraduate, is called up and becomes a pilot in the Battle of Britain, their younger children are still at school, their home is bombed; they even have to face a German parachutist. Mrs. Miniver (Greer Garson) endures it all; she sees her young daughter-in-law (Teresa Wright) killed, sees her husband (Walter Pidgeon) take his small boat across the sea to Dunkirk. The problem of this film was that sincerity of feeling collapsed too readily into middle-class sentimentality, and sentimentality into false social values. To the British people involved in a war, it was just such comfort-loving people who had appeared to be most responsible through their prolonged blindness to the nature of fascism during the period of appeasement. The film was all the more embarrassing because it was made with great skill and panache in manipulating the emotions, and because both Greer Garson and Walter Pidgeon had innately charming personalities. The trouble also lay in Mrs. Miniver's "social inferiors," who were all too frequently given the characterization of morons or comic dolts. Yet these were the very people who formed the vast majority on the beaches of Dunkirk, the very people fighting the war and with no comfortable riverside homes to return to if they survived it. Wyler and his scriptwriters (Arthur Wimperis, George Froeschel, James Hilton, Claudine West) accepted an outdated and in some respects unrealistic concept of Britain. Nevertheless, it made at least some sections of the British public cry and think a little better of themselves. The appeal, however, was solely emotive; there was no appeal to social reason. In the closing words spoken by the local village rector at the memorial service for the village dead at the end of the film:

> The homes of many of us have been destroyed, and the lives of old and young have been taken; there's scarcely a household that hasn't been struck to the heart. And why? Surely you must have asked yourselves this question. Why, in all conscience, should these be the ones to suffer? Children, old people, a young girl at the height of her loveliness—Why these?—Are these our soldiers? Are these our fighters? Why should they be sacrificed? I shall tell you why! Because this is not only a war of soldiers in uniform. It is a war of the people—and it must be fought not only on the battlefield but in the cities and in the villages, in the factories and on the farms, in the home and in the heart of every man, woman and child who loves freedom! Well, we have buried our dead, and we shall not forget them. Instead, they

will inspire us with an unbreakable determination to free ourselves and those who come after us from the tyranny and the terror that threatens to strike us down. This is the people's war! It is our war! We are the fighters! Fight it, then! Fight it with all that is in us—and may God defend the right.[9]

However it was the American reaction that mattered most to *Mrs. Miniver*. Although James Agee said, "one look at the *Miniver* stills was enough to keep me away,"[10] Talbot Jennings speaking at the Writers Congress in Los Angeles in October 1943 said, "She was just the right British for us, and came at just the right time, too—that critical time when many people in this country were, for one reason or another, indifferent to Great Britain, even hostile."

Another American film that presented England at war was adapted from Eric Knight's best-seller, *This Above All*. Knight was a Yorkshireman by birth who, after a hard upbringing in poverty, had emigrated to the United States at the age of fifteen. He became eventually a journalist and author. While he loved the United States, he continued to have a strong feeling for Britain, and *This Above All* (a novel published in 1941) was intended to show this. As a wartime writer, Knight dedicated himself to Anglo-American understanding; he served in the United States Army, and was eventually killed in 1943. According to his close friend, Paul Rotha, *This Above All* was "credited with doing more to cement Anglo-American understanding in the United States than any piece of conscious propaganda because it represented to the American public Britain's ability to examine her own faults and virtues with equal objectivity." Knight wrote to Rotha that he had "tried to raise all the problems concerning war that face the young man of today, brought up on 'no more war' and pre-Munich laissez-faire."[11] Though the film failed to match the qualities of the book (Knight was too disillusioned with Hollywood to expect anything else), it was by no means negligible. It was the story of a Dunkirk hero (Tyrone Power) of humble origin who deserts in order to think out his position, reexamining the "ideals" (in the film) or values (in the book) for which he is expected to fight. He falls in love with a WAAF (Joan Fontaine) who belongs to the upper classes and who befriends him; she restores his faith, persuading him in the end to surrender to the authorities. On the way he is severely injured while rescuing a woman and child in an air raid. The film certainly emphasizes the distinctions of class in Britain, and the need for the "working class" to win a higher place in the society of which they form by far the greater part. But the arguments became oversimplified, and the solution involving the hero's return to duty was too facile.

Less emotionally pretentious was *Journey for Margaret,* which handled with tenderness the sensitive subject of children uprooted by war. The wife of an American war correspondent based in Britain is injured in an air raid, and learns that in consequence she can never have children. Her husband, remaining alone in London, decides with her consent to adopt two British war orphans, for whom he successfully manages to secure space on a plane. This film, though much concerned with emotional effects, avoids sentimentality in its appeal to American audiences to understand the plight of such children in wartime Britain.

The war action films achieved a reasonable degree of realism— *Desperate Journey* and *Wake Island.* The first involved the escape from Germany of certain members of the crew of a Flying Fortress bomber who had baled out over the Black Forest. They escape to Holland and steal a captured British bomber. Raymond Massey plays a somewhat sneering Nazi officer responsible for interrogating the captives, and Errol Flynn appears as a razzle-dazzle American serviceman. *Wake Island* transfers action to the Pacific, and claims to be a true story. It concerns the defense of the island in December 1941 after Pearl Harbor; only a small American force defends it from heavy Japanese attack. Lewis Jacobs praised the film for "its lack of bluster and bravado and for its harsh expressiveness."[12]

Other important American films of 1942 include *Casablanca* (Michael Curtiz, with Humphrey Bogart, Ingrid Bergman, Paul Henreid, Conrad Veidt, and Peter Lorre), *Saboteur* (Alfred Hitchcock, with Robert Cummings and Priscilla Lane), *Once upon a Star* (or, *Once upon a Hangman,* Leo McCarey, with Cary Grant and Ginger Rogers), and *To Be or Not To Be* (Ernst Lubitsch, with Carole Lombard and Jack Benny).

The primary aim of all these films was, of course, entertainment. But they involved also a serious and responsible use of war themes. Lubitsch's and McCarey's films both illustrated the hazards of developing comedy from a contemporary situation involving so much suffering. Lubitsch's burlesque satire was produced in association with Alexander Korda in the United States; it was set in occupied Warsaw. Its purpose was to deride the overweening Nazi conquerors. The story involves a husband and wife, members of a company of Polish players who, before engineering their escape to free territory, manage to bring about the death of a German secret agent who has posed as a free Pole, and to outwit the Nazi authorities. The actor (Jack Benny) is both vain and ridiculously jealous of his beautiful wife (Carole Lombard); the light comedy turns on their relationship, and the satire lies in a barbed attack on the Nazis, led by Sig Rumann as Colonel Ehrhardt. Edwin Justus Mayer's script and Lubitsch's masterly direction ensured a fine balance in the delicate handling of the comedy of the situation alongside the tragedy of conquered Poland, but the timing of the film's release (March 1942 in the United States) led to some criticism by those who preferred humor (even "serious" humor) to be kept strictly segregated. 1942 was long before the period in which audience taste for "black" humor had been developed, and the moods created in films still remained relatively uncomplicated.

Leo McCarey's film, *Once upon a Star*, is less happy in maintaining the delicate balance of contrary moods. It weaves its way between comedy, romance, thrills, and sheer tragedy. The leading character is an American radio correspondent (Cary Grant) who eventually exposes the fifth column activities in Austria, Czechoslovakia, Poland, and Norway of an Austrian baron (Walter Slezak) whose wedding to an American showgirl (Ginger Rogers) he originally came over to report. The film ends with the romantic association of Grant and Rogers once she realizes the nature of the baron's activities, and their final escape together to New York. But the film lacks deep feeling for the plight of the betrayed countries, and leaves the tragedy to such brief moments as the situation of a German-Jewish servant (Natasha Lytess) working in a Warsaw hotel.

Saboteur, released mid-1942, is not one of Hitchcock's favorite films; in discussing it with Truffaut he considers it undisciplined in story line, cluttered with too many incidents and locations, and lacking true star value in its leading players. It concerns a young man on the run because he is wrongfully suspected of sabotage in a war plant; his purpose is to find the real culprits, and the long chase ends with one of the villains (Norman Lloyd) suspended by his tearing coat-sleeve on the top of the Statue of Liberty. A girl who becomes converted to the hero's case is teamed with him during the chase. The film, set during 1941 before American entry into the war, was intended to expose the strongly entrenched, pro-German fascist element in the United States, and this was obscured to some extent when the popular American actor Hitchcock wanted to lead this wing of the cast, Harry Carey, refused the part as unsuitable for his "image." The "counterpoint" this would have given (the popular, sympathetic actor in the ultimately unsympathetic role) was therefore lost, and the political point covered over by having a conventional actor-villain in the villainous part.

Casablanca (released at the beginning of 1943) used serious melodrama to expose the situation of refugees waiting in Casablanca to reach Lisbon and cross the Atlantic; only those with money escape eas-

ily. The story turns on the relationship of Renault, prefect of Police
(Claude Rains), Strasser, a Nazi agent (Conrad Veidt), Lazlo, head
of an underground movement (Paul Henreid), his wife (Ingrid Bergman), and Rick, her former lover, proprietor of a café where visas can
be obtained (Humphrey Bogart). There are many sharply observed
small parts—by Peter Lorre, Sidney Greenstreet, Dooley Wilson (Rick's
Negro attendant), and Leonid Kinsky's barman. This was one of the
prolific Michael Curtiz's most brilliant films; the script (J. J. and P. G.
Epstein, with Howard Koch), impeccably rich in undertones and right
in its dramatic emphasis, was supported by the shadowed camerawork
of Arthur Edeson and the apt score of Max Steiner. *Casablanca* remains in the memory as one of the supreme examples of creative team-
work in the 1940s style. In so far as an emotionally orientated melodrama would catch the spirit of the period, *Casablanca* achieved just
this.[13]

Another film was Jules Dassin's *Nazi Agent* (1942), a serious melodrama. Conrad Veidt played the dual role of German twins, one,
Baron Hugo, a Nazi agent in the United States, the other, Otto, a refugee, now a dedicated American who detests the Nazis. After a showdown between them, Otto kills Hugo and then, in order to frustrate
the spy ring, impersonates his twin at the German consulate, where
Hugo had organized his work as saboteur. Everyone is deceived in him
except Kaaren De Relle (Ann Ayars), who had loathed the first brother
but finds herself attracted by the second. In order to save her, Otto
is finally forced to give himself up.

With these few films the United States began the difficult task of
dealing with war themes responsibly in the field of entertainment. The
record in official documentary was to be much more considerable.

The March of Time: Canada Carries On: World in Action

The March of Time, its pioneer work done in aligning American
public opinion with the struggle in Europe, settled in 1942 for a relatively conventional magazine approach to the world war situation.
There was in general a marked fall-off in technical quality, though not
necessarily in informational value. Among the issues for the year were:

> *Battlefields of the Pacific* (Special issue: February 1942). A geographical
> and economic commentary on Japan, the Philippines, the Dutch
> East Indies, Australia, and what Japan could gain by swift aggres-
> sion.
>
> *America at War* (VII, 9: March 1942). Largely a reedited version of
> *The Ramparts We Watch*. The United States' part in the 1914–18
> war.

The Argentine Question (VII, 10: March 1942). The Argentinian economy, her relations with the United States and Europe, and the problem of her neutrality, in spite of known Axis plans for aggression in Latin America to be initiated from the Argentine. The threat this represents to the United States.

America's New Army (VII, 12: May 1942). The reorganization of the United States war machine under General George Marshall. General MacArthur's announcement of his command of the Pacific offensive on his arrival in Australia.

India in Crisis (VIII, 1: July 1942). Disunity in India, and Gandhi's policy of passive resistance; the threat of invasion by Japan. The vast potential of India with its four hundred million population. The evils of the caste system. India's determination to throw off British rule.

India at War (VIII, 2: August 1942). India's mobilization, and her great industrial potential, which needs organization and transport.

Men of the US Navy (VIII, 4: October 1942). The importance of the American fleet; recruitment and training. Propaganda designed to increase enlistment.

G-Men at War (VIII, 5: November 1942). How the FBI fight sabotage by the pro-Nazi Fifth Column in the United States, and seizure of stockpiles of arms. Enactment of a staged incident by a Bund member.

The Fighting French (VIII, 6: December 1942). Both actuality and studio enactments show the work alike of resistance in France, and the work of the Free French under de Gaulle.

The full story of official sponsorship of documentary in the United States, primarily through the War Department's film section (established in December 1941 under Major Frank Capra), the Office of War Information (established in June 1942), and the Field Photographic branch of the United States Navy (established in 1942 under John Ford) will be told in the next chapter since, although production began in 1942, the work only developed fully in 1943. According to Owen Lattimore of the Office of War Information, Americans appear to have been dubious at first of the value of direct propaganda. Speaking later, in 1944, at the Writers Congress, he said:

There are still many people who feel somehow that to resort to the warfare of ideas is a little beneath the dignity of Americans, that this is in some way an unbecoming and unprofessional approach to the business of war. There are others who believe, or who try to make others believe, that the work of the Office of War Information is something that was dreamed in Washington by a lot of long-haired, New Deal bureaucrats, and that this work has no rational bearing on the winning of the war. . . . We are not, like propaganda agencies of the German and Japanese type, staffed with a carefully chosen elite of highly conditioned, war-indoctrinated servants of a limited power-holding group.[14]

Pride of place was taken in American production by the service departments; in fact, the production budget of the Office of War Information was cut in 1943 from $1,226,000 to $50,000 on the plea that it would be better for Hollywood to make the films needed for the war effort. Nevertheless, certain civilian documentaries were made, notably *Tanks*, on tank production, with a sonorous commentary by Orson Welles. Disney made *The New Spirit*, showing Donald Duck as a ready taxpayer, and *Get the Scrap*, on conservation of raw materials. OWI concentrated on distributing films of American life or of propaganda, such as the film of Toscanini conducting, *Hymn of the Nations*. The films were released in both the commercial and non-theatrical fields. Other theatrical films were *War Town* (about Mobile, Alabama, a war-boom town) and *Troop Train* (propaganda to discourage excessive civilian travel). The US film industry, like that in Britain, accepted the principle that there should be weekly releases to the cinemas of short films related to the war. OWI films alternated with those produced by the industry itself. In the non-theatrical field the OWI released many effective American films, such as *Henry Browne Farmer* and Disney's Donald Duck cartoon, *The Spirit of 1943*. Non-theatrical exchanges we made with British and Canadian films. These included general descriptive documentaries of American life and culture, such as *The Town* (Josef von Sternberg, 1941), *Cowboy, Autobiography of a Jeep, Valley of the Tennessee*, and *Hymn of the Nations*.

The Canadian equivalent to *The March of Time* was the bimonthly *Canada Carries On* (known in the United States as *World in Action*), first released in 1941. It was, of course, produced by the National Film Board; the Board had its headquarters in Ottawa and a staff by September 1942 of some 250, among them several filmmakers well-known in England, and including Stuart Legg, Stanley Hawes, Raymond Spottiswoode, John Ferno, Joris Ivens, and Norman McLaren.[15] Stuart Legg was producer-in-charge of *Canada Carries On*, and titles of earlier issues (each two reels, or up to twenty minutes in length) included *The Battle for Oil, The Strategy of Metals, Food—Weapon of Conquest, Churchill's Island, This is Blitz*, and *War Clouds in the Pacific*. As summarized by *DNL* (May 1942) the characteristic approach to production was:

Behind each of these items one can detect not merely the brain of the experienced propagandist but also certain attributes without which any widely-based film cannot be more than superficially convincing. These attributes are:—
(i) Constant, intensive and imaginative research work;

(ii) Close attention to history, to immediate strategic considerations, and to the various possibilities as regards the future;

(iii) Elimination of makeshift visuals, and concentration on welding picture and commentary into an integral whole;

(iv) A strong sense of screen journalism;

(v) Fearlessness and forthrightness—both of which are impossible unless based on the preceding attributes. . . .

To sum up their main achievement, it is probably just to say that they are not merely interpreters of policy but actually the pacemakers of policy; and this remark is a tribute not merely to the makers of the films but to the far-sightedness of one of the most powerful of the United Nations, the democracy of Canada.

The films enjoyed considerable box-office success in both the United States and Canada, and were only prevented from doing the same in Britain through the idiocy of maintaining until 1942 the validity of a clause in the Film Act (1938), which classified these Commonwealth products as "alien" and therefore ineligible for British quota. Grierson had determined from the first that the series should stand on its own feet commerically—"We were selling it commercially because if it was good, it was good enough to sell commercially, and if it wasn't good enough to sell commercially, we weren't any more interested in it than the industry." Its success led to production being stepped up to one issue a month in April 1942, and by October it was being distributed not only in North America, but in Britain, Australia, New Zealand, India, South Africa, and Latin America, with dubbed tracks. In addition, Canada developed a strong, nontheatrical production program similar to that in Britain, a proportion of which was distributed by the MOI in Britain.

Russia

On the day before Pearl Harbor the Russians launched their counter-offensive against Hitler. This was 6 December 1941, in the height of the winter that took such toll of the ill-prepared German armies, which had been ordered to withstand any assault at whatever cost in lives. The Germans themselves were unable to renew their own assaults until the summer of 1942; then Hitler struck again, mainly in the south. Here the armies pushed forward some 450 miles into the Caucasus as far as the oil territory of Maikop. Hitler also pushed past Rostov-on-Don toward Stalingrad on the Volga. Russian defense of both stiffened, while the German forces, divided between these two campaigns far to the southeast of Moscow, were weakened. Finally, with the winter returned, the German armies stretched round Stalingrad were surrounded, and Paulus, a replacement general who had just taken over, surrendered. Stalingrad is commonly regarded as the turning point in Hitler's fortunes. His armies were never to move farther east than this point.

Back in June and July 1941, no one could have foreseen these events.[17] Nevertheless, the Cinema Committee controlling the Russian film industry left Moscow for Novosibirsk, situated beyond the Urals in Siberia. Cameramen were mobilized to cover the warfronts. Short propaganda films were rushed into production. The studios at Tashkent, Stalinabad, and Alma-Ata were alerted to anticipate increased production as units in threatened areas were moved to them. The final evacuation of the great Lenfilm and Mosfilm studios took place in October to the small studio stages in Alma-Ata in Kazakstan. The Kiev studios had already moved to Tashkent. Others moved elsewhere. Only the Central Newsreel Studios remained in Moscow; early short-record films of war included *In the Line of Fire* (Dziga Vertov), Troyanovsky's films about the Red Air Force and the defense of Odessa, and *Black Sea Marines* (V. Belayev). Mobile projectors, common in the USSR, were set up everywhere in improvised premises, such as the large air-raid shelters in the Moscow Underground.

The production of short-story films became the order of the day, films which, joined together, could make up new and telling wartime programs. These grouped films were called albums, produced monthly for immediate screening. Twelve of these collections appeared during 1941–42, the work alike of the celebrated and the less celebrated filmmakers—among them Pudovkin, Gerasimov, Kozintsev, Barnet, Alexandrov, Yutkevitch, Donskoi, and Perelstein. Eisenstein, on the other hand, went with Mosfilm to Alma-Ata to prepare for the production of his final great films, *Ivan the Terrible Parts I and II*, to be made during the war years.

Jay Leyda, in *Kino*, describes a typical album; when exported to the United States it was called *This is the Enemy*:

> Two of its five items were written by V. Belayev and Mikhail Rosenberg, the latter from the team that wrote *The Girl from Leningrad*, and its director, Eisimont, made another of the items. The climactic fourth item, a bitter drama of Yugoslav hostages, was directed by Herbert Rappoport. The close was a 'gag' by Grigori Kozintsev: 'Incident at the Telegraph Office' shows a warning being sent to Hitler by Napoleon.[18]

The first short feature-length compilation, playing virtually an hour, was *The Defeat of the Germans near Moscow* (February 1942), the

A Day of War (1942), directed by Mikhail Slutsky.

A Day of War (1942), directed by Mikhail Slutsky.

69th Parallel (1942), directed by Vasili Belayev.

combined record of the 1941 December campaign.[19] It was supervised
by D. Varlamov and I. Kopalin, and showed the advance of the Red
Army, the recapture of villages and towns, the German atrocities against
both servicemen and civilians, and the German dead, the price paid
for the initial advance.[20]

Writing at my invitation immediately after the war, the distinguished wartime documentary director, Roman Karmen, said:

> From the first hours, after fascist Germany treacherously invaded our
> peaceful country, we film reporters became military men. Cameramen
> were in the forward lines of fire on every sector of the front. In the
> fullest meaning of the word, they were soldiers, armed with a camera.
> They followed the infantry on foot, filming them as they went in to
> attack, they flew over enemy territory, filming the bombing, they
> filmed the strafing of German columns from diving 'Stormoviks', they
> took pictures on the warships of the Baltic, Black and North Seas and
> on submarines. They went into attack, sitting with their cameras inside
> tanks, made parachute landings on to enemy territory, filmed and fought
> with the partisans of the Ukraine, Byelorussia and the Baltic territories.
>
> Our cameramen were among the last detachments of troops to leave
> the heroic towns of Odessa and Sebastopol. They fought on the out-
> skirts of Moscow and at Stalingrad. The cameramen of Leningrad did

not abandon their beloved city when it was blockaded. Exhausted by hunger and privations, they filmed the heroic defence of Leningrad, day in day out, during the 900 days and nights of the siege, constantly under artillery fire and air bombing. When the Red Army began its broad offensive, the cameramen were again in the front ranks. They were among the first to rush into the liberated towns, they accompanied the first soldiers and tanks that crossed the German frontier, they stormed Berlin and filmed the hoisting of the red flag of victory over the Reichstag.

Many of our friends died a hero's death on the battlefields. Many perished with the partisans. Often cameramen had to exchange their cameras for an automatic or a grenade. Even in the last days of the street fighting in Berlin, when it had become clear that only a few blocks of houses and a few hours separated the men from victory, the cameramen were in the thick of the fighting, facing death. In many European towns you can find modest tombstones, always decorated with fresh flowers, with the inscription: 'Newsreel cameraman so-and-so died a hero's death during the liberation of our town'.

Other feature documentaries of 1942 were:

Siege of Leningrad (or *Leningrad Fights!*; seven reels, July). Supervised by Roman Karmen, and deriving from the work of a large number of cameramen, showing life in besieged Leningrad with its four million inhabitants, the defenses built in the streets, work in the factories, the bombing and destruction, food brought to the starving people by lorry over the frozen waters of Lake Ladoga. The English-language version was narrated by Edward R. Murrow.

69th Parallel (1942). Director, Vasili Belayev. The arctic operation linking up with the Allies through the Berents Sea and Murmansk.

A Day of War (October 1942). Supervised by Mikhail Slutsky. Jay Leyda quotes the director's own description of the making of this eight-reel film, which was widely shown in Britain and North America: "From headquarters in Moscow, assignments for the film were sent to all parts of the Soviet Union. We asked that the cameramen strive for outward effect, in preference to inner significance or film dramatizations. Everyone was told of the exact date only two days in advance. Early in the morning of the thirteenth work was begun by 240 cameramen at 140 'filming points' scattered throughout the Soviet Union."

The first major feature production of the war years was the Vasiliev Brothers' *Defence of Tsaritsin* (Spring 1942), a film of the civil war period in 1918, when this city on the Volga (later called Stalingrad) became a key area of combat leading to the Revolution. Stalin was military commissar and Kliment Voroshilov the general in command of the Red forces. The film, though historical in context, was a timely

Defense of Tsaritsin (1942), directed by Sergei and Georgi Vasiliev.

Defense of Tsaritsin (1942), directed by Sergei and Georgi Vasiliev.

reminder of past battles. Ivan Pyriev's *Russian Guerrillas* (or *Secretary of the District Committee*, 1942) and *Guerrillas and Heroes* (1942), a combined album film by L. Lukov, V. I. Pudovkin, and M. Sadkovitch, alike celebrated the heroism of the partisans, the latter through interlinked stories covering both Yugoslavia and Russia, and concentrating realistically on the hardships of occupation. Another early feature of the period was *Georgi Saakhadze* (Part I September 1942) directed by Mikhail Chiaureli; Saakhadze was a Georgian of the seventeenth century who is shown as a champion of liberation. Feature films of 1942 that more directly touched on the war itself included Yuli Raizman's *Maskenka*, a film about nurses, and Donskoi's adaptation of Ostrovsky's novel of 1930 about the civil war, *How the Steel was Tempered* (September 1942), begun in Kiev and completed in Arkhabad. This showed partisan warfare with the White Army and the Germans who in 1918 occupied the Ukraine, a theme Dovzhenko had dealt with in his film, *Shors* (1939).

Italy

1942, the final full year of Mussolini's regime, was remarkable in

Secretary of the District Committee (1942), directed by Ivan Pyriev.

Italian production for two events only—the challenge offered the Italian fascist censorship by Luchino Visconti's first film, *Ossessione* (*Obsession*), and the emergence of Rossellini as a director of some initial importance. *Ossessione*, a film with only indirect political implications, was the work of an Italian aristocrat whose Marxist convictions had been confirmed by working in France prewar with Renoir on *Une Partie de Campagne* and *Les Bas Fonds*. Visconti (aged thirty-six in 1942) felt for a while, at least, committed to social realism, obviously a dangerous commitment in a fascist country, largely as a result of his four years' association with Renoir. The film, suggested initially by Renoir and loosely based on James Cain's *The Postman always Rings Twice* (and therefore dogged by a second campaign of repression because the film rights to the novel were never to be cleared), was wholly Italian in the outcome; more than this, it belonged, according to Geoffrey Noel-Smith in his sensitive study of Visconti's work, to "a kind of artistic resistance movement," made up of young critics and filmmakers with a partisan background, and with a devotion to Verga's novels because of their *verismo*, or naturalism of treatment.

Because of its dual history of suppression (both during and after the war), *Ossessione*'s reputation has become distorted into a legend. (I was shown it privately, but still behind locked doors in Rome during the late 1940s.) The view of Italian society it offers—the lover a born wanderer; the woman, once a prostitute, but married now to an unloved husband because of her innate need for security, which she risks direly when she induces her lover to murder him—was a view few in Italy wanted—certainly not the fascists, the Church, or for that matter the exhibitors. The legend that it was reprieved from banning by Mussolini himself is apparently apocryphal. Its importance lies rather in its sheer existence in 1942, and the encouragement this offered to the "neo-realist" directors of the future waiting their opportunity once Italy was liberated.[22]

One of the foremost of these, of course, was to be Roberto Rossellini (also aged thirty-six in 1942). His father, an architect, had built cinemas that young Roberto haunted during the 1920s, later entering the industry while at the same time making amateur films in a small studio in his villa. Finally involved in professional cinema during the late 1930s, he had (as we have seen) found himself involved in "official" filmmaking, with Geoffredo Alessandrini in *Luciano Serra, pilota* (1938). After this he had become associated with the fascist supporter, Francesco De Robertis, who preferred to make story films in a marked documentary style, even using nonprofessional actors. De Robertis made *Uomini sul fondo* (1940) on board a submarine, another film which, in spite of its official sponsorship, helped to consolidate the younger director's interest in *verismo*. De Robertis, as head of the film department of the Naval Ministry, commissioned Rossellini to direct a documentary about a hospital ship, a film which developed into a feature—*La Nave Bianca* (1941)—made, like *Uomini sul fondo*, entirely with nonprofessional players. The story involved a wounded sailor who is cared for on a hospital ship by a nurse who turns out to be the "pen pal" he has never met. The treatment of the ships and their movements was in a documentary style; the sailors, however, are humanized, and the situation of the pen pal is even to some extent sentimentalized and idealized. The serious propaganda value of the film appears to be twofold—to show how every care was lavished on the wounded, and how these floating machines of war work under efficient leadership. The less serious side is the romantic element, possibly largely introduced by De Robertis, who shared in the scripting.

The success of this film ensured further productions for Rossellini. These were *Un Pilota ritorna* (*A Pilot Returns*, 1942) and *L'Uomo*

L'Uomo della Croce (1943), directed by Roberto Rossellini, with Alberto Tavazzi.

della Croce (*Man of the Cross*, 1943), set on the Russian front during the summer of 1942. The first (made under the supervision of Vittorio Mussolini, brother of the Duce, under the name of Tito Livio Mursino) is the story of a young pilot who escapes from a British prisoner-of-war camp and reaches home at the time of the surrender of Greece to Axis forces. *L'Uomo della Croce* concerns the selfless acts of heroism of an Italian army chaplain who is killed while helping Italian soldiers, their prisoners, and displaced local people in a village suffering bombardment alike from the Italians and the Russians. Their virtue as films is the apparent desire of their director to come as close as possible to actuality in the treatment of the *mise-en-scène* of war.[23] On the other hand, according to José Luis Guarner, in his study of Rossellini's work, *L'Uomo della Croce*, though technically falling into the category of propaganda for the fascist cause and for Catholicism in the saintly figure of the chaplain, appears also, with its lyrical opening and close, to celebrate the universal desire of mankind for freedom from the hideous pressures and confinements of war. The beginning, with its panning shot of a flight of birds rising above the violence below, and the ending, with a similar panning shot of runaway horses galloping unfettered over the battlefield, contrasts with the soldiers and civilians hemmed in and subject to injury and death, while the chaplain ministers alike to all, whether Italian or Russian. His actions assert the brotherhood of man. There is some limited Marxist stereotyping in the characterization, but on the whole the film fairly presents the enforced confrontations of warfare, and an end-title states a somewhat crudely put antipathy to the Soviet regime, with Italian soldiers fighting a war for "truth and justice" in territory ruled by barbarism. Guarner sums up this period in Rossellini's career: "Roberto Rossellini's first three films, then, appear entirely subject to the demands of Fascist propaganda; they praise sailors, airmen, priests, the army, country and religion. In spite of all this, two at least display a remarkable feeling of directness. However, because of their 'ideology' they are not valued very highly and remain almost unknown."[24] In the career of an average director, the presence of these "patriotic" films would probably pass as normal wartime exercises, but in the light of the coming fame of Rossellini as the great protagonist of the Italian Resistance in *Rome, Open City* and *Paisa,* their production remains something of an embarrassment.

Japan and the Conquest of Asia

In Asia this period was one of almost total collapse before the widespread pressure of Japanese forces. Simultaneously with the attack on Pearl Harbor, the Japanese bombed Hawaii and British Malaya; in the same month, December 1941, Hong Kong was surrendered to Japan. The following month, January 1942, the Japanese invaded Burma and the Dutch East Indies; Kuala Lumpur was taken. In February Singapore passed into enemy hands and the Japanese landed in Java. In March Rangoon fell, and the Japanese onrush in Burma and seizure of the Andaman Islands threatened India itself. In April Bataan surrendered. In May Mandalay was taken, and the British forces withdrew to India. In June came the battle of the Midway Islands, defended by the Americans, who in August landed in Guadalcanal, the center of bitter fighting during the year. While on the other side of the world, Anglo-American successes in North Africa seemed to lighten the prevailing darkness, the situation in Asia was profoundly disturbing. However, the same month (January 1943) that saw the German surrender at Stalingrad, the Americans managed to drive the Japanese from Guadacanal, while in Africa the British Eighth Army entered Tripoli.

Captured footage from British newsreels appeared in Japanese war documentaries of the period, such as *Malay Taken*, an account of the fall of Singapore.[25] In *Capture of Burma* a Japanese heavenly choir accompanies the dropping of bombs, Western music being used in all Japanese films for popular audiences in this war with the West. Jay Leyda notes that Haydn was used in support of scenes of the camouflage of planes in *Occupation of Sumatra*, Wagner's "Die Walküre" for scenes of parachuting arms and troops, Tchaikovsky to give emotional force to the wrecking of an airfield, and "Meistersinger" for the "finale of destruction." The evident models were the German documentaries, which used such orchestral emphasis with far greater skill and judgment. Japanese combat coverage, however, could be extremely effective. Leyda, who has had the opportunity of viewing several Japanese war films, instances specially *Gochin*, a film of battle on the Indian Ocean—"filmed [he writes] almost entirely in a Japanese submarine during a hunting cruise, a camera feat I have never seen equalled."

The Japanese successes were celebrated in a number of notable feature films. *The War at Sea from Hawaii to Malaya* (December 1942, the anniversary of Pearl Harbor) was directed by Kajiro Yamamoto, a highly experienced filmmaker who had been working in the studios since 1920. Made at exceptional cost (almost ten times the average budget for a first-line feature) it celebrated "the spirit of the Navy which culminated at Pearl Harbor," reconstructing in a documentary style the building up of the navy over the years to a level capable

Hawai Marei Oki Kaisen (The War at Sea from Hawaii to Malaya) (1942), directed by Kajiro Yamamoto.

Hawai Marei Oki Kaisen (The War at Sea from Hawaii to Malaya) (1942), directed by Kajiro Yamamoto.

Hawai Marei Oki Kaisen (The War at Sea from Hawaii to Malaya) (1942), directed by Kajiro Yamamoto.

of achieving so great an assault. Anderson and Ritchie claim that its use of special effects and miniatures was so effective that, after the war, sections filmed in this way were accepted by the American authorities as if they were real. Meanwhile, other theaters of war were featured in Tetsu Taguchi's *Generals, Staff and Soldiers* (1942), filmed in North China under strict control of the Japanese military authorities and reflecting war as experienced at every level in the army. Tadashi Imai made *The Suicide Troops of the Watchtower* (1942), an action film in the documentary style produced in cooperation with the Korean film industry, in which the Korean guerrilla resistance forces were represented as "bandits." Anderson and Ritchie also point out that the Japanese antiespionage campaign films began at this period, exposing with greater or lesser effect American use of spies (Chinese, Filipino, and so forth) all of whom come to a bad end at the hands of the Japanese or the Americans themselves; such a film was Kimisaburo Yoshimura's *The Spy Is Not Dead Yet,* which was actually criticized as showing too much sympathy for the spy. In later films established Japanese actors impersonated American and British

Shogun to Sanbo to Hei (General, Staff, and Soldiers) (1942), directed by Tetsu Taguchi.

spies, speaking normally in Japanese with nothing comparable to the thick accents of German or other spies in equivalent American or British films. No attempt was made to parallel the extreme type of violent anti-Oriental caricature so frequent in British and American films, stemming from the old, melodramatic image of the cunning, sub-human Asiatic or from Sax Rohmer's Fu Manchu stereotype, the mad villain with a mastermind.

Propaganda against the British tended to be seen in a historical context—the British as intruders into Asia, with the Japanese fulfilling a long-term mission to drive them out. This was to be seen, for example, in Shigeo Tanaka's *The Day England Fell* (1942), a hostile study of British "imperialistic and anti-Oriental attitudes" in Hong Kong during the period of the Pacific war up to the Japanese occupation. In Daisuke Ito's *Kurama Tengu Appears in Yokohama* (1942) and particularly later in Masahiro Makino's *The Opium War* (1943) the British, among other international intruders, are alleged to exploit the Chinese by encouraging the use among them of the drug. This campaign culminated in a film of 1944, Daisuke Ito's *International*

Smuggling Gang, in which the head of the British consulate in Yokohama is involved in a similar design to weaken the Japanese through the exploitation of the opium habit.

China

A brief survey of Chinese production in wartime was presented to the Society of Motion Picture Engineers in New York in December 1942 by T. Y. Lo of the Film Section of the Political Department of the Military Affairs Commission of the Government of the Chinese Republic.[26] He described a small industry functioning as much below ground during air raids as above, and supplying films to China's 375 theaters, the majority in coastal cities, and supplemented by traveling units. Early, prewar (1937) nationally conscious films had protested against oppression from outside China, following Japanese invasion of Manchuria (1931), including *The Fisherman's Song,* directed by Tsai Chosheng, and *The Road to Life,* directed by Sun Yu. After 1937, those concerned with filmmaking, along with others in industry, had joined in the great migration west, including some fifteen hundred executives, technicians, and artists from Shanghai. Just before the fall of Hankow (1938), which had some of China's best studios, the equipment was with difficulty moved away by boat and barge up the Yangtze, settling finally in Chungking, where filmmaking began again under bombardment.

In Chungking three studios were established—the China Film Studio, the Central Studio, and the Educational Film Studio, all under government control, and using film and much equipment imported from the United States. Films for military training were made alongside feature films with war themes, such as *Good Husband* (about military service) and *Victory Symphony* (about a Chinese victory as Changsha), both directed by T. S. Shih. The film continued to be shown in 1942 by traveling units and in free China's remaining cinemas, in that year only some 112. The traveling units worked their way even into what was technically Japanese-held territory. The principal slogan of the Chinese studios and projection units alike read: "Remember—one foot of film properly used is as deadly as a bullet fired against the enemy." T. Y. Lo describes the film units at work in wartime Chungking:

> Of course, not all the work is done in dugouts. The sound stages, for example, are on the surface. But the laboratories, and editing and storage compartments are built in the tunnels which in some parts reach as far as thirty feet below ground. As soon as an air-raid alarm

is sounded, things start to move. Studio lights, cameras, sound equipment, even portions of studio sets and important 'props', are carried down into the dugouts. Once there, work is resumed. Directors confer with scenarists on scripts, actors and actresses study and rehearse their parts, editors work at their benches, cutting and splicing furiously to the horrible hum of approaching enemy raiders. One of our great worries is the possible destruction of stages or studio sets by Japanese bombs. The worst problem, however, is the destruction of the water mains. The China Film Studio is situated at the highest point in Chungking. When electricity supply is cut off, we can still use our own generators as a makeshift. But when the water supply is cut off, as it was in 1939, we are compelled to carry water from the river at the foot of the hill up to the studio, and by this painful means fill a reservoir made specially for the purpose. About 200 people were needed for this task alone.

Germany

With the invasion of Soviet Russia, anti-Russian films began to appear once again. The first notable example was Karl Ritter's *GPU* (1942), in which a White Russian girl refugee from the Bolsheviks joins the Soviet GPU to trace the murderers of her parents. More typical of the production of the midwar years are the strongly nationalist films designed to promote the morale of the German people. Among them was the epic-scale film directed by Veit Harlan, *The Great King* (*Der Grosse König*; 1942), one of the cycle of films about Frederick the Great; set in the period of the Seven Years War, it had contemporary significance because it showed the old king, played as usual by Otto Gebühr, seizing control of the army from his recalcitrant generals and winning victory in the teeth of defeat. Another favorite historical precedent for Hitler lay in the Bismarck cycle, represented in 1942 by Wolfgang Liebeneimer's *The Dismissal* (*Die Entlassung*); in this film the aged but all-powerful statesman opposes the incompetent Wilhelm II. Another film with national prestige was *Secret File WB1* (*Geheimakte WB1*; 1942), directed by Herbert Selpin; this told the story of the German inventor of the submarine, Wilhelm Bauer, and the sabotage of his work by the British in 1834. Anti-Semitism was maintained in *Wien 1910* (1942), directed by E. W. Emo, in which Jewish-inspired financial speculation is shown to be ruining the city's economy at that period, with the mayor, Karl Lueger, uncovering these machinations. As for more contemporary themes, Roger von Norman's *Bloody Dogs* (*Himmelhunde*; 1942) emphasized the importance of absolute discipline for youth in a story concerning a gliding competition. Another

GPU (1942), directed by Karl Ritter.

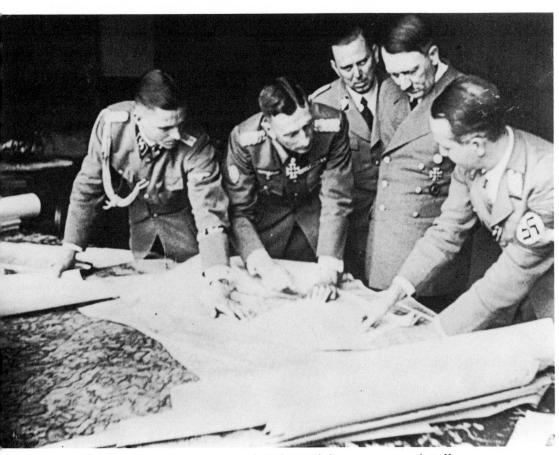

German wartime newsreel, Hitler and the army general staff.

film by Veit Harlan, by now the premier director of Nazi film, was *The Golden City* (*Die Goldene Stadt;* 1942) which contained anti-Czech propaganda; the golden city is Prague, but a young Sudetan girl goes to that city only to be seduced in a film with a tragic end. Made in Agfacolor, the film was an award winner at the Venice Film Festival.

It is of some interest to note that among the anti-British films planned for production during this period some were abandoned—*The Opium War*, which was intended to show British exploitation of opium in their commercial dealings with India and China (this theme was apparently left to the Japanese), a film on Thomas Paine and his opposition to Britain in support of Washington, and *The Great Game*, a film designed to expose terrorism in the British secret service. Another film made in 1942–43 and completed but withdrawn as a result of the circumstances of war was Karl Ritter's *Garrison Dora* (*Besatzung Dora*), showing the exploits of a German company on the African, French, and Russian fronts. The principal anti-British film of 1942 proved to be *Titanic* (released 1943), directed by Herbert Selpin and Werner Klinger. In this, the villain is represented as Ismay, President of the White Star Line, who causes the disaster through his blind desire to win the Blue Riband at grave risk to the safety of the ship and those aboard, whereas the hero is a survivor, a German ship's officer, who does his best to bring about an exposure of Ismay's guilt, and fails.

1942 was the year in which Goebbels sought most strongly to dominate European film production in the occupied countries. In 1941 he had founded the International Chamber of Film in Berlin, with UFA as the central force representing the cinema in Germany. The infiltration of German capital into foreign film concerns meant that the German film industry gained relatively invisible internal control without overtly assuming open control in such important centers of production as France and Italy.

4
The War: III. Victory in Europe and Asia, 1943–45

The two and a half years between the fall of Stalingrad and the defeat of Hitler in Europe and of the Japanese in Asia is a record of the gradual retrieval of lost territories until finally both Germany and Japan became occupied by the various Allied armies. Events during these thirty-one months of action were timed as follows; it is useful to keep this in mind when considering the many films these actions occasioned:

1943. Heavy raid by RAF on Berlin, following up the 1,000 bomber raids of previous year. Bombing of Germany a vital factor from 1943 to end of the war.
May. German army surrender in Tunisia.
June. Americans land in New Guinea.
July. Allies land in Sicily. Fall of Mussolini's regime, succeeded by the Badoglio government.
September. Allies land in S. Italy. Russians, having recaptured Kharkov, cross the Dnieper and take Smolensk.
November. Russians capture Kiev.

1944. January. Leningrad relieved.
March. Russians force the Dniester.
May. Monte Cassino taken; Hitler's defense line in Italy broken.
June. D-Day landings in France.
July. Russians take Minsk. Failure of attempt by German Army Resistance group to assassinate Hitler. Liberation of Poland begun by Russians.
August. De Gaulle enters Paris following its liberation by Allied armies.
September. Americans cross German frontier in the West.

October. Americans land in the Philippines. Russians enter Belgrade. Russians advance into Hungary.

December. N. Burma cleared of Japanese by the British.

1945.   January. British offensive in Burma. Russians take Warsaw. Russians reach the Oder.

February. 14th Army enters Mandalay. Allied armies cross the Rhine. Russians cross the Austrian frontier.

April. Americans take Okinawa; naval victory at Kyushu. Russians reach Berlin. Assassination of Mussolini by Italian partisans (28 April). Suicide of Hitler in Berlin (30 April).

May. Germans surrender in Italy. Capitulation of Germany in the north.

June. Occupation of Germany by Allied forces.

July. Three-power occupation of Berlin.

August. Atomic bombs dropped on Hiroshima and Nagasaki. Japan surrenders. Occupation of Japan by US forces.

November. Trial of the Major War Criminals by the Allied International Military Tribunal begins at Nuremberg.

British War Films, 1943–45

The main emphasis in British war films during the last phase of the war was on the documentary approach. In a sense, it made comparatively little difference if the films were reenactments of events using professional actors speaking consciously developed forms of dialogue with carefully planned characterization (as in *Nine Men, We Dive at Dawn,* or *San Demetrio, London*), or whether nonprofessional actors were called upon to re-create real events within their own experience (as in *Western Approaches* or, alongside a number of professionals, in *Journey Together*). Actors, many of them seconded from the services to perform parts reflecting their service lives, were in many cases as close to what they were interpreting as the nonprofessional servicemen who appeared along with them or, in certain documentaries, managed to sustain performances in their own right unleavened by professional assistance.

It is particularly interesting to contrast *San Demetrio, London* (1943)—Charles Frend's studio film made at Ealing, which reconstructs an actual event concerning a burning tanker that is temporarily abandoned by its crew, but later rejoined by a small group and sailed safely to port—and the wholly documentary approach of Pat Jackson's film, *Western Approaches* (1944), which concerns a boatful of men who have also abandoned ship. Filmed in color, *Western Approaches* used real merchant seamen who were called upon to reenact an incident on the high seas with which they were all familiar. The script of *San*

Nine Men (1943), directed by Harry Watt.

Western Approaches (1944), directed by Pat Jackson.

Demetrio, London was fully developed to allow its professional actors to establish the contrasting range of English, Welsh, Scottish, and even American characters among the captain and crew of the tanker; *Western Approaches* depended entirely on the simple speech worked out between Pat Jackson and his chosen group of men; they were never asked to say more than they could compass naturally before camera and microphone, and the strong characterization they achieved was, of course, entirely their own.

San Demetrio, London was reconstructed almost entirely within the studios and involved liberal use of models and the tank. The story was the true one of an oil tanker that caught fire following action at sea; she was abandoned by her crew, and then reboarded by the group on a single lifeboat when she was resighted still burning, but apparently seaworthy. They considered the great risk involved well worth it. The remaining fires were put out, and the ship brought safely to port in the Clyde by this small band of men who salvaged a great part of her precious cargo of oil. The characters were played in a wholly naturalistic style, but with a scriptwriter's due consideration for neat balance and contrast—Walter Fitzgerald as the humane, strong-minded chief engineer: Mervyn Johns, restrained and sympathetic as a greaser who dies of his injuries and is buried at sea; Robert Beatty, toughly independent as an American who had been working his passage over the Atlantic to join the RAF. An utterly unpretentious film, *San Demetrio, London* stayed as close as possible to the facts of the official report on this heroic incident, and emerged as one of the most sincere as well as one of the simplest reenacted films of the period.

Other films made in this style and tradition were *We Dive at Dawn* (1943; Anthony Asquith, with John Mills and Eric Portman), an account of the attack undertaken by a British submarine on a new German battleship, Ealing's *For Those in Peril* (1944; Charles Crichton, with David Farrar and Ralph Michael), a story of an incident from the Air Sea Rescue Service, *The Way Ahead* (1944; Carol Reed, with notable performances by a large, professional cast including David Niven, Billy Hartnell, James Donald, Stanley Holloway, Raymond Huntley, and a script by Eric Ambler and a very youthful Peter Ustinov), about the development into an effective fighting unit of a group of disparate, and mainly unwilling late recruits to the army, *The Way to the Stars* (1945; Anthony Asquith, with Michael Redgrave, John Mills, Rosamund John, Douglas Montgomery, Renee Asherson), and *Journey Together* (1945; John Boulting for the RAF Film Production Unit, with Richard Attenborough and Edward G. Robinson). The last film had a fine psychological study by Richard Attenborough of the young work-

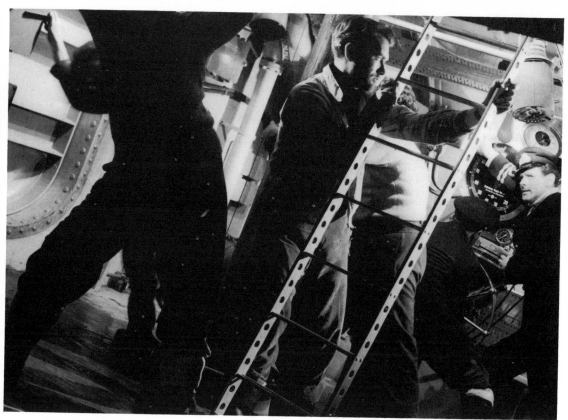

We Dive at Dawn (1943), directed by Anthony Asquith, with John Mills.

The Way Ahead (1944), directed by Carol Reed, with David Niven.

The Way to the Stars (1945), directed by Anthony Asquith, with Trevor Howard.

ing class corporal-fitter in the RAF whose ambition is to become a pilot but who has to reevaluate himself and recognize the importance of his qualities as a navigator after failing to qualify as a pilot following training in Britain and the United States. Terence Rattigan worked on both *Journey Together* (story only) and *The Way to the Stars* (story and script). The latter handled with sensitivity the problems arising from relationships, both British and American, established by men of the RAF and USAAF in daily danger of death with women in the locality of their airfield. Among these relationships is that of a war widow (Toddy) with Johnny (a married United States airman). As such films as these pass into the final phase of the war, or indeed overpass its conclusion in Europe, they tend to search more deeply into the kind of purely human and psychological problems of the time which so many members of the audiences in Britain had themselves been forced to experience in one form or another.[1]

Reviewing *Journey Together* at the time, I wrote:

This is a beautifully made picture, restrained in its treatment of the real emotional problems of very young men who are ambitious to pilot aircraft and yet have to learn the disciplines involved in operational flights. Richard Attenborough, who plays Wilton, has proved already on the stage (*Brighton Rock*) and on the screen (*In Which We Serve*) that he is an imaginative character actor, which is rare among players technically classed as juveniles. Edward G. Robinson's mature, humane strength gives Attenborough precisely the right foil, as he shows Wilton's struggle towards emotional maturity. There is nothing pretentious or unnecessary about the general direction of the film. It makes its points, mainly psychological, at leisure and yet never seems slow. It derives its sense of tension from the drama of actual events, without the heroics or artificial respiration of some American air pictures. [*Monthly Film Bulletin*, 1945, p. 117]

Ernest Lindgren, reviewing *The Way to the Stars*, said:

Has a man who is daily courting death the right to marry? (a question answered in the affirmative, but only by the emphatic assertion of Toddy, not because it is really resolved). But another subject hardly less important which obtrudes itself is the question of Anglo-American relationships, of which several facets are shown. Then again there is the problem of Johnny and his friendship for Toddy, although it was implied in only the slenderest of hints. And finally, much emphasis is laid on the last line of a poem to a dead airman, 'Johnny Head-in-air'— 'see that his children are fed', was that the film's main point? The truth is that this film was presumably conceived, and must be judged, not primarily as one of idea, or plot, or character, but as a film of atmosphere, and so regarded, it is so successful and so entertaining that it must rank as one of the outstanding British films of the war years. No other film has so subtly and so truthfully portrayed the life of the airman in war, its problems, its hazards, its exaggerated casualness towards death, its courage, its humour, its comradeship. [*MFB* 1945]

Closer to *Western Approaches* in its documentary recreation of a war incident was Harry Watt's small-budget picture, *Nine Men*, made much earlier for Ealing. Shot largely on location on a deserted beach in South Wales, it reconstructed the adventures of a small British detachment lost in the North African desert in an area held by the Italians, and it depended for its effectiveness on the character-playing of a group of largely unknown professional actors carefully chosen by Harry Watt, and used partially improvized dialogue. Ernest Lindgren claimed at the time that the film came "as near to a native style of British film-making as anything which has yet been seen."[2]

Before his death on the flight from Lisbon, Leslie Howard directed the first of a series of feature films dedicated to the part women were playing in wartime Britain. This was *The Gentle Sex* (1943), with Joan Gates, Jean Gillie, Joyce Howard, Rosamund John, and Lilli

The Gentle Sex (1943), directed by Leslie Howard.

Palmer. The story, documentary in treatment, concerns seven girls of varied social background who join the Auxiliary Territorial Service (ATS), meeting for the first time on the train like the men in *The Way Ahead*, and staying together, separating, reuniting during their varied lives in the service. This film, introduced by Leslie Howard himself as he pinpoints in the opening sequence each girl in the crowd at Victoria Station, keeps in sympathetic contact with them as they pass through real ATS centers for training and service. The professional actresses (including Lilli Palmer as a Czech refugee) had to blend inconspicuously with the real servicewomen.

Frank Launder and Sidney Gilliat followed this film with their account of women in wartime industry—*Millions Like Us* (1943), with Eric Portman, Patricia Roc, Anne Crawford, and Gordon Jackson. In spite of a documentary background in the aircraft factory, the emphasis tended to be on the love relationships of two girls—the "working-class" Celia and her young husband, who is a pilot later reported missing, and Anne Crawford as an "upper-class" girl drafted into war work and, in spite of her snobbishness, falling in love with the works foreman (Eric Portman). The film was restrained in mood, and quiet as all the later British war films tended to be. In the same year Maurice Elvey made *The Lamp Still Burns* (with Rosamund John, Stewart Granger, Godfrey Tearle) about a successful woman architect who dedicates herself in wartime to nursing. This film, too, had a semidocumentary treatment in its presentation of life in a hospital. Nevertheless, it had a platitudinous close implying duty is duty now, but one day everything will again be "all right."

In 1945 Sidney Gilliat wrote and directed *Waterloo Road* (with John Mills and Stewart Granger), employing a similar authenticity in its portrayal of wartime civilian life. The story dealt with a young soldier who goes absent without leave in pursuit of his wife, who he gathers is having an affair with a civilian philanderer in the area where they live in the Waterloo Road in London. A reconciliation follows after he has beaten up his rival in a fight, and he then surrenders himself to the military authorities. This again was a situation the audience thoroughly understood, and the hot sincerity and urgency John Mills brought to the character of the soldier gave the film great sympathy as well as quick action. The film forecast what the documentary approach might mean if it could be sustained in postwar subjects, when the war-action films were over.

In 1943 the British Army Film and Photographic Service had extended to some eighty cameramen and eight directors distributed over the various fighting fronts, while the Army Film Unit had its headquarters in Pinewood Studios, near London, under Hugh Stewart.[3] All material shot was sent initially for censorship and classification to a department known as Public Relations 2 (PR2), operating under Ronald Tritton, who was responsible for army film propaganda, and who maintained liaison with the civilian Ministry of Information. Much of it was then forwarded to Pinewood, where individual directors would return to finish their films. The newsreel companies received service material free of charge.

The staff of the Film Unit was divided into various sectors. No 1 Unit (four directors and forty cameramen) was assigned to the Eighth Army and served under David MacDonald with headquarters in Cairo; the Unit was responsible for coverage of the whole Middle East (Syria, Iran, Iraq, etc.). No 2 Unit, under Geoffrey Keating (three directors and thirty cameramen) was with the First Army in Tunisia; responsibility here was to the Public Relations at army headquarters, but leaving initiative very much in the hands of the Unit. No 3 Unit (three cameramen) was attached to Home Forces, and No 4 Unit (one director—Paul Fletcher—and four cameramen) was attached to an Airborne Division; both had freedom of initiative, but like the rest kept naturally in close liaison with the divisional headquarters where they were operational. Independent cameramen also operated in Gibraltar and Malta. All cameramen held the rank of sergeant, and had battle training in order to maintain equality with the men they were filming. Many were cameramen in civilian life, but the majority were new to the work and had been trained specially for it.

Pinewood acted as the center for other service and official units, including the RAF Unit and the civilian Crown Film Unit. In addition to the Army Film Unit there were the various branches of the Army Kinematograph Service, concerned with the army's own film production, including training films, centered on the Fox Studios at Wembley, It was here that Carol Reed made *The New Lot* (later developed into the feature film, *The Way Ahead* for release to the general public); Thorold Dickinson was for a while attached to the AKS, and (as we have seen) made *Next of Kin* at Ealing for this Service. The production of training films amounted to around one hundred annually at this period. AKS was also responsible for the exhibition and distribution of films for army use, screened in centers equipped with thirty-five-millimeter projectors or shown by means of some 150 mobile units.

The admiralty limited its own production to training films, its public relations being left to the MOI or the newsreel companies. Training films were made either by outside professional units, or by the Royal Naval Film Section based on Plymouth. The RAF, however, worked in a manner roughly equivalent to that of the army, sharing the base at Pinewood, and making training films through the RAF Film Production Unit. The RAF made extensive use of film records in the analysis of the effectiveness of their planes in action.

1943 was to be a year of achievement in officially sponsored documentary. Productions included *Desert Victory,* on the war in North Africa, Humphrey Jennings's two finest war films, *Fires were Started,* on the Fire Service, and *The Silent Village,* shot in a Welsh mining village in tribute to the martyrs of Lidice in Czechoslovakia, Jack Lee's *Close Quarters,* a study of submarine warfare, and Paul Rotha's possibly best film, *The World of Plenty,* which had a profound influence on audiences in wartime Britain and elsewhere. Other documentaries of 1943 were the RAF film Unit's *Operational Height,* a short feature on the work of the balloon ships, and *The Volunteer,* Michael Powell and Emeric Pressburger's short feature about the Fleet Air Arm and in particular Pat McGrath, Ralph Richardson's peacetime theatrical dresser who became a skilled engineer in the Fleet Air Arm in which

Greek Testament (1943), directed by Alberto Cavalcanti.

Richardson, who narrates the film, was a pilot.

Desert Victory (March 1943), an hour-long film by the combined talents of the Army Film and Photographic Unit and the Royal Air Force Film Production Unit, was primarily the directional and editorial work of Roy Boulting; the photography was by combat cameramen attached to the Eighth Army; the outstanding music score was composed by William Alwyn. The action, which was handled with a dramatic artistry which lifted the film well above the average war record documentary, covered the campaign in Egypt and Libya from the blockade at El Alamein to prevent Rommel's advance into Egypt and the great assault which broke the German general's line in October 1942 and led to rapid advances first to El Agheila, and then to Tripoli. This film of Britain's first major victory against Hitler was directed with such imaginative, dynamic skill that its value to public morale in the darker days of the European war was incalculable. Its wonderful night photography as the British wait, their watches synchronized, for the barrage to open up, offers close portraits of men poised for action. Alwyn's music reinforces this, as the faces, alert and tense, alter-

Desert Victory (1943).

Road to Russia (c. 1943).

nate with shots of the tanks and guns, standing silent, massed and ready. Alwyn introduced a single, sustained note for the sequence which rose octave by octave like a nerve stretched to breaking point, finally snapping as the barrage begins with prolonged, vibrating thunder. The commentary, quiet spoken and factual, was written by J. L. Hodson.

Desert Victory had its successors in the same tradition—*Tunisian Victory* (1944; a combined operation of the British and United States Service Film Units, co-directed by Roy Boulting and Frank Capra), a lesser film that covered the North African campaign from the American intervention in 1942 to the final capitulation of the German armies in this theater of war. The commentary made marked use of alternate British and American actor-type voices—actually Bernard Miles and Burgess Meredith—and is important as an early example of the British combining to produce a film record with their new Allies.[4] The film lacked the imaginative emotional unity that made *Desert Victory* outstanding, and that was to appear again, though with an entirely different atmosphere, in *Burma Victory*, for which Roy Boulting was

Desert Victory (1943).

wholly responsible. And there was a grave miscalculation at the close of the film, with its Capra-like touch of "pie in the sky" when the war is over and everyone is happy to "bring back smiles to the children's faces again."

Burma Victory (November 1945), an hour long, had to explain the complex action in Burma between 1942 and 1945, interlocked with the China campaign. It did so brilliantly, making abundantly clear the wholly alien difficulties of jungle warfare against a strange and implacable enemy. The British are seen at first forced back to Imphal and Kohima. Then comes Stilwell's campaign from the north to reopen the land route to China from Northern Burma, while Central Burma is invaded by the Chindits under Wingate. The Japanese are finally pressed back by an Allied counterinvasion under Mountbatten; Mandalay falls to Slim; the British move down to Rangoon, and Allied forces are finally massed to relieve Malaya and Singapore when the Japanese capitulation takes place. Again music brought particular atmosphere to the film—for example, the cool, melodic score by Alan Rawsthorne was most effectively combined with sound effects at the moment when the Chindits are landed by gliders in Central Burma far behind the Japanese lines. The gliders, towed in the air over mountains eight thousand feet high, land in a clearing to the cries of jungle creatures and the watchful stare of birds of prey perched in the trees.

The True Glory was the film that marked the climax in combined film operations between the British and Americans, in this case the British Ministry of Information and the United States Office of War Information.[5] Directed by Carol Reed and Garson Kanin, its team of script and commentary writers included Eric Maschwitz and Gerald Kersh. Again the music was by William Alwyn, and the film made outstanding use of multivoiced commentary. It is described by Paul Rotha as "an emotional as well as a factual resumé" of the war in Europe following the D-Day landings. The prolonged and massive action in Europe is given throughout a detailed and human perspective—men and their equipment waiting in the summer sunshine of the English countryside, the tension of the landings themselves given magnificent coverage by combat cameramen, the Normandy bridgeheads stubbornly contested, the liberated peasants and townsfolk, the scene of the Teheran conference of the war leaders set against a face here, a soldier lying dead in Caen, or scenes on the roads leading through to Paris, to Brussels, to the German frontier itself. The problems of supplying the rapidly moving forces—traveling at unexpected pace as the Germans fall back to defend their Fatherland—is pinpointed by the agonized frustration of the crew of a British tank run out of fuel and

The True Glory (1945), directed by Garson Kanin and Carol Reed.

left stationary near Metz. The whole complex operation moves forward with a tempo matched by that of the film itself, while the commentary works on several levels, at some moments almost Homeric—"they looked across the heaving sea"; "the steel-encumbered ships"; "on the green banks of the Elbe we watched for the East and West to meet"—at others reflecting the blunt speech or the personal observations of dozens of men and women enduring the campaign as a firsthand experience. Occasionally Eisenhower himself injects an overall description of what was going on, insisting on the range of the Allied effort—"Anyone who wants to take a bow by himself—he's nuts." The music, overused if anything, is dramatically impressionist, up-pointing the excitement and feeling of the action. The views of the representative participants are spoken by men and women alike (servicemen, civilians, correspondents) in every kind of tone, ironic, human, passionate, and in every kind of accent, English, Welsh, American (White and Negro), French, Canadian. A soldier says on seeing Belsen—"I had to fall out and be quickly sick in the courtyard." "If you'd only given up in 1940 none of this might have happened," is a comment quoted by a soldier from a German woman. The film ends with the ancient prayer that gives the film its title.

Writing in *DNL* (issue 49, 1945), Donald Bull, then a British Staff Officer with the Film and Photographic Section of SHAEF, Eisenhower's Supreme Command, explained that official coverage of the European campaign resulted in some 5.5 million feet of film being shot by five hundred cameramen belonging to more than twenty different services and government departments. It was, he says, "the most lavishly equipped and planned photographic campaign in history." Censorship of the material, as shot, was centralized by SHAEF in a single viewing center in Davies Street, London. The aim was "to survey the whole field of coverage of the SHAEF operation, to allocate this great camera force with economy and efficiency, to secure complete recording of every phase of the operation, both front-line and rear echelon." He adds:

> From the beginning, the scene was dominated by the vast numbers of American service cameramen sent into the field. After the admittedly poor results achieved in North Africa, the Americans turned to the statistical, or herring-spawn, method. The idea was that every formation from army groups downwards should have a given degree of coverage, ensured by the attachment of a given camera force to operate within the area of that particular formation. With a certain amount of reshuffling, this system held from D-day to VE-day. There is no doubt it yielded results. The US War Department now possesses an unsurpassed record of its army's activities in Europe.

The British method differed in organization:

> . . . the use of small combat camera teams attached to formations as necessary . . . very mobile, able to tie on to any formation that looked as if it were doing something interesting and record what was going on; the use of special coverage units, briefed from a higher organization . . . to secure broader and more organized footage on particular subjects; free use of newsreel photographers to shoot as and how they pleased, to satisfy their own particular requirements.

The United States put some four hundred cameramen in the field, and shot 3.5 million of the 5.5 million combat footage from the campaign. Overlapping could not be wholly avoided. The British teams, small in mumbers and unaccountably short of film and equipment, covered the war thinly rather than in depth; on the other hand the RAF material was superb, with its wing camera material revealing the results of daytime strafing and of mass bombing at night. The material from the navies excelled only at the beginning when their work was most in evidence. Automatic cameras were also attached to landing craft, achieving remarkable shots to judge by the small amount (some three hundred feet only) that survived the action; most of this particular coverage was lost. To this must be added the work of the European crews—of camera directors such as John Ferno covering the Netherlands, the Norwegian covering of the Walcheren landings, the units covering civilian life—and the independent work of the newsreel cameramen. Donald Bull singles out for the highest praise the shots of the liberation of Paris by the brothers Mejato and Gaston Madru, later killed by a sniper while filming street fighting in Leipzig. Madru filmed the last days of occupied Paris using a camera concealed in a carrier-basket on a bicycle. In the end, for all the elaborate planning of the Service units, everything depended on the initiative and the instinctual eye of individual cameramen who could catch the full flight of battle on the wing. The collective resulting material, viewed and censored in London, gave the newsreels their coverage from D-Day to the collapse of Germany, as well as a number of special films, such as *A Harbour Goes to France*, showing the celebrated sectional harbor, *Mulberry*, which was towed across the Channel and subsequently battered after its arrival by unexpectedly heavy seas. The whole vast collection of shots forms an archive to be forever drawn upon in visual surveys of the war, primarily now for television. Only *The True Glory* had used it at the time for a primary feature documentary, though the French material as we shall see, appeared in a remarkable short feature, *Le Journal de la Résistance*, first shown in England in January 1945.

In British civilian documentary, Humphrey Jennings was the "poet militant"; a Cambridge man, like Elton, Wright, and Legg, he believed in the gradual evolution of culture in such a country as Britain, and combined an intense, observer's visual sense with a literary student's response to words; these qualities are reflected (though his critics have said, near-parodied) in his early short, *Words for Battle*. For him, the war represented Britain defending her great heritage of culture against the destructive barbarism of the Nazis, the censors and destroyers of books and art.

Jennings's best war films, apart from the short *Listen to Britain* already mentioned, were *The Silent Village* (1943) and the short feature, *Fires were Started* (1943, *I Was a Fireman*, fullest version, eighty minutes).[6] His producer at this time, Ian Dalrymple, has written that "no work recalls the atmosphere and feeling of the times more poignantly than Humphrey's films." I can testify personally that they were the ones of all we constantly showed that most immediately stirred emotions not only in the West Country but in the far tougher Northeast of Britain (the Tyneside) which I also came to know well

Fires Were Started (1943), directed by Humphrey Jennings.

Fires Were Started (1943), directed by Humphrey Jennings.

at the time. Today they may well appear at times overtraditional—at rare moments, even a touch chauvinistic, like the "Rule Britannia" chorus sung at the close of *Listen to Britain.* But Jennings's sensitivity to the deeper traditional feeling in Britain, relating to culture rather than to class, was intuitive and emotional, and emerged impressionistically in the films, embedded in point of view, behavior, landscape, whether the green beauty of Downs or the rubble of cities. It inspires the simple yet extraordinary sequence of the assembly of the auxiliary firemen, coming together to face the night's danger of raids on London's docksides under a full moon, and singing in turn as they arrive with their fire-fighting equipment the traditional English song, "One man to mow, went to mow a meadow . . . Two men . . . Three men . . ." and so on till the siren announcing the coming of the bombers stops them. *Fires Were Started* was the story of the varied team (workmen, artisans, a middle-class scholar) who work and die together during the great fire raids of 1940–41, told with the help of real firemen who reenact their life together, and the labor involved in fighting fires during one of the heavier raids. It is wrong, possibly, to call such a film a documentary. Rather it is an evocation of a genuine group of people in a real environment as they appeared to an artist permeated by the cultural history of the British people.

Jennings also conceived the unique film, *A Silent Village*, as a tribute to the people of the Czech mining village of Lidice, who had been massacred by the Germans in retaliation for the assassination of SS General Heydrich, Hitler's plenipotentiary in Prague during May 1942. Jennings made the film in a very similar mining village in South Wales, Cwmgiedd. The film, recorded largely in Welsh and English, yet with its action abundantly clear, was made in cooperation with the Czech Ministry of Foreign Affairs in exile, the South Wales Miners' Federation, and the people of Cwmgiedd and the Swansea and Dulai's valleys. The idea of using the Welsh language (symbolically representing Czech) was an inspired one. It linked the Czechs closely with the whole British people. The Czechs themselves were deeply touched by this imaginative tribute; I saw the film myself for the first time at a private screening with a Czech army officer, who was unable to restrain his tears. Genuine emotion was seldom held back during these times.[7] Jennings made the official record-film of the German V1 rocket ("doodlebug") attack on London and Southern England—*The 80 Days* (1944). The style of this film reverted to that of the early blitz films, with a commentary in this case by Ed Murrow, who speaks of the "steadiness of the people of London," whose "sacrifices were speeding victory." "The Battle of London," says

Murrow, "was part of the Battle of France." Elderly men playing bowls, civilians working in the fields, children in the streets turn their faces up to the sky at the distant but on-coming sound of the V1, with its crude, vibrating pulse. Some of the flying bombs are intercepted and blown up in flight, while some reach their target, where civilians scatter to the shelters and listen in silence for the chug of the engine to cut-out preparatory to explosion. Smoke rises slowly from the heart of the city panorama, while a camera on the site covers rescue operations.

Against the standards of authenticity set by the documentaries and the documentary styled features, the rest of the wartime subjects with a few exceptions appear colorless. It seemed difficult to imagine the war by this time wholly in the context of entertainment, but such films continued to appear. Among the better were *The Silver Fleet* (1943, directors Campbell Sewell and Gordon Wellesley, with Ralph Richardson and Googie Withers), which was about a Dutch shipbuilder who poses as a collaborator in order to bring about major sabotage, ultimately at the cost of his own life. In this film the local Gestapo chief was played by Esmond Knight, who had been blinded while serving in the navy. Other such films were *The Bells Go Down* (1943, Basil Dearden, with Tommy Trinder, James Mason, and Finlay Currie), a comedy about rivalry in an East End Auxiliary Fire Service Unit during the blitz, *Undercover* (1943, Sergei Nolbandov, with John Clements, Godfrey Tearle, and Mary Morris), set in occupied Yugoslavia, with another resistance hero posing as a collaborator, *Escape to Danger* (1943, directors Victor Hanbury, Lance Comfort, and Mutz Greenbaum, with Eric Portman and Ann Dvorak), set in occupied Denmark, with an Englishwoman working initially for the Danish resistance while posing as a collaborator, *2,000 Women* (1944, Frank Launder, with Phyllis Calvert, Flora Robson, Patricia Roc, and Renee Houston), set in a women's internment camp in France, where a group organize the escape of some British airmen who have baled out in their area, and *Johnny Frenchman* (1945, Charles Frend, with Françoise Rosay, Tom Walls, Patricia Roc), a romantic comedy in which war unites the former "enemies," the Breton and Cornish fishermen. *Johnny Frenchman* was shot at Mevagissey in Cornwall, where certain of the Breton fishing boats that escaped from occupied France were based and appeared in the film.[8]

The more romantic films with a war background were headed by *The Demi-Paradise* (or *Adventure for Two*, 1943; Anthony Asquith, with Laurence Olivier and Felix Aylmer), *Perfect Strangers* (1945, Alexander Korda, with Robert Donat and Deborah Kerr), and Herbert Wilcox's *I Live in Grosvenor Square* (1945, with Anna Neagle, Rex Harrison, Dean Jagger, Robert Morley). These films reflect much of the past obsessions of the British, including devotion to the foibles of the upper classes. Anthony Asquith's comedy pokes affectionate fun at this, with English life seen through the wary, disorientated eyes of Laurence Olivier as a visiting Russian engineer coming to what terms he can with a wayward-seeming English shipbuilder (Felix Aylmer), whose attention appears to be more on gracious living than on business. Like so many of these "affectionate" self-portraits, such films are in the end a form of national vanity that appears now both whimsical and dated. Similarly, *I Live in Grosvenor Square* places a middle-class American airman (a sergeant) in the arms of a WAAF corporal who is also a duke's granddaughter, so rivaling an English major who is already her fiance. Each gives her up in turn for the other, and the American is finally killed in action, but not before he has enjoyed the (to him) fascinating spectacle of ducal living. This was English class-consciousness at its most extreme—it had become almost an obsession for Herbert Wilcox and Anna Neagle. However, *Perfect Strangers* stays strictly lower middle class in spite of being directed by Alexander Korda,[9] whose previous films made in Hollywood, *Lady Hamilton* (in the United States, *That Hamilton Woman*, 1941) had become an unlikely box-office success in wartime Russia, and (by drawing a romantic parallel between Britain facing Napoleon and facing Hitler) had acted as effective propaganda in prewar Russia. Churchill saw it often, and is rumored never to have ceased weeping at its splendors.

Perfect Strangers saw the transformation effected in a dyspeptic clerk and his mousy wife when they are separated and join the services. They have modest, unconsummated extramarital love affairs, and become so glamorized they scarcely know each other when they finally meet again. The inevitable quarrels are patched up, and marriage reestablished on sound romantic lines. The domestic propaganda line was obvious—a husband or wife in the services is worth two in civil life.

The most unusual film of the period was Michael Powell and Emeric Pressburger's *The Life and Death of Colonel Blimp* (1943, with Roger Livesey, Anton Walbrook, Deborah Kerr), the first production of their new company, the Archers, and based very loosely indeed on the cartoon character developed by Britain's greatest political cartoonist, David Low. Blimp was a myopic member of Britain's most reactionary upper-crust and imperialistic class, the equivalent, in fact, in English terms, of the right-wing nationalists who had helped

Hitler to power in Germany. Michael Powell's original intention had been to get Laurence Olivier to make a character part of Blimp—"vicious, slashing, cruel, merciless." But the MOI so disapproved of the project in 1943 that Olivier, who was serving at the time in the Fleet Air Arm, was denied to them. They made do with Roger Livesey, who turned Blimp into a sentimental bumbler—a quite different figure from Low's recalcitrant old reactionary. The result was that "everybody loved him,"' except, it would seem, Winston Churchill, who went to the premiere in the summer of 1943 and thought the film "disgraceful."

It certainly caused some controversy, and might well have caused more if the original interpretation of Blimp by Olivier had been introduced. Powell still claims he would have preferred Olivier, but Pressburger was very happy with Livesey's far softer, more endearing interpretation. Clive Candy is a young, highly decorated officer of the South African Boer War who fights a duel afterward in Germany because the Germans claim the British committed atrocities against the Boers, with whom the Germans traditionally sided. However, he makes friends with his opponent, although he loses to him the girl he loves, marrying instead another woman during the 1914 war who reminds him of his original love. A brigadier by the time of the Second World War, he is a widower and his German friend, who has become an anti-Hitler refugee, lives with him on the friendliest terms. Deborah Kerr, as the three successive women in Candy's life, reemerges in the 1940s representing a young girl in the services.

The film was one of the most ambitious productions of the war years, shot in Technicolor when the great majority of films remained in black and white. Its length, too, was prodigious—163 minutes when most films were ninety. The designer was the brilliant German refugee, Alfred Junge, and the photographer the Frenchman, Georges Périnal; altogether the film emerged as a distinctively European portrait of the British, with a somewhat obscure "message" in 1943. Critics even disagreed about the color—"admirable," said the British Film Institute's reviewer, "the worst seen for a very long time," said the critic of *DNL*.

The *DNL* review reflects what contemporary opponents of the film thought:

> . . . the Blimp of this film is the Englishman that a certain type of emigré would like to think exists—stupid, brave, amiable, kind to animals and domestics, and, *au fond* eminently amenable to reason, particularly if put forward by someone of another nationality.

> Unfortunately the type does not exist; the nearest approach being not the diehard, who sincerely and openly professes his intentions and

does not try to be nice about it, but rather the quisling or Munichite who conceals his venom under the facile charm of you-know-who.

The best thing *Blimp* can do is to reassure the reactionaries by making it clearer that they are, as they have themselves so often suspected, the salt of the earth. And it is remarkable, if you think back over the film, that not one single ordinary person, such as you may meet in the street or a bus in England, has anything more than a walking-on part in the entire film. But the people are perhaps not important in comparison with the huge collection of financiers, soldiers, diplomats, judges, etc., who pat our Prussian hero on the back in 1919 and promise to put Germany on her feet again. Note, too, that it is the Prussian who reneges on the Nazis, while the financiers, soldiers, diplomats, etc., as we well remember—carried on the good work of backing up Hitler.

As one sees Blimp reunited to his German friend, and being taught by him a few elementary facts about international affairs, one wonders who is the real hero of the film—the German who doesn't like Hitler or the Old Soldier who refuses to die?[10]

1943 was a watershed year for sociopolitical thinking in Britain. While those who were politically "conscious" were raising an increasing demand for our "war aims" to be stated by those in authority, authority itself, as we have seen, led by Churchill as war leader, thrust such demands aside as untimely and likely to be divisive when all that mattered was to maintain a united front with a single slogan— "win the war." While the "simple message" of the film might have been, as Charles Oakley put it twenty years later, "presumably that mankind unites to resist brutal intolerance," many felt that the film in effect sentimentalized the very social structure that had given Hitler his greatest opportunities to establish tyranny. The gracious presence of Deborah Kerr as the girl of three generations only served to reinforce the idea that the upper middle class were the salt of British society.

Only one officially sponsored film stood out at the time as representing this growing, conscious desire to define something of the social values for which Britain was expending her blood. This was Paul Rotha's *World of Plenty* (1943), a combined compilation film and specially shot "argument" brilliantly edited to shock people into realization that while whole areas of the prewar world were starving, other areas (notably North America) were suffering from unmarketable overproduction. Using journalistic techniques learned in part from America's prewar *Living Newspaper*[11] by involving the audience in the give-and-take of argument about social problems, it was scripted by Eric Knight and Rotha, and incorporated the challenging opinions of Sir John (later Lord) Boyd Orr on nutrition, backing its statistics with mobile Isotype diagrams. The American material and interviews were specially filmed for Rotha by *The March of Time* unit. *World of Plenty* was therefore an officially sponsored documentary of argument coming at the very time when argument tended to be officially frowned upon. Above all, it put a spotlight on the area that seemed to relatively unthinking people most obscure—the world to come at the end of the war. I was present at numerous screenings of this film, both in cinemas and projected nontheatrically during the period 1943–44 for British audiences of every kind, rural, urban, industrial, as well as specialized, and it never failed to stir them to prolonged applause. It presented social thinking not only in absolute contrast to the world of Adolf Hitler, but in contrast to the bitter experiences we had known in the flaccid "democracies" that tolerated prolonged unemployment and depression, the unresisting societies on which Hitler had stamped the jackboots of his armies.

Nevertheless, *World of Plenty* was only achieved with the greatest difficulty during the period 1942–43.[12] It made quite plain what it meant, time and again. The voice of the man-in-the-street constantly

World of Plenty (1943), directed by Paul Rotha.

interrupted the impersonal newsreel voice of E. V. H. Emmett, who delivered the mainstream commentary: of the United States, "the wealthiest nation in the world and a third of it ill-nourished. Laugh that one off with a diagram, mister"; "they are throwing back fish into the sea! Why, in God's name, why?"; "D'you know, they actually poured away down the drains a lot of my milk, so as I could get a decent price for what was left" (British farmer); "Out of every twenty people receiving income in the United Kingdom before the war, one got £26 a week, another one got £6, six got £4 and the remaining twelve got only £2 a week or less." The film stressed the internationalism represented by Lend-Lease, the new attempt at equalization in food rationing, the improved health of the British people. Looking to the future, it stressed the need for organized, scientific farming without gluts or bankruptcy and organized, world distribution of the food produced. "So soon as the shooting war is finished, we're pledged to win the other war— we're pledged to go on fighting until we have fulfilled the promise to bring freedom from want to all men in all lands. Tell me, what are we fighting for if not for something revolutionary?" (Sir John Boyd Orr). And the film ended with the recorded voice of Henry Wallace, vice-president of the United States: "I say that the century in which we are entering, the century which will come into being after the war, can be and must be the Century of the Common Man. The peace must mean a better standard of living for the Common Man, not merely in the United States and England, but also in India, Russia, China, Africa and Latin America—not merely in the United Nations, but also in Germany, Italy and Japan. There can be no more privileged people."

United States—Victory in Europe and Asia

Frank Capra, who had volunteered his services to the War Department in December 1941, was established as head of the film production department with the rank of major.[13] The initial result was the celebrated *Why We Fight* "orientation" series, work on which was begun in Washington early in 1942, the year in which the first two titles, *Prelude to War* and *The Nazis Strike*, were completed. The Hollywood team was a close-knit one (working at first in Washington and later in the old Fox studio on Western Avenue, Hollywood), staying together for the whole series from 1942 to 1945. Editing was in the hands of Captain, later Major, William Hornbeck, the music composed by Dmitri Tiomkin, and the principal narrator Walter Huston, while the research was conducted by an expert team headed by Sergeant Richard Griffith, later to become well-known as a film historian and curator of the film department at the Museum of Modern Art. Griffith has described their purpose succinctly: "The problem in 1942 was how to turn the youth of a nation, so recently and so predominantly isolationist, into a fighting force not only effectively trained and equipped but armed, too, with the conviction that his country's entry into a world war was not only just but the inevitable answer to serious wrongs."[14]

The full list of the series is as follows:

1942. *Prelude to War.* Directed by Maj. Frank Capra; written by Maj. Eric Knight and Capt. Anthony Veiller. 52 minutes. The first part of a series filling in the historical background up to 1941. This compilation film dealt with the rise of fascism in Italy, Germany, and Japan, and their designs for territorial aggression. The film received a late theatrical release in May 1943. Its purely Service audiences were reported to have reached nine million by 1945.

The Nazis Strike. Directed by Lt.-Col. Frank Capra and Maj. Anatole Litvak; written by Maj. Eric Knight, Capt. Anthony Veiller, and Robert Heller. Five reels. Second part in background historical series. The Nazis initial actions in Europe.

1943. *Divide and Conquer.* Directed by Lt.-Col. Frank Capra and Maj. Anatole Litvak; written by Capt. Anthony Veiller and Cpl. Robert Heller. 56 minutes. Third part in background historical series. The story of Nazi blitzkrieg, and the invasion of the North and West in Europe up to Dunkirk evacuation and the emergence of de Gaulle.

The Battle of Britain. Written and directed by Capt. Anthony Veiller. (Frank Capra was in London working on the American section of *Tunisian Victory.*) 55 minutes. Shows how, after the collapse of France, Hitler's plans for the invasion of Britain were frustrated by the RAF; the bombing of Britain. Its service audiences were reported to have reached eight million.

The Battle of Russia. Directed by Lt.-Col. Anatole Litvak; written by Lt.-Col. Anatole Litvak, Capt. Anthony Veiller, Cpl. Robert Heller. 83 minutes. The German campaign in Russia up to the defeat at Stalingrad.

Prelude to War has a powerful, emotive beginning—"Why are Americans on the march?" asks the commentator. "Is it because—" shot of Pearl Harbor; "or because—" shot of British cities on fire; "or because—" France, China, Czechoslovakia, Norway, Poland, Holland, Greece, Yugoslavia, Russia, with shots of tanks moving as if over prone bodies as a prolonged dissolve. References to the historical tenets of freedom culminate in the Declaration of Independence and a shot of the Liberty Bell— "government of the people, by the people, for the people shall not perish from the earth."

The dictators' rise to power is traced—Hitler, Mussolini, Hirohito—with shots showing the sacrifice of individual liberty by their peoples through mass regimentation, all backed by heavy, discordant music, and massive gunfire. The Nazi "philosopher" Rosenberg declares the churches must go, and a stained glass window shows a portrait of Hitler. Enacted shots of German children at worship of the new god —"Hitler is our Saviour"—with acted parallels for Italy and Japan. With a crescendo of crashing march effects, young men are seen goosestepping; inset is a caption (a frequent technique): "I want to see in youth again the gleam of the beast of prey" (Hitler). The disarmament movement in Europe and isolationism in the United States, coupled with domestic troubles blind the democracies to the dangers of Hitler; American choirboys sing, "Onward Christian Soldiers" while German children prepare for war.

With the aid of maps, Axis expansion is shown. Axis threat to the United States exists through possible invasion of Alaska in the north and Latin America in the south; the Japanese hope to march down Pennsylvania Avenue (strong, discordant music). Germany expands her population with her military budget, while in a series of historical flashes Japan is seen invading Manchuria, quitting the League of Nations, invading China, where opposition is sustained by Chiang kai-shek. Meanwhile Mussolini attacks Ethiopia. The Japanese and Nazi Germany plan to divide the world. "It's us or them," says the commentator. "The chips are down."

The Battle of Russia begins with tributes to Russia by Knox, Marshall and King. This is followed by clips from Eisenstein's *Alexander Nevsky*, Petrov's *Peter the Great*, a film of the Napoleonic invasion, and newsreels of the First World War to show how Russia has been subject to invasion throughout the centuries. Her vast scale, three times that of the United States, is demonstrated, with flashes showing the variety of peoples and cultures the Soviet Union represents. Then comes Hitler's plan for invasion (though Russia's part in the invasion of Poland is glossed over); the Russo-German pact is represented as giving time to change her peacetime industries into war industry; Russia's war with Finland is seen as an attack on a dangerous ally of Germany with a neighboring frontier that threatens Leningrad.

With the German invasion, Russia loses half a million square miles of territory to the occupiers, but "the blitz spluttered—and finally died": "the Germans came across a country [shot of Russian guns] that would not submit." The Russian strategy of defense in depth is shown by means of animated diagrams—the Russian defense lines give way, bend back, retreat strategically to strengthen the next lines

The Battle of Russia (1943), directed by Anatole Litvak.

Battle of Russia (1943), directed by Anatole Litvak.

of defense behind them, until eventually a massed, collective line is formed inside the cities—forcing the Germans out of their armored vehicles and into the city streets. The Russians are prepared to sacrifice their cities and their lands through a policy of scorched earth. In this part of the film the commentary is backed by heroic music with Russian themes, while on the screen the diagrams are cut in with brilliantly selected and timed key shots.

Behind the German lines the resistance builds up; Hitler's armies are held before Moscow, where services are seen taking place in the churches. The winter onslaught on the German lines is shown, with white-clad soldiers. Very quick cutting emphasizes guns, low-flying planes, tanks; massive sounds of explosion are orchestrated with the music. The film leaves the war momentarily to dwell on Russian culture—Tchaikovsky, Tolstoy (whose house is vandalized by the Germans). Shots of mutilation of Russian victims (results of mass murder, rape, hanging) lead to the Russian oath of retaliation—"blood for blood," "death for death."

Leningrad holds out, a bare two miles from the German lines; men, women, and children build the barricades. To a barrage of anti-aircraft guns the German planes come, the searchlights pinpointing them, while below the fires are fought and extinguished. The siege of Leningrad is conducted by mixed German and Finnish forces and the city is bombarded by long-range guns. Leningrad starves, without transport, without food, without water. But relief comes with fleets of lorries traveling over the frozen lake Lagoda; even a railway track is laid over the ice to bring in the supplies. When spring comes, the streets return to life, though wooden crosses from the graves of the dead float on the spring floods. A woman spits vehemently on a passing group of German prisoners.

As the United States lands forces in North Africa, the Russians counterattack, culminating in the great assault on Stalingrad, with the flash of Russian rockets, plunging tanks, and the skies halating with explosive fires. The Germans, led by Paulus, capitulate—twenty-two divisions are taken prisoner. The rhetoric of statistics follow—captured men, captured equipment.

The shadows are beginning to withdraw from the Russian map. The USSR stands for attack. Heroic Russian songs fill the sound track.

After completion of the first five films in the series, army film production was put under the Signal Corps, and the department was renamed the Army Pictorial Service, with joint studio facilities in the old Paramount Studios at Astoria, New York as well as the Fox Studio in Hollywood. Capra left the series in the capable hands of Litvak, since he had to supervise the whole range of army production including training films (some thirteen hundred produced between Pearl Harbor and the end of the war), *Know Your Ally* and *Know Your Enemy* (both projected as a series), and the important war series for the general public, such as *Report from the Aleutians* (1943) and *The Battle of San Pietro* (1944), directed by Major John Huston. Capra's brilliant editorial skill is revealed particularly in the early issues of the *Why We Fight* series; according to Griffith, "many

The Battle of San Pietro (1944), directed by John Huston.

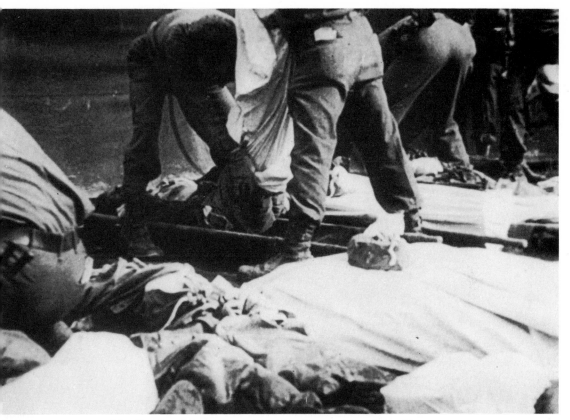

The Battle of San Pietro (1944), directed by John Huston.

times he would take it [the film] away to the cutting room" where it "acquired a magical coherence and cogency which testified eloquently to Capra's editing capacity." Rotha testifies in *The Film Till Now* that the Russian filmmakers admired the films and analyzed them in detail.[15]

Meanwhile, the various series continued to the end of the war:

1943.   *Know Your Ally: Britain.* Directed by Capt. Anthony Veiller; written by Maj. Eric Knight. An attempt to explain British characteristics to the Americans who are to be based there,

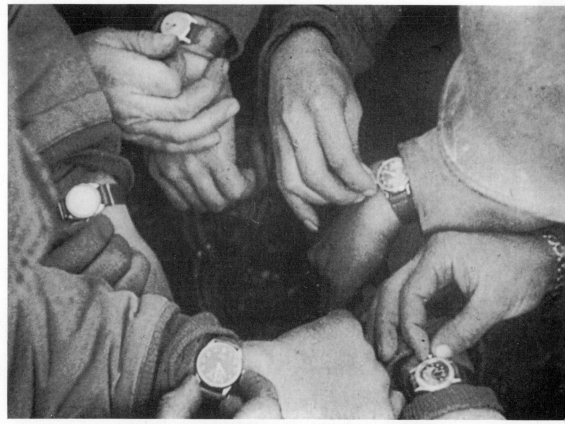

The Battle of San Pietro (1944), directed by John Huston.

and to overcome possible prejudices. (A reciprocal film, *United States*, was written and directed by Maj. Eric Ambler, for British soldiers who had to work with the Americans.)

1944–45. *Why We Fight: The Battle of China* (1944). Directed by Col. Frank Capra and Lt.-Col. Anatole Litvak; written by Maj. Anthony Veiller. Griffith wrote subsequently: "The Battle of China was regarded as the least satisfactory of this series. Though notable for its visual record of the vastness of the Chinese land and people, it was forced to omit any reference to the Communist armies, and to balance accounts it omitted more than passing reference to Chiang Kai-shek. The resulting incomplete assessment of the total Chinese situation was also judged to be impolitic: the film was not seen by the general public and was ultimately withdrawn from circulation to the armed forces."[16]

Why We Fight: War Comes to America—I (1945). Directed by Lt.-Col. Anatole Litvak; written by Lt.-Col. Litvak and Maj. Anthony Veiller. Griffith describes this as a "detailed

examination and recapitulation of the tremendous changes in
American opinions and attitudes, as well as of the conflicting
impulses and ideologies that shaped them."
Know Your Enemy: Japan (1945). Directed by Col. Frank
Capra and Joris Ivens; written by Allen Rivkin, Sgt. Robert
Heller, and Maj. Anthony Veiller. Not released.[17]
Know Your Enemy: Germany (1945). Directed by Sgt. Gott-
fried Reinhardt; written by Sgt. Reinhardt and Maj. Anthony
Veiller.

The newsreel archive material on which these films largely drew
was principally located in New York (some of it in the Museum of
Modern Art Film Library) and after initial attempts to produce outline
scripts and then struggle to locate the footage to fit what seemed to
the writers to be the essential themes, it was found better largely to
reverse the process, and let the necessary themes emerge from the
available footage, which often inspired its own lively comment. It is
a major, if elementary temptation to write the commentary first, and
then plaster over the wise (or perhaps only journalistically rhetorical)
words with less than relevant "wallpaper" shots.[18]

The *Why We Fight* series at its best was brilliant "packaged" history, conceived in the broadest terms, with frequent well-designed ex-
planatory maps in which animated arrows and other devices showed
the territorial movements that aggression represented or stategy involved. The maps were produced by the Disney animation studios.[19]
This was not "scholarly" history; but as Richard Griffith has described,
background indoctrination for the United States serviceman who knew
little or nothing of contemporary events in either Asia or Europe, in
which he was drafted to take part, and as a result might even die. It
was for this reason that the authorities preferred to place production
policy in the hands, not of a tried documentary man, but of a director
(a first-generation immigrant from Sicily) who had proved his devotion
to accepted American ideals in *Mr. Deeds Goes to Town* (1936) and
Mr. Smith Goes to Washington (1939). Capra, president of the Screen
Directors' Guild, understood the "common audience," and knew how
to appeal to their emotions in a way directors who had worked solely
in the documentary field might have failed to do. In Capra's case the
authorities, for once, were proved right. He went straight for an emotional drive in his films, a convincing continuity of argument expounded
through the commentary in Walter Huston's dry, but humane, American voice keeping up the pace against, or in counterpoint to, the music,
traditional, established, or composed specially by Tiomkin, together
with the often massive use of sound effects. The best of the films never

slackened pace; they were cut succinctly and meaningfully, working always for mood, atmosphere, or sheer rhetoric. Parallel or reflected movement was used to link the shots together, to drive home the significance of the great world-shattering conflict that was the underlying reason for the series. Film material from the aggressor nations was constantly introduced—the Nazis and fascists shouting, orating, drilling, marching, blitzkrieging their way to power. The sheer, overwhelming actuality of ninety-nine percent of the footage is only occasionally threatened by the use (surely misjudged) of enacted material when the archives did not provide what some preconceived point in the commentary demanded—such as the German, Italian, and Japanese schoolchildren singing hymns to their respective dictators in *Prelude to War*. This use of production footage is only justified in what the audience can accept as a genuine context, in film reconstructing past history, for example, when the cinema did not exist to make records, as in the scenes of the early "historic" invasions of Russia by Germany, Sweden, and France. But clips from *Confessions of a Nazi Spy* go ill with actuality footage in *War Comes to America*.

Among other official war productions, the most important combat films included:

1942. *The Battle of Midway*. Directed by Lt.-Commander John Ford, USNR; commentary written by John Ford, Dudley Nichols, James Kevin McGuinness. 20 minutes. The first direct United States combat film, winning an Academy award. Ford, though wounded, kept in action with his camera. Later, he lost the use of his left eye. (When Ford became chief of the Field Photographic Branch of the United States Navy, he took with him such well-known filmmakers as Gregg Toland, Budd Schulberg, Garson Kanin, and Robert Parrish. Among the films of the war period Ford worked on or supervised were *Torpedo Squadron* (1942, an eight-minute record film taken on a PT boat, prepared by Ford for private distribution to the families of the men involved when the boat and most of the crew were lost in action), *December 7th* (1943) (an Academy-award winning film about Pearl Harbor), and *We Sail at Midnight* (1943) (a co-production with the British Crown Film Unit on merchant ships in the combat zones).[20]

1943. *Report from the Aleutians*. Directed by John Huston. 45 minutes; color. The occupation of the strategically important island of Adak in the Aleutian group, and the construction in eleven days of an airfield on the drained surface of a lagoon. The life of the servicemen on this desolate and rain-sodden base, and the bombing of the Japanese-held island of Kiska.

The Fighting Lady (1944), produced by Louis de Rochemont.

1944. *The Battle of San Pietro*. Directed by Maj. John Huston. A shortened version, *San Pietro*, introduced by Gen. Mark Clarke. Described by Richard Griffith as "the most poignant picture of the war," it is summarized below.
Attack! The Battle for New Britain. Supervised by Frank Capra.

The Fighting Lady (1944), produced by Louis de Rochemont.

52 minutes. The arduous preparations, and the final victorious assault on the Japanese at Arawa and Cape Gloucester in New Britain.

Memphis Belle. Directed by Col. William Wyler. The American equivalent of *Target for Tonight,* this film covers the planning and execution of a USAAF raid.[21]

Fighting Lady. Produced by Louis de Rochemont for Twentieth Century-Fox. 61 minutes. Shot in 16mm color under the supervision of Edward J. Steichen USNR on board the aircraft carrier, the *Fighting Lady* during actions in the Pacific, notably off the Marianas and Guam, including attack by Japanese planes, and rescue of the pilots of damaged and burning planes. The commentary, written by John Stuart Martin, is spoken by Lieut. Robert Taylor.

The Negro Soldier in World War II. Directed by Lt.-Col. Frank Capra and Maj. Stuart Heisler. An attempt to overcome any racial prejudice present in white American soldiers, but weakened, however, by its terms of reference that precluded any mention of the difficult position of the Negro as a civilian in American society.

1945. *Two Down—One to Go.* Directed by Lt.-Col. Frank Capra. Written by Maj. Anthony Veiller. On the problems of bringing soldiers back from Europe. Frank Capra in his autobiography, *The Name Above the Title,* claims that General Marshall personally approved this film for showing to all units.[22]

Fury in the Pacific. Produced jointly by the American Army, Navy and Marine Corps. The story of the landings on Pelelieu and Anguar in the Palaus. The work of 39 combat cameramen, of whom one was killed and nine were wounded.

To The Shores of Iwo Jima. Produced by the American Navy, Marine Corps and Coast Guard, supervised by Lt. Com. John McLain and Lt. Lothar Wolff. The work of 109 cameramen.

Let There Be Light. Directed by John Huston. A film still kept on the restricted list, dealing with the treatment given in an army hospital to battle casualties of a neuropsychiatric nature, such as battle neurosis. (A postproduction transcript of this film, which contains records of psychiatric interviews, is given in *Film: Book 2, Films of Peace and War,* edited by Robert Hughes [1962].) Huston's interest in psychiatry appeared in one of his best feature films, *Freud: The Secret Passion* (1962), and his concern for the experience of fear by soldiers in *The Red Badge of Courage* (1951). Griffith writes of *Let There Be Light:* ". . . the camera like an invisible spectator recorded the facial expressions, uncontrollable weeping and tics, and the voices of half-a-dozen men being given their initial interviews by psychiatrists: it followed treatments by hypnosis, by narco-synthesis, and continued through to the final group-therapy and

The Fighting Lady (1944), produced by Louis de Rochemont.

group discussions in which the men participate. The purpose of this film was to convince the general public and potential employers of such men that they are not 'nuts' or dangerous. But its implications are deep. One was the intolerable strain that combat puts on men; one was that amnesia, speechlessness, loss of the use of limbs and other symptoms which they show stem often not only from the battle experience itself but from far deeper emotional conflicts dating back to childhood experiences. Perhaps most striking of all is the tacit implication that everyone needs (and an ideal society would provide) security and that this would include readily available psychiatric treatment for everyone."[23]

The Battle of San Pietro, even in its recast form, remains a strong and deeply moving film, an almost personal account by Huston, whose voice is heard making the terse but eloquent commentary. General Mark Clarke introduces the film, explaining that this action in midwinter was primarily concerned to draw away enemy forces prior to the D-Day landings. Maps show the strategic position of the village of San Pietro in the Liri valley, lying between Naples and Rome; each peak above the valley had to be fought for. San Pietro lay directly in the main Nazi line of occupation, and was strongly garrisoned. There is much close-in combat photography as the combined United States and Italian forces move in, the camera constantly shaken by the bombardment. Heavy casualties were sustained for an advance of only six hundred yards; the infantry are "forced to take such cover as the quaking earth could offer."

The Germans, faced with the loss of their footholds, make heavy counterattacks, but eventually the empty streets of San Pietro are reached, patrols creeping warily and skillfully from house to house. The Germans, driven out, set up new positions five kilometers away, while the Americans bury their dead during the respite. One by one the people come back to their ruined homes—the old people and the children, thin, hollow-eyed, and staring. Now and then one smiles at the man behind the camera. A woman carries an empty coffin on her head; others sit on the stones, suckling their babies and weeping. "Yesterday they wept, today they smile," for the army brings them food. Behind the lines the ploughing begins again, and a church procession forms to pray to the patron saint of San Pietro, whose image is a statue half buried in the rubble. The film is supported by music played by the Army Air Force Orchestra, while a Mormon choir accompanies the final scenes in San Pietro.

Other films of special interest in the vast output of American war propaganda include:

Samuel Spewack: *The World at War* (1943). A compilation study of aggression in Europe and Asia from the Japanese invasion of Manchuria to Pearl Harbor. (70 minutes)

Office of Strategic Service and United States Navy: *Brought to Action* (1944)

Warners production: *Appointment in Tokyo* (1944). The use of captured Japanese film to project the second battle of the Philippine Sea.

Office of War Information: *The Russian People* (1942) Joris Ivens and Helen van Dongen. *Russians at War* (1943) about Russia behind the lines. *News Review No. 2* (1943), a survey of the world battlefronts. The latter two directed by Helen van Dongen.

War Department: *Twenty-Seven Soldiers* (1944), a documentary of Allied soldiers of twenty-seven nationalities serving together in harmony on a sector of the Italian front, *Your Job in Germany* (1945), a film warning soldiers not to trust or fraternize with the Germans, and *Thunderbolt* (1945) on aerial warfare in Italy, which was never shown.

Leonard Spigelgass: *Army-Navy Screen Magazine*. A bi-monthly, twenty-minute newsreel for the armed forces, produced from the spring of 1943. Of this Griffith wrote: "More and more the *Screen Magazine* turned into a mirror of the soldier mind (thanks to Spiegelgass's courageous fight for its independence of customary restrictions)." Spiegelgass was a Hollywood scriptwriter; he introduced a "By Request" section in which particular soldiers' needs were met, such as news of his home town. One issue, *The Battle of the United States*, commentated in this case by J. Edgar Hoover, concerned espionage and sabotage in the United States.

The total budget of the War Department alone on production and distribution of film was, according to Richard Griffith, estimated at fifty million dollars annually. To this should be added the Navy's lesser expenditure, which was not revealed. Griffith also speaks of Lt.-Col. Pare Lorentz's Air Transport Command's Overseas Technical Unit, which was responsible for air reconnaissance by film operating under strict security; the unit produced strategic air studies, briefing for pilots, and the like. Staff reports on film (restricted to commanding officers) were produced regularly. Griffith estimated the total library of uncut American war film at 13.5 million feet. Griffith criticizes many of the general combat films released to the army and to the public: "There was little or no adventitious comment, no reference to ideas or causes, facts or consequences, outside the actual events portrayed. For the most part, the films reached a level of communication which one would like to see attained in current newsreels but no more. Technically, they ranged from the crudest juxta-position of not very significant shots and bald verbal description, as in a typical Film Communiqué like *Normandy Invasion,* to the well-planned, skilfully executed, singularly eloquent study of a single bombing raid, *Memphis Belle.*"

In contrast to the outstanding war combat films, the work of the Office of War Information was concerned with civilian subjects for use both at home and abroad. Their production program was carefully coordinated with representatives of the State Department, the army, and the navy, as Owen Lattimore pointed out in his speech to the Writers' Congress, held in October 1943 at the University of California in Los Angeles.

The March of Time and World in Action

During the final war years *The March of Time* continued its regular issues. Among the more significant war subjects were:

1943. *Prelude to Victory* (VIII, 7: January). Preparations for the allied landings in North Africa.

Mr. and Mrs. America (VIII, 8: February). How the United States is being transformed by involvement in war, shown in the form of a letter written by his parents to a son away in the services.

The Navy and the Nation (VIII, 9: March). How the navy is maintained while in action.

Inside Fascist Spain (VIII, 11: May). A parallel is drawn between Franco's Spain and Hitler's Reich, the threat represented by raising a generation of Spanish youth dedicated to restoring Spain's lost empire through the use of force.

Food and War (VIII, 12: May). The United Nations faces the problem of the fair distribution of food after the war; knowledge of this objective in occupied countries as one of the key factors in psychological warfare.

Preparation for Invasion (IX, 1: August). The enormous problem of preparing the organization needed to supply the forces who will assault occupied Europe.

1944. *South American Front* (IX, 10: May). This issue showed North American consciousness of the importance of South America in the global strategy of the war, as reflected alternately in fascist Argentina, orientated to Germany, and democratic Brazil, orientated to the United States with its "Good Neighbor" policy.

The Irish Question (IX, 11: June). Reveals the passionate nationalism and independence of the Irish now that they control their affairs after centuries of oppression and want. Their indifference both to the Allies and to the war.

Underground Report (IX, 12: July). Using film smuggled out through Norway and France, this issue exposed Germany's use of collaborators (such as Quisling and Laval) in every social grade, using food and social position as bribes, and Nazi exploitation of the labor of some twelve million foreign workers. Germany's seemingly impregnable position is threatened by widespread resistance everywhere, including Yugoslavia and Poland. The grave cost of breaching Europe must not tempt the Allies to make a peace that would only enable Germany to create another war machine in the future.

Back Door to Tokyo (IX, 13: August). This film summarized Joe Stilwell's success in Burma with a mixed force of Chinese and American soldiers, and the importance of this to maintaining Chinese resistance which since 1942 had been supplied only by air from Northeast India. Now the Burma supply road to China has become a reality once again.

Later issues began to look ahead to the problems facing the Allies after the war—*Racial Problems* (X, 2: September 1944) posed in particular the "liberal" view in the States over equal rights for Negroes, while *British Imperialism 1944* (X, 1: September 1944) gave an American view of the British Empire and its future problems, showing that even if its origins betrayed much violence and injustice, the Empire remained, "the widest system of organized freedom which has ever existed in history." *What To Do With Germany* (X, 3: October 1944) restated Germany's brutalization under Hitler and asserted that this indoctrinated nation must be taught a stern lesson so that those dedicated to Nazism will not secretly reorganize once the war is over.

In 1945, with victory either in sight or in certain territories already achieved, *The March of Time* broadened its themes. *Post-War Jobs* (X, 5: December 1944) dealt with the problem of realigning American industry for peace, while later, in 1945, *The Returning Veteran* (X, 11: June) dealt with the importance of proper rehabilitation through the G. I. Bill of Rights, the Veterans Administration, and service centers. *Inside China Today* (X, 7: February) contrasted Chiang Kai-shek's China, which although still in a state of dictatorship ruled by a single party, is said to be looking forward to the establishment of a democratic constitution after the war with Japan is over, with that of Mao Tse-tung, who controls at this time some eighty million Chinese in the North in defiance of Chiang. *Report on Italy* (X, 8: March) studied the problems facing the Italian people as they adjust themselves to peace under the Allied Control Commission, and set about their economic and political reconstruction. *Profile of Britain* (X, 10: May) was an American tribute to Britain's part in the war. *Palestine Problem* (X, 13: July), however, reflected only the Zionist case to the virtual exclusion of the Arab position, or the problems facing Britain in trying to administer the mandate.

During the same period, 1943–45, Grierson and Stuart Legg used the best issues of their Canadian Film Board *World in Action* series to create a symposium of subjects that in many instances faced postwar issues with greater insight than *The March of Time*. Stuart Legg was not only a brilliant producer and editor, but also a commentary writer with a sufficient sense of authorship to make words sound stylish without being too inflated or literary. The series was distributed internationally with great success, reaching in the end some seven thousand theaters in Canada, the United States, and Britain. *World in Action* banished any suspicion of the "provincialism" of Canada. It was as Forsyth Hardy put it, "a widely circulating medium . . . for the discussion of international affairs."[24] Or as Grierson himself said: "We are concerned in these films primarily with the relation of local strategies to larger world ones. This is partly in reaction to what some of us regard as a dangerous parochialism in English-speaking propaganda; but also because Canada is moving as swiftly towards a world viewpoint as England in recent years has been moving away from it." He is quoted as saying at the time of the initiation of this work in Canada: "This isn't a documentary war, it's a newsreel war," meaning time was no longer on the side of considered, specialized shooting, but that creative comment must be developed through the use of day-to-day shooting from the war fronts.

World in Action did first-rate work, like the other series, in presenting the battlefronts and homefront, from *Inside Fighting Russia* and *Inside Fighting China* (1942) to *The Gates of Italy* (June 1943), The *Labour Front* (August 1943), *The Battle of Europe* (April 1944), and *Fortress Japan* (July 1944). But it also risked a look ahead in *The War for Men's Minds* (May 1943, an initial, somewhat overvague attempt to oppose totalitarianism to the democratic purpose), *Tomorrow's World* (October 1943), *Global Air Routes* (May 1944, on the revolution in communications opened up by the war), *When Asia Speaks* (1944, on the future for a free Asia), *John Bull's Own Island* (March 1945, on Britain's economic future), *Now—the Peace* (April 1945, the hopes for the future of Europe with Nazism gone), and *Food, Secret of the Peace* (July 1945, on a key problem for postwar Europe).[25]

United States—The War Feature Film, 1943–1945

Many films of the period concentrated, naturally, on combat. Some did this for excitement alone, deeming it sufficiently patriotic to squeeze the last ounce of drama out of the battlefronts—for example, *Bataan* (1943, Tay Garnett, with Robert Taylor, Thomas Mitchell, George Murphy, Lloyd Nolan). In this extravaganza of the American retreat to the Bataan peninsula, a small unit left to keep the Japanese from repairing a demolished bridge face horrific deaths through mutilation or through such suicide missions as crashing an aircraft into the bridge, while Robert Taylor, the sergeant in charge of the unit, is the last survivor and digs his own grave, sets up his own cross, and pronounces his own freedom funeral oration while killing Japanese with a machine gun.

Action in the North Atlantic (1943, Lloyd Bacon, with Humphrey Bogart, Raymond Massey, and Alan Hale) at least kept the excitement on a more plausible level. The captain (Massey) of an American Liberty ship decides to use his vessel as a decoy to lure a U-boat away from a convoy bound for Russia. He finally rams the U-boat and, after other adventures, reaches Murmansk. The film managed to draw the audience into the excitement of the action and maintain a reasonable standard of characterization in the Captain and his mate (Bogart). Howard Hawks in *Air Force* (1943), with John Garfield, centered his expertise in flying on the crew of a Flying Fortress during the Pacific war after Pearl Harbor, with action in Manila, the Coral Sea, and, after a crash-landing in Australia, in another plane bound for Tokyo. Made in cooperation with the United States Air Force, the authenticity of the action scenes was of the highest order for a reconstruction and the artificiality of the star performances was entirely avoided, though heroics in the action were piled high. Robin Wood holds it to be "one of his [Hawks's] greatest works; in feeling perhaps the noblest . . . informed by a deep commitment"; while agreeing that the action is far-fetched at times, he feels the film, seen morally and thematically, "communicates a magnificently realized sense of fulfilment and wholeness."[26] The emphasis, as in several of Hawks's films, is on the group, the team—in this case the crew of an aircraft, to whom the individuals, without loss of genuine though unstressed personal identity, give all their energies and loyalty. This powerful group feeling is something the rear-gunner, Winocki (John Garfield) has initially to learn; it is he, later, who crash-lands the plane when the wounded captain has ordered the others to bale out.

So Proudly We Hail (1943, Mark Sandrich, with Claudette Colbert, Paulette Goddard, Veronica Lake) showed the experiences of nurses serving with the men in the Philippines, and retreating with them up the Bataan Peninsula and finally to the fortified island of Corregidor.

Although somewhat muted in their uniforms, the stars give star performances, and the actuality of war, though stresssed, does not exclude powerful love themes—mother love enduring the loss of a son, wife love the loss of a husband, and a girl the loss of her sweetheart, all killed elsewhere in action. As Richard Winnington (beginning in this year to write his astringently sincere reviews for the London *News Chronicle* wrote of the emotional dialogue—there is "nothing left unsaid and nothing said"; stock studio responses survived in a film patently well meaning in its attempt to pay tribute to courageous women.

Commandos Strike at Dawn (1943, John Farrow, with Paul Muni, Cedric Hardwicke, Anna Lee) was another film that aims at reasonable authenticity within the framework of drama. An English admiral is on holiday in a Norwegian fjord village with his son and daughter in 1939; the girl falls in love with Torensen (Muni), who after the German invasion becomes a local resistance leader and escapes to England in order to guide a British commando raid on a German airfield in the locality of the village. He dies during the raid. The film was shot on location in Newfoundland, with Canadian troops simulating the raiding party, who sail in a ship commanded by the admiral. Here character counts for much of the force of the film—the conversion of the quiet, thoughtful Torensen into a dedicated and ruthless resistance activist. On the other hand, *Five Graves to Cairo* (1943) can scarcely rank as a combat film—rather it is a fictional espionage thriller with its setting in the Libyan campaign. It is remarkable most for the people who worked on it—Billy Wilder, Charles Brackett, Lajos Biro, and Erich von Stroheim. Filmed on location in a Californian wildlife reserve in the Mojave Desert and also in Arizona, it was, as it happened, remarkably timely; first released in May 1943, it included at the close of its story the British advance from El Alamein. Erich von Stroheim played Rommel in the guise of Erich von Stroheim. Seeing it later, Brackett claimed it had "a dreadful smell of propaganda."

One of the more celebrated of the American combat features, *Guadalcanal Diary* (Lewis Seiler, with Preston Foster, Lloyd Nolan, William Bendix, Richard Conte, Anthony Quinn), based on Richard Tregaskis's eyewitness account, was completed in 1943. It shows the part played by the Marines in the Guadalcanal action, and the difficulties and hazards of jungle warfare, fighting a genuine, not a caricatured, Japanese enemy. The film was used as propaganda for recruitment, with recruiting stations placed near the movie theaters. The following year saw Zoltan Korda's *Sahara*, with Humphrey Bogart in a story of an isolated unit defending a desert well from a large force of Germans, and Delmer Daves's *Destination Tokyo,* with Cary Grant and John Garfield, about a submarine sent into Tokyo Bay to radio information to enable General Doolittle to lead an attack; both were efficient action pictures, but neither of them free from patriotic and even religious "homilies" in the dialogue. *Thirty Seconds over Tokyo* (1944, Mervyn Leroy, with Spencer Tracy, Van Johnson, Robert Walker) concerned the fate of the crew of a bomber sent after special training on a highly secret mission over Tokyo. After successfully completing it, their aircraft is damaged and eventually they are forced down in occupied China. They finally reach home after treatment of the injured, including the newly married captain (Johnson), in a Chinese hospital. *The Purple Heart* (1944, Lewis Milestone, with Dana Andrews, Richard Conte, Farley Granger) reconstructs what it was surmised happened following a parallel mission over Tokyo; in this case the crew is handed over by collaborationist Chinese to the Japanese for interrogation, torture, mock-trial, and execution. The film is notable for the venom with which the Japanese (and a Chinese quisling) are portrayed, amounting to hostile "typage" of the kind practiced by the Russians in their portraits of czarist officers in the 1920s.

A foreword explains the significance of the Order of the Purple Heart:[27]

> Established during the War of the Revolution by General George Washington, the Purple Heart is awarded only to soldiers whose blood has been spilled in the defense of our country. It is to those gallant Americans who have given, and are giving, their life's blood for the United States, that this motion picture is humbly dedicated.

The hearing in the Japanese court takes place before members of the Axis and neutral press; the captives are charged with murder of civilians under civil law, and are held to be guilty unless they can prove their innocence. The hearing has an interesting climax in which Mitsubi, a general in Military Intelligence, feels forced to commit suicide because he has failed to blackmail the fliers into revealing where their aircraft came from. Ross, the captain among the group, challenges the Court to do its worst:

> *Ross.* It's true we Americans don't know very much about you Japanese, and never did—and now I realize you know even less about us. You can kill us—all of us, or part of us. But, if you think that's going to put the fear of God into the United States of America and stop them from sending other fliers to bomb you, you're wrong—dead wrong. They'll blacken your skies and burn your cities to the ground and make you get down on your knees and beg for mercy. This is

your war—you wanted it—you asked for it. And now you're going
to get it—and it won't be finished until your dirty little empire is
wiped off the face of the earth!

It is at this point that Mitsubi accepts defeat and commits hara-kiri.
Of the best of these action films, Lewis Jacobs has written:

> . . . there was implicit a rationale that attempted to define the moral
> consequences of the fighting and dying. . . . To express the imperatives
> of an ideological and global war demanded scripts with characters
> coming from every economic level and representing almost every racial
> strain in American society. . . . This kind of national collective hero,
> who wanted the Axis destroyed and a good society created, clearly
> sprang from the liberal social attitudes of the Thirties that questioned
> prejudice and social injustice and focused attention on those wronged
> or victimized by society.[28]

In 1945 British critics and audiences reacted strongly against *Objective Burma!* (Raoul Walsh, with Errol Flynn), a documentary-style
picture with brilliantly staged combat scenes about the adventures of
a group of American paratroopers who are cut off in the Burmese
jungle after successfully completing a raid on a Japanese radar station.
Some of the group are killed or tortured to death; the others, after
great hazards, survive. The film reveals a "down-beat" attitude towards
war. The British, unusually touchy about their "neglected" Burma
campaign, felt slighted because no mention was made of the major
British fighting in this area. Delmer Daves directed *Pride of the Marines,* with John Garfield, as Marine Sergeant Al Schmidt, a war
hero blinded in action. More formidable as an example of action
filmmaking was John Ford's *They Were Expendable* (1945), made
while he was still a Lt.-Commander in the USNR, with Robert Montgomery (Capt. USNR) and John Wayne. Set back in the period of
Pearl Harbor, the film shows the variety of arduous service undertaken by the small motor torpedo boats based on the Philippines before the American defeat in this area.

"Of course, they *were* glorious in defeat in the Philippines—they
kept on fighting," Ford said to Peter Bogdanovich. The film was made
around the character of his friend, Johnny Bulkeley,"the most decorated man of the war" (Lieutenant Brickley in the film, played by
Montgomery) while Wayne played a fictional character (Lieu. Rusty
Ryan) based on Bulkeley's second-in-command, Lieu. Robert Balling
Kelly. Montgomery had served with Bulkeley, and so brought
authenticity and a recognizable service philosophy to the film—a mixture of fatalism and unquestioning acceptance of duty. The film, though

They Were Expendable (1945), directed by John Ford, with John Wayne (center) and Robert Montgomery (center right).

ostensibly about defeat, is really about victory—the victory of sheer character inspired by loyalty and naval discipline. Ford, in his moving opening caption quotes, "I speak for the thousands of silent lips, forever stilled among the jungles and in the deep waters of the Pacific which marked the way."

Yet while accepting the fatalism bred of combat conditions, Ford brings out the ancient ethos of war, the aspiration to heroism, a profound acceptance of self-sacrifice for the "cause" of the nation, the near-worship of the charisma of military authority implicit in such terminology as *high command* and *supreme command*. This is revealed most directly in the near-mystical presentation of MacArthur (unnamed, but clearly impersonated as a visitant passing through during these melancholy days); he brings the indefinable aura of one carrying the highest authority and responsibility. Yet it is felt that these men set low in the scale of rank are linked to this Supreme Being who knows all, but says nothing to those who are in no position to reason why; they

must simply live or die at his command. The men face death with a
kind of iron sorrow; the loss of a comrade is the loss of some part of
themselves, yet within a moment or two the psychological balance
is restored with the palliative of humor, and the essential humanity
of these men, so dear to Ford, shines through everything, the "joshing,"
the deflatory talk, seemingly to belittle what they most value, the
emotionalism of supreme comradeship, bred of true professionalism
in the service. This, they would say, is what the civilian has to learn
when admitted to the brotherhood of war. It is understood and accepted, too, by women, represented in this film by Donna Reed as a nurse
who is in love with the lieutenant, played by John Wayne. It is also
understood by the pioneer breed of civilian, represented by the "old-
timer," the boatyard owner who refuses to leave the property that
represents his life's work although he knows the Japanese are coming.

No American film reflects more profoundly the age-old tradition
of war than *They Were Expendable*. It is little wonder that Ford
retired with the highest rank of all those men from Hollywood whose
war service was expressed in filmmaking; he was granted the rank
of admiral in the United States Naval Reserve. The experience of
war and its link, in his view, with the traditional human virtues became
reflected in many of the films he made subsequently, such as *She Wore
a Yellow Ribbon*, *Fort Apache*, *The Long Gray Line*, *The Horse Soldiers*, and *Sergeant Rutledge*.[29]

Two films with a factual approach to the portrayal of the American
infantryman were released in 1945 after the war—*The Story of G. I.
Joe* (William A. Wellman, with Burgess Meredith, Robert Mitchum)
and *A Walk in the Sun* (Lewis Milestone, with Dana Andrews, Richard
Conte, Herbert Rudley). The first developed the celebrated American
war correspondent, Ernie Pyle, into a screen portrait by Burgess Meredith; Pyle-Meredith lives and marches with a company that starts as
a group of untried men and develops, in spite of losses, into a unit of
battle-scarred and battle-hardened veterans as they move from North
Africa to Sicily, and from Sicily to Italy, finally reaching Rome itself;
they celebrate Christmas 1943 below Monte Cassino. The film concentrates very much on effects achieved through acting—Burgess Meredith with his laconic, quizzical style; Robert Mitchum as a sergeant
whose personal interest lies in hearing on a seemingly unmendable
gramophone he has picked up the voice of his infant son recorded
on a record sent him through the mail. In spite of the vigorously cine-
matic effectiveness of the action scenes, what emerges from this film
is what is meant to emerge, the highly individual characters of the

The Story of G. I. Joe (1945), directed by William Wellman, with Burgess Meredith.

men developed collectively by director, scriptwriters, and actors, a miscellany of personalities, anchored by the overall presence of Ernie Pyle as both protagonist and chorus. [Another, but highly fictionalized "true life" film was *The Story of Dr. Wassell* (Cecil B. De Mille, with Gary Cooper) tracing the experiences, and frustrations, of a medical missioner who becomes a naval doctor serving in Java and evacuating his cases to Australia.] *A Walk in the Sun* goes even further in its stylized actuality, achieving a unique kind of succinct poetry in both form and language. Again it is the veteran combat unit, detailed to take a farmhouse six miles inland which may or may not be a German strongpoint at the time of the Salerno landings in 1943. It epitomizes the strain placed on men in war; the lieutenant in charge is killed, the sergeant who succeeds to the command collapses in battle hysteria, while another sergeant who takes over uses his initiative to develop a strategy that is in the end successful. The whole action is tightly controlled: the beachhead landing, the dive-bombing of the platoon, the successful attack on an isolated German armored car, and the cli-

A Walk in the Sun (1945), directed by Lewis Milestone, with Herbert Rudley (center) and Dana Andrews (right).

A Walk in the Sun (1945), directed by Lewis Milestone.

A Walk in the Sun (1945), directed by Lewis Milestone, with Dana Andrews.

mactic taking of the farmhouse. Again the emphasis is on the very differing characters of the men, and the impact of war upon now one, now another of them. The dialogue (script by Robert Rossen, following closely the novel by Henry Brown) has beeen criticized for its "heightened" literary quality, using repetitive phrases, recurrent thematic ideas, almost turning the men at moments into universalized symbols. Neither of these impressive films had moved over into the position that could be called anti-war; rather they accept war as a grim necessity, but at the same time present it as an infliction that can break as well as make good men. For some, including the writer, *A Walk in the Sun* is one of the most memorable of American war films, not for any great profundity in its ideas, but because its atmosphere and tension, its sheer artistic unity, catches with a fine seriousness the mood of a period that still accepted war with disillusionment but without fundamental protest—and certainly not from the pacifist standpoint of Milestone's profoundly pacifist film of the First World War, *All Quiet on the Western Front*, made only fifteen years earlier.

The large number of dramatic films of the period 1943–45 with a war background can be dealt with more briefly. They divide into groups with kindred themes or geographical locations, the first being those which attempted to deal with morale on the home front. Edward Dmytryk's *Tender Comrade* (1943, with Ginger Rogers) deals rather sentimentally with a group of "typical" American war wives who, in the absence of their husbands, work in war factories and set up house together with a refugee housekeeper (Mady Christians)—the script was written by Dalton Trumbo. More alarming was *Since You Went Away* (John Cromwell, 1944; script by David O. Selznick); it was dedicated specifically at the outset to "an unconquerable fortress, the American home," which is presided over here by an hygienically idealized American wife expertly played by Claudette Colbert, with an adolescent daughter (Jennifer Jones). The daughter falls most responsibly and correctly in love with the grandson of the lodger (that sentimental old crust, Monty Woolley), who has been taken in to ease the household economy. Claudette Colbert becomes a welder when her husband is posted missing, and the boy is later killed at Salerno. Such a film is a Hollywood-devized emotional confidence trick practiced on the deepest feelings and experiences of the many American women separated from their men. There seems a kind of indecency that men still living in the comforts of Hollywood should devise such an entertainment at such a time in American history—although no doubt millions of women everywhere got what they regarded as momentary consolation from this so-called woman's film.

It provided a wartime emotional narcotic since, with all the polish of its expert professionalism, it glided from one emotional peak to the next, with everyone behaving with a kind of packaged perfection.[30]

In *Tomorrow, the World!* (1944, Leslie Fenton, with Fredric March and Skippy Homeier) the American home of a widowed university professor faced up to political ideology in the shape of an orphaned nephew from Germany, who turns out to be a thorough-going juvenile Nazi despising the memory of his German father, who died in a concentration camp. This child brings dissension into the kindly household to which he is unwillingly introduced. Based on a play, and with Ring Lardner, Jr. as co-scriptwriter, the film rubbed home as hard as possible the contamination that dedicated Nazism could bring to decent values, though the miniature Nazi is finally reduced to childish tears and, one is led to assume, some kind of repentance. Films that dealt with the development of fascist espionage in the United States itself included *Watch on the Rhine* (1943, Herman Shumlin, with Bette Davis, George Coulouris, Paul Lukas, scripted by Dashiel Hammett from a play by Lillian Hellman), in which the German husband (Lukas) of an American wife (Bette Davis) feels forced to return to prewar Germany to combat Nazism;[31] Otto Preminger's *Margin for Error* (1943, based on Clare Booth Luce's play, with Preminger and Joan Bennett) exposed the sabotage a German consul was preparing in a prewar American town; while George Cukor's *Keeper of the Flame* (1943, with Spencer Tracy and Katharine Hepburn) had an intelligent script by Donald Ogden Stewart, and went so far as to suggest a fascist dictator could take over in the United States itself under the guise of a respected political figure. Spencer Tracy plays a journalist who unravels this man's merely potential threat to the United States, after his death in a car crash. The film, in its way, parallels *Citizen Kane* and anticipates *All the King's Men*.

Nor is the German threat all the United States has to contend with. *Betrayal from the East* (1945, William Berke) exposes on a commonplace level Japanese intelligence and counterintelligence in the United States before Pearl Harbor. Later a far superior production appeared, Henry Hathaway's film for Louis de Rochemont, *The House on 92nd Street* (1945, with William Eythe, Lloyd Nolan, Signe Hasso), in which the documentary approach was adopted with success in a story involving considerable detail about the methods used in countering espionage when the FBI allows a German-American to receive training in Nazi Germany so that he can act as their agent when he returns to the United States. The whole paraphernalia of scientific, technological investigation made this film a fascinating exercise, recalling the enacted episodes of the earlier *March of Time* series. The FBI gave its active cooperation.

However, Hollywood's major interest at this period lay in Germany itself, and occupied Europe.[32] With very varying degrees of success, the German-based film dramas and melodramas included *Hitler's Children* (1943, Edward Dmytryk, with Tim Holt, Bonita Granville), which reduced the conversion of a Gestapo official through love of an American-German girl to a quite incredible level, *Address Unknown* (1943, William Cameron Menzies, with Paul Lukas), a drama of revenge against a man whose actions in Vienna lead to the death of a Jewess and, rather later, *Hotel Berlin* (1945, Peter Godfrey, with Helmut Dantine, Raymond Massey, George Coulouris, Peter Lorre), with its tangle of hunted Nazi and anti-Nazi characters and theme of German militarism. In *The Hitler Gang* (1944, John Farrow, with Robert Watson, Alexander Pope, Martin Kosleck) an attempt was made to reconstruct Hitler's career and the rise of the Nazi. The script was by Francis Goodrich and Albert Hackett. This was a commendable

The Hitler Gang (1944), directed by John Farrow, with Robert Watson as Hitler.

attempt to create a genuine document, if not documentary, about a most complex span of history. Unfortunately Robert Watson proved a totally inadequate Hitler; apart from this, the film offered at least interesting impersonations by eminent German actors of the German nationalist and Nazi leaders—for example, Reinhold Schunzel as Ludendorff, Fritz Kortner as Otto Strasser, Martin Kosleck as Goebbels, Alexander Granach as Streicher.

Above Suspicion (1943, Richard Thorpe, with Joan Crawford, Fred MacMurray, Conrad Veidt) remained prewar, and set an Oxford don and his bride the task of tracing a vanished agent in Hitler's Germany in a film of the crudest propaganda;[33] *The Seventh Cross* (1944, Fred Zinnemann, with Spencer Tracy, Signe Hasso) also set in prewar Germany was far better, with Tracy as the sole survivor of a group who get away from a concentration camp, and who manage, with underground help, to escape the country. Other films in this category included *The Moon is Down* (1943, Irving Pichel, with Cedric Hardwicke, Harry Travers, Lee J. Cobb), which led up to the shooting of hostages in a small Norwegian town after sabotage has taken place; *Hostages* (1943, Frank Tuttle, with Luise Rainer, Arturo de Cordova, William Bendix, Reinhold Schunzel, Katina Paxinou, Oscar Homolka, Paul Lukas), a stagey story of hostages held in Prague; *The Edge of Darkness* (1943, Lewis Milestone, with Errol Flynn, Ann Sheridan), a well-made melodrama of the Norwegian resistance; and *Hitler's Madman* (1943, Douglas Sirk, with John Carradine as Heydrich), reconstructing the assassination in 1942 of Heydrich in Prague and the massacre at Lidice that followed. This subject of Heydrich's assassination recurred in more imposing form in Fritz Lang's *Hangmen also Die* (1943, with Brian Donlevy, Hans von Twardowsky, Walter Brennan), a fictional development of the killing by Lang and Berthold Brecht, with an atmospheric evocation of life in an occupied country.[34] Jean Renoir in *This Land Is Mine* (1943, with Charles Laughton, Maureen O'Hara) also tried his hand at reconstructing life under occupation in a French town.[35] But all these films, even when they gained from the touches of distinction given them by skilled directors and fine actors, created cumulatively only propaganda stereotypes that meant little or nothing to audiences. Most Nazi officers were portrayed smooth, brutal, pseudo-cultured, and given to liking classical music, anticipating a later taste for setting murder to Bach. They operated in the old us-versus-them world of studio fiction, and contributed little or nothing to any real evaluation of what Nazism meant either in Germany or the world outside. Two films, released in the summer of 1945, dared to deal very early with the problems arising from the American presence in territory formerly occupied by the Germans—one was *The Master Race* (Herbert J. Biberman, with George Coulouris), in which a former Nazi colonel impersonates a Belgian returning to his country in order to foment trouble there for the Americans and reindoctrinate German prisoners-of-war who now want to help restore the country they had ravaged. The other film was *A Bell for Adano* (Henry King, 1945), a moving film about the close relationship established between a sympathetic United States Affairs administrator (John Hodiak) and his sergeant (William Bendix) and the citizens of the Sicilian town of Adano.

More interesting were the various shy attempts by Hollywood to pay tribute to America's ally, the Soviet Union. These films were to be the cause of considerable embarrassment when, in 1947, the Un-American Activities Committee began its investigations into alleged Communist influences in the film industry. The key films were *Mission to Moscow* (1943, Michael Curtiz, with Walter Huston, Ann Harding, and a script by Howard Koch based on the published reminiscences of America's ambassador to the Soviet Union 1936–38, Joseph E. Davies), *North Star* (1943, Lewis Milestone, with Anne Baxter, Dana Andrews, Walter Huston, Erich von Stroheim), the story of a village over-run by the Germans, with a screenplay by Lillian Hellman, and the romantic *Song of Russia* (1943, Gregory Ratoff, with Robert Taylor, Susan Peters), in which an American orchestral conductor visiting the USSR marries a Russian pianist of peasant extraction who, when her village is overrun by the German army, becomes a guerrilla fighter until she is persuaded she can do more for her country if she and her husband return to the United States to work for the Russian cause. Another purely romantic film of Russian guerrilla warfare was Jacques Tourneur's *Days of Glory* (1944, with Gregory Peck and Tamara Toumanova). Of these films the only one of real quality was *Mission to Moscow*, a magnificent propaganda exercise. Lewis Jacobs cites the controversy this film caused, in itself a tribute to its effectiveness whatever we may now think of Stalin, whom the film defends, not least in its recreation of the Bucharin-Radek trials of 1937, and the alleged sabotage of Russia by these men in association with Trotsky. Says Jacobs:

> The picture's missionary zeal to approve the famous Moscow purge trials and to celebrate a country 'long maligned and disgracefully minimized in our press and cinema' [Clifford Odets] evoked a sharp storm of debate. Divergent opinions evaluating the film ranged from 'an epoch making film for America' [text of a statement by 266 leading Americans denouncing disruptive attacks on the picture] to 'The film

Mission to Moscow (1943), directed by Michael Curtiz, with Walter Huston as the American ambassador, Joseph E. Davies.

is anti-British, anti-Congress, anti-Democratic and anti-truth' [John Dewey]. One group of 66 distinguished and prominent commentators, including Anne O'Hare McCormick, Dorothy Thompson, Sidney Hook, Eugene Lyons and W. E. Woodward, took strong exception to the film and sided with the comment expressed by John Haynes Holmes: 'As history it is a lie, as propaganda it is a scandal of the first order'. Another group of equally prominent Americans representing all fields of endeavor, among whom were Representative John M. Coffee, Senator Pepper, Walter Duranty, Theodore Dreiser, Fritz Mahler and more than 200 others, issued a signed statement denouncing the attacks as a 'distinct disservice to the cause of American-Soviet unity during the war and afterward'. *Mission to Moscow*, they declared, 'is more than a motion picture; it is a gesture of international friendship made at the most crucial period of American history with the highly laudable and important object of promoting trust instead of distrust in the Soviet Union.'[36]

Around the same period Hitchcock made his controversial allegorical film, *Lifeboat* (1943, with Tallulah Bankhead, John Hodiak,

Lifeboat (1943), directed by Alfred Hitchcock, with Hume Cronyn, Mary Anderson, and William Bendix.

William Bendix, Walter Slezak, and derived by Jo Swerling from a story by John Steinbeck). The action was set on a lifeboat isolated in mid-Atlantic after a ship has been torpedoed; the surviving passengers prove to be a represenatative group, enhanced by their inadvertent rescue of the commander of the submarine that sank the freighter in which they were traveling, and who has in turn lost his vessel. The group includes a Negro, a woman journalist, a near-communist stoker, and a near-fascist millionaire businessman. Part of the contemporary criticism of the film was that the treacherous Nazi was by far the most resourceful person in the boat. The film, photographed largely in close-shot, was meant to prove that the Nazis were not film villains, but real people, efficient and difficult to beat. It was, said Hitchcock to Truffaut, "a microcosm of war. . . . We wanted to show that at that moment there were two world forces confronting each other . . . and while the democracies were completely disorganized, all the Germans were clearly headed in the same direction. So here was a statement telling the democracies to put their differences aside temporarily and to gather forces to concentrate on the common enemy, whose strength was precisely derived from a spirit of unity and of determination."[37] The film was not successful commercially at the time, but is nevertheless an acute and independent statement for the period it was made, and worth revival and reassessment as a distinctive film in Hitchcock's work.

First of all, *Lifeboat* proves to be one of the rare "nonconformist" films of the war period. Walter Slezak's Nazi is the most interesting character in the group aboard this symbolic lifeboat, and a man worth comparison with the Nazi commandant in *49th Parallel*. Indeed, he is a man of great potential quality, though suffering from the moral disease of Nazi indoctrination, an ultimate characteristic gradually revealed as the film progresses. He possesses knowledge and skills the others do not—he has seamanship, where they (the democrats) have none; a surgeon in civilian life, he amputates the leg of the seaman (William Bendix) whom he is later to murder in cold blood. Above all, he has his own concealed purpose that dominates his whole attitude to the "government" of the boat he "occupies." Further, Hitchcock's portrait of the desperate democracies is by no means favorable; they are infirm of purpose, at loggerheads with each other, and finally become horribly, vengefully violent in the uncoordinated savagery of the retribution they wreak on the Nazi who is, in certain respects, their superior. Robin Wood, one of the rare critics to have analyzed this film in depth, points out that the only man in the boat who shares something of the Nazi's characteristics is the communist stoker:

> The Nazi is dangerous (as so many film Nazis are not) because there is so much to be said for him. Beside him, the morally pure characters are impotent. And it is significant that the character who comes nearest to being a 'hero'—the Marxist stoker (John Hodiak)—is the nearest (the point is made explicitly) to the Nazi in outlook, having a similar ruthless determination whose effect is softened however by our awareness that it springs from warm human sympathies. If Hitchcock shows himself, in *Lifeboat* and in *Rope*, a committed anti-Fascist, he does not on the other hand show himself a committed democrat.[38]

The true democrat-character is, of course, Tallulah Bankhead's journalist, who gradually sheds the psychological affectations of her professional pose as well as the inhibiting trappings of her "wealth" (the bracelet) and reveals her true strength and humanity.

Still within the war period another, though less significant nonconformist film came from Preston Sturges, *Hail the Conquering Hero* (1944, with Eddie Bracken).[39] This film dared to satirize the nation's wartime urge to offer hero-worship to the returning warrior. It is true that the teeth of the satire are to a large extent drawn by making the "hero" (Eddie Bracken) a marine with a perpetual sneeze who has had to be invalided out of the service. But the satire is directed not against him, but against the absurd persistence of the citizens of his native town (Truesmith) to regard him as "their" hero, in spite of his asseverations, between sneezes, that he is not the kind of man they insist on believing him to be. Sturges, precursor of Wilder as a persistent satirist on the American screen, attacks everything from mother love to local politics. The appearance of this film was a healthy sign during a time when the national tendency was to accept all war-imposed values without question.

In this variety of ways Hollywood contributed to American propaganda according to its lights. At the Writers' Congress held in Los Angeles (October 1943), Darryl Zanuck expressed the Hollywood viewpoint uncompromisingly: "If you have something worth while to say, dress it in the glittering robes of entertainment and you will find a ready market. . . . Without entertainment no propaganda film is worth a dime."

Hail the Conquering Hero (1944), directed by Preston Sturges.

Russia: The Years of Ascendancy

Russian war-record films of 1943–45 made the most of the magnificent combat footage pouring into the Central Newsreel Studios in Moscow. The cameramen did not hestitate to show the worst they observed: death on the warfronts, the atrocities committed by Nazis against their Russian victims—scenes presented with restraint (too much restraint) in American films intended for the theaters, where the American dead, when shown, were filmed with a kind of abstract anonymity (avoiding the face), an anonymity not accorded dead Germans. It is true that the death of people unknown to us personally is anonymous, but the Russians did not flinch from showing torn and mutilated bodies, or faces contorted in the final throes of death. The Russians hated the Germans with a profound, agonized hatred. The British and Americans, spared occupation, hated only derivatively, in a sense theoretically, except when after D-Day they experienced by direct observation something of the worst of which indoctrinated Nazis were capable. The "Jerries" were the "enemy," and therefore technical opponents. Real, heartfelt hatred between technical opponents is difficult to achieve; hence the barbarous, hate-inducing drill, the men using bayonets and uttering murderous cries, urged on by their instructor. But real, that is natural, loathing did spring up when German atrocities were discovered in the occupied territories in the West, culminating in the dazing experience of initial contact with the liberated concentration camps. For the Russians, however, the experience of German occupation was so terrible, the accumulated passion of the great films of 1943–45 must be accepted as something that went beyond the experience of British and American soldiers and civilians in the West. The experience of British and American soldiers held in Japanese captivity is another matter.

Working against time, the seven-reel documentary-feature *Stalingrad* was released on March 10, less than six weeks after the German capitulation. It remains a monumental war film, the product of fifteen named cameramen whose work was edited under the superivsion of Leonid Varamov; it covered the six months of the German onslaught— from August 1942 to 31 January 1943, the day of Paulus's surrender. Both the German and Russian strategy was illustrated by animated maps and diagrams. The film shows the civilian evacuation, the street fighting, the mutilated corpses of Russian prisoners discovered in surrendered territory, and gives spectacular scenes of the Russian Katiusha, the multirocket secret weapon, in action. Roman Karmen, himself in Stalingrad at the close of the action, is quoted by Jay Leyda, concerning coverage of the surrender:

Wartime Russian newsreel (1944–45).

We filmed the surrender of Field Marshal von Paulus—a moment we had all been eagerly awaiting. In one sector on the western outskirts of Stalingrad we recorded the surrender of Lieutenant-General von Daniel, Commander of the 376th Division. The camera caught him walking down the street in full dress, followed by a file of luggage-laden officers.[40]

In the wake of *Stalingrad*, other regional battle films, all concerned with victorious strategy and spectacular action, followed as the war of liberation progressed:

1943. *The Peoples' Avengers* (August, 6 reels), Directed by Vasili Belayev. Thirteen named cameramen. Distributed in English as *The Partisans*, this film covered extensive sabotage behind the German lines.
The Battle for Orel. A 55 minute film about the fall of the strongly held German bridgehead at Orel in August 1943.
The Fight for Our Soviet Ukraine (October, 7 reels). Directed by Yulia Solntseva and Y. Audeyenko; supervision, Alexander Dovzhenko, who was in Moscow during the war; Yulia Solntseva

was his wife. 24 named cameramen, and some captured German material. As Jay Leyda comments (*Films beget Films*, p. 68) Dovzhenko managed to make this compilation film "astonishingly *personal*", bringing out his love and passion for his native Ukraine. He wrote the commentary and molded the film to fit his own viewpoint.[41]

1944. *Towards an Armistice with Finland.* Directed by Yuli Raizman, and reflecting a new policy inaugurated by Sergei Gerasimov after his appointment early in 1941 as head of the Documentary Film Studio to bring directors of fiction film in to supervise the more important war documentaries, a decision perhaps influenced by the American choice of Capra, whose war documentaries the Russians so much admired.

Sebastopol. Directed by V. Belayev, who had made an earlier record of the 1942 defence of Sebastopol called *Black Sea Marines*.

The Kharkov Trials (Justice Is Coming). A straight, seventy-minute newsreel record of one of the first trials of Nazi war criminals—three Germans and a Russian traitor responsible for mass murder and atrocities in Khakov. Their cross-examination is shown, and the film ends with their execution. The prisoners are articulate, plead to be allowed to go free and express their newly-acquired anti-Nazi views, but their impassive faces conceal a form of neurosis. As they speak in the courtroom, the hideous film record of their crimes is cut in. The public showing of this film in Britain revealed, virtually for the first time, what Nazi atrocities really looked like.

1945. *Victory in the Ukraine and the Expulsion of the Germans from the Boundaries of the Ukrainian Soviet Earth* (mid-year; 7 reels). Directed by Alexander Dovzhenko, Yulia Solntseva, assisted by F. Fillipov. Twenty-one named cameramen. Speaking of this film at a Congress in Moscow convened to discuss the technique of the American *Why We Fight* series, Dovzhenko said:

> Once we needed shots of mud—just the sort of shot that directors usually reject and for which cameramen are growled at. When these shots of mud—in themselves saying nothing at all were joined together in a sequence about the difficulties of the 1944 offensive on the left bank of the Ukraine, they acquired point and meaning. Now they are accompanied by a commentary on how these infinite examples, washed in the blood of Soviet people like the fields under spring floods, saw the destiny of mankind decided; for here the military art of Nazi Germany was crushed and the liberation of Europe assured. And instantly this vast stretch of mud begins to gleam like something precious. One does not need pathos to express deep emotion—pathos can be born not from a raised voice but from a profound and truthful assembly of materials.[42]

The Kharkov Trials (Justice Is Coming) (1944).

Liberation of Czechoslovakia. Directed by Ilya Kopalin and Pera Atasheva.

Berlin (June; 9 reels). Directed by Yuli Raizman and Yelezaveta V. Popov, was shown in Britain later in 1945.

Vienna. Directed by V. Poselsky.

Budapest. Directed by V. Belayev.

Defeat of Japan. Directed by Alexander Zarkhi and Josef Heifitz.

Liberated France. Directed by Sergei Yutkevich, using Allied and captured German footage. Eisenstein, in a long review, praised the film for the dynamic "passion" by which it was governed, with the fate of France presented as a classic tragedy of retribution—instancing the "mute suite" when the Germans enter a Paris of deserted streets, and the contrast later of the crowded boulevards when the liberators arrive.

One celebrated cameraman who was killed on active service, Vladimir Sushchinsky, had a documentary made about his work, *A Cameraman at the Front* (1946). Sushchinsky's celebrated final shot, made by his still-operating camera after his death, the lens pointing to the sky after he had been killed at Breslau, was included in this film. (A Brit-

Stalingrad (1943).

Victory in the Ukraine (1943), directed by Alexander Dovzhenko.

Stalingrad (1943).

Stalingrad (1943).

Stalingrad (1943).

Stalingrad (1943).

Stalingrad (1943).

Stalingrad (1943).

ish parallel to this tribute was Len Lye's one-reel documentary, *Cameramen at War*, made 1943–44.) In all, over four hundred documentaries of a technical, instructional and informational nature, mostly linked directly with the war, were made by the Russians during the war years.

The feature films in Russia from 1943 reinforced in their own way the message of the combat documentaries, though few were actually outstanding. There were films of the Partisans—such as Pudovkin's *In the Name of the Fatherland* (from *Russian People*, a play by Konstantin Simonov) and Frederic Ermler's *She Defends her Country* (*No Greater Love*, in the English-language dubbing, 1943), about a woman who, after losing husband and child, becomes a Partisan leader. This last film was a war melodrama, but done with passion and verve, as was Lukov's *Two Soldiers* (1943), a story of two friends on the Leningrad front, and Yuli Raisman's comedy, *Moscow Skies* (1944), set on the Moscow front of 1941, about a trainee in the Air Force who has more luck bringing down German planes than he has with his girlfriend. These latter films are Russo-Hollywood, sincere enough but lacking fundamental seriousness; but there were interesting racial overtones. V. Pronin's *Son of the Soviet East* (1942), in a melodrama of friendship developing after mutual distrust between two army volunteers of different races, Hafiz from Tadjik, and Ivan from Russia. It is left to Hafiz to avenge Ivan's death on the battlefield. Ivan Piriev puts the war in an altogether gayer context in *Six P. M.* (*1944*), the title referring to the time when the guns fire victory salvoes; this is almost a musical, with song and dance, and a connecting theme of the meetings and separations of wartime lovers. The Russian equivalent of Hollywood sentiment lies in the simple story behind *Wait For Me*, about the loyalty of a wife as she waits for her much-loved husband, away at the wars and reported dead—though he is in fact organizing partisan warfare behind the German lines.

A film dealing seriously with the home front and evacuated war industries was Gerasimov's *The Great Earth* (*The Ural Front*, 1944), which I reviewed at the time:

> The main story largely concerns the problems of the management of the evacuated factory in their efforts to increase production. The film possesses all the virtues of unenlightened realism; there is verisimilitude of characterization and considerable discussion of production and morale. But realism in this bare form is not enough. . . . The imagination is not caught up into the action or stirred by the humanity of the characters as in the great Russian films. . . . The most human person in this film is the recalcitrant old mother who hates to see strangers

in her Russian home, though even she, in the interests of propaganda, ends up in the plant, though we see nothing of the hours of persuasion which must have been necessary to get her there. Only once does the film achieve the warm touch of poetry, in the silent emotional face of the beautiful Tamara Makarova as she dances with her husband for the last time before he goes to the war. This opening sequence of the film has a vitality which only returns at the end, when the husband comes back and Anna sits on the bed smiling at him with quiet delight.[43]

On a different plane were the few films that more nearly matched the great documentaries. There was Victor Eisimont's film dealing with children in wartime Leningrad, *Once there Was a Girl* (1944). And there were the better-known films dealing with German treatment of Russian women and children, *The Rainbow* (Mark Donskoi and R. Perelstein), based on a novel by Wanda Wassilewska, *Zoya* (1944, Lev Arnshtam), dedicated to a Soviet war heroine, Zoya Kosmodenyanskaya, played by Galina Vodianitskaya, and *Girl 217* (1944, Mikhail Romm). Girl 217 is Tanya (Elena Kuzmina), a Russian slave worker bought for fifteen marks to be abused and maltreated in a German household; finally she revolts, is imprisoned and tortured, and

Once There Was A Girl (1944), directed by Victor Eisimont.

The Rainbow (1944), directed by Mark Donskoi.

The Rainbow (1944), directed by Mark Donskoi.

Zoya (1944), directed by Lev Arnshtam.

returns to exact vengeance by killing the son in the German household and his friend, both soldiers home on leave. She escapes and
mingles with a trainload of prisoners being transported to Russia. Not
only is Elena Kuzmina's performance remarkable for its insight into
this young girl's transformation under stress, but the Germans are portrayed with a similar psychological insight unmarred by "typage."
Equally outstanding, *The Rainbow*, set in a small Ukrainian village
under occupation, portrayed the Germans with insight; Donskoi went
to the trouble of studying actual German prisoners, officers, and soldiers, whom he interviewed. The German commandant is played by
Hans Klering, while the women are interpreted by Natalia Uzhvi, as
the pregnant Partisan trapped when she returns to the village to have
her child, Nina Alisova, as the commandant's Russian mistress, and
Yelena Tyapkina as the woman whose house he has taken over. The
only thing marring this film is the insistent music, which on occasion
resorts to choral effects, while the sudden liberation of the village
by the Red Army is not well integrated. Lastly, *Zoya* tells a true story
of an eighteen-year-old girl who, as a young Komsomol, was sent
behind the enemy lines to join the partisans. She was caught by the
Germans, tortured, and, refusing to give information, finally hanged.

The film is a sensitive, even poetic biographical study, showing her childhood as well as her war service. A Russian critic, writing contemporaneously describes the end of the film:

> When Zoya is shown on her last road, at night, walking through the snow, we first see her bare feet and slender legs, then her whole figure in vague outline against a background of whirling snow, and then her radiant and inspired face, seeming lit from within by the flame of her thoughts and emotions.[44]

These films were the first reconstructing the disasters of war as they overcame the civilian population in occupied countries. They remain in the memory as experiences that cannot be forgotten, produced as the Germans were still being driven back to their own borders, and affecting to a degree that nothing made after the war was over could quite equal. The makers of these films, writers, directors, and actors alike, were projecting experiences that were still only too real to them.

The Russian view of propaganda was expressed succinctly in the message sent to the Writer's Congress held in Los Angeles in October

Unconquered (1945), directed by Mark Donskoi.

1943. Signed by Mikhail Sholokov, Alexei Tolstoy, Ilya Ehrenberg, Konstantin Simonov, and Leonid Leonov, the cable urged that true propaganda existed to:

> promote nations' increased vigilance, mobilize public opinion for fierce struggle against subversive acts all shades of pro-Nazis and reactionaries at home and front, against all attempts racial discrimination and isolationism. At the same time writers—and this is what we are attempting to do—should reflect this war not only in direct works of propaganda but also in books and films which abide through ages as witnesses of this struggle. . . . Our experience has shown us that only means of uniting writers for common cause is by mergence with peoples' lives, with their cherished yearnings and interests. Only that artist is capable of creating genuine masterpiece who merges in his war efforts with all his people, who dedicates himself wholly to struggle. And it therefore seems to us that your task is to indefatigably, persistently, daily and hourly appeal to American people to the struggle.

Japan

The final phase of wartime Japanese filmmaking saw a distinct revolt by certain filmmakers of repute against subjects dictated by national or war policy.[45] Heinosuke Gosho, for instance, attempted to concentrate on any element of love story in the subjects he was given; so also did Keisuke Kinoshita. But the State had a hold over the companies through the rationing of raw stock; production was substantially cut in 1943, and the companies were consolidated; this was followed by partial closure of cinemas when the air raids intensified in 1944.

In 1943 a film about naval air cadets appeared—*Toward the Decisive Battle in the Sky* (Kunio Watanabe)—and this was followed by a similar film produced by Shochiku for the Army Air Corps, *Flying South in His Plane,* and a film about Pearl Harbor, *Navy* (Tomotaka Tasaka). Kajiro Yamamoto, the leading director of war films, made *General Kato's Falcon Fighters* (1944), a tribute to the army's fighter planes in Malaya, Burma, and Thailand, following this with *Torpedo Squadrons Move Out* (1944) about the human torpedo force, and the sinking of a battleship by three young officers. Other films looked back to the immediate past to attack Britain and the United States in their alleged attempts to weaken Japan, such as *If We go to Sea* (1943, Masanori Igayama), *Army* (1944, Keisuke Kinoshita), and *The Angry Sea* (1944, Tadashi Imai), about international restriction placed on the Japanese navy. Teinosuke Kinugasa's *Forward! Flag of Indepen-*

Rikugun (Army) (1944), directed by Keisuke Kinoshita.

Kessen No Ohzura He (Toward the Decisive Battle in the Sky) (1943), directed by Kunio Watanabe.

Raigekitai Shutsudo (Torpedo Squadrons Move Out) (1944), directed by
Kajiro Yamamoto.

Raigekitai Shutsudo (Torpedo Squadrons Move Out) (1946), directed by
Kajiro Yamamoto.

dence (1943) was designed to encourage Indian independence from Britain; a young prince in India helps the Japanese to expose a British spy ring. One film, Daiei's *You're Being Aimed At* went so far as to suggest the Americans were spreading bacteriological infections in Japan.

The American anthropologist, the late Ruth Benedict, wrote *The Chrysanthemum and the Sword* while she was working for the American Office of War Information. This was a popular study of Japanese culture intended to help the Americans when they came to occupy Japan, and in it she commented briefly on the characteristics of Japanese war films. She pointed out certain sharp differences between the popular conception of entertainment in the United States and Japan. The Japanese do not ask for "happy endings"; they do not, like American audiences, want everything neatly resolved. Indeed, they expect unhappy endings, since for them the supreme task of life is fulfilling one's obligations, to the State, to the family, to the business or institution to which they are attached. Referring to many traditional films, she says:

Guadalcanal Diary (1943), directed by Lewis Seiler, with Richard Conte, Robert Taylor, and Barry Nelson.

Japanese popular audiences sit dissolved in tears watching the hero come to his tragic end and the lovely heroine slain because of a turn of the wheel of fortune. Such plots are the high points of an evening's entertainment. . . . Their modern war films are in the same tradition. Americans who see these movies often say that they are the best pacifist propaganda they ever saw. This is a characteristic American reaction because the movies are wholly concerned with the sacrifice and suffering of war. These movies therefore in Japan were propaganda of the militarists. Their sponsors knew that Japanese audiences were not stirred by them to pacifism.[46]

Italy after the Fall of Mussolini

Italy's production of war films ceased with the arrival of the German army of occupation. Mussolini, deposed in July 1943, was rescued by German parachutists the following September and installed as puppet ruler in German-occupied northern Italy—the so-called Italian Social Republic, or Salò Republic. Naples passed into Allied hands in October, Rome in June 1944, and the surrender came in May 1945. It was a hard and bitter war; the Italians had to deal with a recalcitrant former ally in Germany, while at the same time establishing some form of relationship with former enemies, Britain and the United States, who were not exactly trusting of a people who had changed sides, as it appeared, overnight. It was a period of the greatest difficulty for many—for Visconti a period in a fascist prison under sentence of death, for Rossellini and De Sica a period of profound emotional and intellectual experience. Rossellini has said of it that it was "an extraordinary moment during the war when the invader arrived. We were dominated by the Germans, the Fascists, experiencing persecutions etc. and then, one fine day, the other arrived. Like enemies. Three days later they noticed that we were not enemies since we were men, and their equals."[47] And De Sica, who had been offered the position of head of the film industry of the Salò Republic, based on Venice, and refused it, has said: "The experience of the war was a determining one for all of us. Everyone felt a mad desire to throw into the air all the old stories of the Italian cinema, to plant the camera in the middle of real life, in the middle of everything which struck our astonished gaze. We sought to liberate ourselves from the weight of our faults, we wanted to look each other in the eyes and tell the truth, discover what we really were, and seek salvation."

It was De Robertis who went north to Mussolini's province to supervise for a few months film production under the fascist banner at the

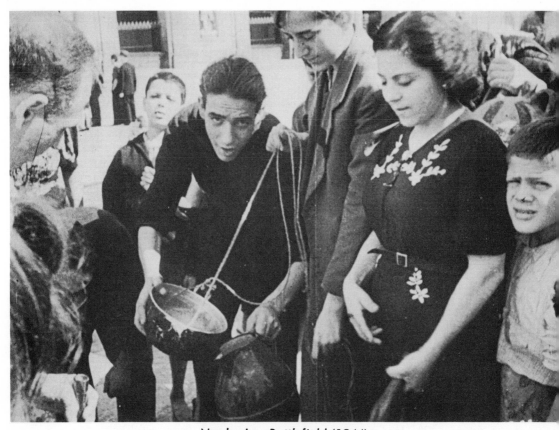

Naples Is a Battlefield (1944).

Newsreel still: allied bombing of Mt. Cassino (1944).

Scalera Studios in Venice. Italian partisans were to assassinate two notorious actresses, Osvalda Valenti and Luisa Ferida, who were thought to have indulged in sadistic orgies at the expense of prisoners. On the other hand, south in Rome Rossellini helped (as a Christian Democrat) in establishing the Cinema Workers' branch of the Committee of National Liberation. Neo-realism in the Italian film, to be so closely linked initially with Italian resistance to the Germans, was in gestation during this interim period, influenced, but no more than influenced, by Visconti's completely apolitical film of 1942, *Ossessione* (*Obsession*), which belonged, in these swiftly changing times to the previous period. In 1944, a year in which the Italians made only sixteen films, all escapist, Rossellini, shortly after the German evacuation of Rome and using odds and end of equipment and raw stock, set about the production of *Rome, Open City*, which was to inaugurate postwar studies of the war not only for Italy, but for the filmmakers of the world.

Germany

During the period of the gradual collapse of Germany, the number

Naples Is a Battlefield (1944).

of feature films made with direct State support dwindled—four only in 1943, three in 1944, and one only in 1945. They were headed by national-historical subjects—*The Endless Road* (*Der unendliche Weg*, 1943, Hans Schweikart), the story of Friedrich List, pioneer eighteenth-century economist, *Young Eagles* (*Junge Adler*, 1944, Alfred Weidenmann), about a rich aircraft manufacturer's son who is apprenticed to his father's firm, and works under the strictest discipline, and Goebbels's special *tour de force* in wartime production—Veit Harlan's *Kolberg*, a color spectacular started in 1944.[48] Kolberg featured the heroic resistance to defeatist and corrupt forces in the army of the mayor of Kolberg on the Baltic coast during the Napoleonic wars of 1806–9. Goebbels's interest in the film could be explained on the grounds that, as Gauleiter of Berlin, he saw himself as the successor to this hero of the past who revived the spirit of Germany when defeat was staring them in the face. Goebbels himself scripted the final speech rousing the people to resistance. In January 1945 Hitler had appointed him officially Defender of Berlin. The film was, however, completed so late it was never released in Germany. Its premiere was spectacular; a print was dropped by parachute to be shown to German forces besieged in Brest; this made news.

More significant was the documentary record footage of the final phases of the war, which Goebbels ordered to be shot, during the so-called *Götterdämmerung* period when Germany was on the verge of collapse. Goebbels ordered his cameramen to cover everything, including any scenes revealing the collapse of morale among the civilian population. These were the people who had, in his view, betrayed the Führer. Goebbels was the sole member of the higher Party leadership (Hitler, Göring, Goebbels, Himmler) who was always prepared at this bitter stage in the war to appear in public, tour the streets, meet the people, make fighting public speeches and broadcasts. It is his image we see in the later film records—making his celebrated oration on the total war in the Sportpalast in February 1943, after the fall of Stalingrad, or challenging audiences when Germany was nearer defeat by saying that the foreign cities occupied by the Germans may fall, but that the enemy will find it difficult to apply the same treatment to Germany itself. These were the scenes that German audiences were forced to see in the lengthy newsreels shown in those cinemas still standing and active. The bombing of the final year reduced a high proportion of the cinemas in the bigger cities to rubble.

More revealing still were the Nazi official records of certain of the worst acts—there survives, for example, the record footage of the Warsaw Ghetto shot in 1942, and the film of the trial of

Shadow of the Ruhr.

Shadow of the Ruhr.

Shadow of the Ruhr.

Shadow of the Ruhr.

the principal defendants in the summer of 1944 following the abortive attempt on Hitler's life, including records of the actual execution by hanging. This film record (said to run some twenty-five hours) was made by order of Hitler, and sections survive, but (as far as we know) nothing of the footage of the executions themselves, which Hitler is said to have viewed privately and ordered to be incorporated into a film to be made for restricted showing to army audiences. According to Allen Dulles in *Germany's Underground*, when service audiences rejected the film by walking out, Goebbels withdrew it. A written record remains however, of the scene of the hangings, the room at the *Plötzensee* prison brightly lit for the cameras:

> Imagine a room with a low ceiling and whitewashed walls. Below the ceiling a rail was fixed. From it hung six big hooks, like those butchers use to hang their meat. In one corner stood a movie camera. Reflectors cast a dazzling, blinding light, like that in a studio. In this strange, small room were the Prosecutor General of the Reich, the hangman with his two assistants, two camera technicians, and I myself with a second prison warden. The convicted men were led in. One after another, all ten faced their turn. . . . The camera worked uninterruptedly, for Hitler wanted to see and hear how his enemies had died.

5
Aftermath: The First Postwar Years

The first postwar years were inevitably the "difficult years" as the titles of the films of the period themselves showed—*Rome, Open City, Anni Difficili, No Peace among the Olives,* and in Germany itself, *The Murderers Are Among Us, Birds of Migration, Germany Year Zero.* The remaining months of 1945—following Germany's unconditional surrender of May 7 and the Japanese capitulation of August 14 after the atom bombs dropped on August 6 on Hiroshima and August 9 on Nagasaki—were the months that saw the military occupation of the enemy nations, and the first attempts to bring some sort of "international justice" to bear on the aggressors. The Allied Control Commission took over Germany on June 5, dividing the nation, and its capital Berlin, into four occupational zones, while General George Marshall began the United States occupation of Japan on August 28. On October 24 the United Nations was founded with twenty-nine nations initially ratifying its charter.

On November 20 the legally unprecedented trial of the leading Nazi war criminals began at Nuremberg before an International Military Tribunal convened by the United States, Britain, France, and the Soviet Union. This was the period of severe "nonfraternization" between Allied nationals and the German people, the period of mass "de-Nazification," of subsidiary trials and executions for war crimes in each zone, of the transfer of millions of people back to their homelands, where only too many had no homes— the return to Germany of prisoners-of-war crossing with the melancholy exodus from Germany of the victims of the Nazi policy of slave labor back to their native countries. It was also the period of the mass movement of some ten million German refugees from East to West, and the savage massacre of large numbers of Germans

The True Glory (1945), directed by Carol Reed and Garson Kanin.

The World Is Rich (1947), directed by Paul Rotha.

Your Freedom Is at Stake (1946), directed by Theodor Christensen.

The World Is Rich (1947), directed by Paul Rotha.

by those in the East whom they (or their Nazi rulers) had once oppressed—crimes against humanity committed by the other side, but never brought to trial. During the next ten years, the newly established West Germany absorbed in all some 12.5 million expelled Germans, and by 1961 (the year of the construction of the Berlin Wall) an additional four million voluntary refugees escaping from East Germany. The divided Germany had to learn not only to live with the conquerors, but to live with itself, and with the chain of socialist states established under Soviet pressure along the total length of Germany's and Austria's eastern frontiers. Russia was determined never again to risk German invasion.

Meanwhile, the formerly occupied countries had to resettle their own affairs, political, social, economic. There was recrimination against those who had collaborated with the Germans. There was also the need to establish new forms of government. While Poland, Czechoslovakia, Hungary, Romania, Bulgaria, Yugoslavia, and Albania with varying degrees of strife established socialist regimes between 1945 and 1948, Charles de Gaulle became president of the French Provisional Government in November 1945 and in June 1946, with Alcide de

The World Is Rich (1947), directed by Paul Rotha.

Gasperi, leader of the Christian Democrats, as provisional head, Italy became a republic, having rejected by referendum continuation of the monarchy. In both countries there were, and still are, strong communist parties. In Asia, communism won in China; in July 1949 Chiang Kai-shek began to evacuate his nationalist forces to Formosa, and in October the Communist Peoples' Republic of China was proclaimed at Peiping under Mao Tse-tung.

Britain

In postwar Britain, comparatively few films were made during the immediate postwar years about a war that most people wanted to forget—at least in the sphere of entertainment. Perhaps the most revealing films were Humphrey Jennings's documentaries, *A Diary for Timothy*, a poetic meditation made during the final period of the war about Britain and its people, written by E. M. Forster and addressed as if to a baby born on the fifth anniversary of the outbreak of war. It tries to reflect the feelings of Timothy's parents at the close of the European war, the need for founding a more just society for those who have not only endured the war (such as the fighter pilot featured in the film), but for those who have suffered bad working conditions in the past (the miner of the film), and the hopes for other representative workers, such as the farmer and railway engine driver also featured in the film. *A Diary for Timothy* is more emotional than intellectual, and recalls *Listen to Britain* in its impressionistic use of the traditional sights and sounds of Britain, and inclusion of moments from wartime concerts (Myra Hess) and plays (John Gielgud).

Of *A Defeated People* (March 1946) I wrote at the time:

It attempts . . . to answer sensibly those who say: leave the Germans alone; let them suffer and die as they have brought suffering and death to others. The film emphasizes the danger of doing this, of leaving millions of temporarily more or less helpless people to be driven by want and suffering to become a disease and a scourge to Europe and the World. The wreckage of the bombed cities is terrible, but the people are alive and moving about in it. The communications are battered, but the bare essentials of train services are running. Thirty million people are seeking each other, covering the walls with little cards, 'I am looking for my wife, my husband, my daughter. . . .' The station platforms are crowded deep with people who clamber with quiet orderliness into cattle-trucks and empty coal-wagons. Meanwhile, the search goes on as the German Army is demobilized and the camera records an interview in which a German suspect is denied his liberty. The film is an excellent piece of visual reporting, ably assembled and edited with a pointed and impartial commentary. There is no attempt to work up pity for the Germans, only a desire that we should realize what the war they started has brought back to them on recoil. The film ends with shots of children dancing in their schools, alternated with shots of German judges being sworn in to administer justice in the new Germany of democratic control.[1]

Other British documentaries of the period that reflected the war years included a one-hour film shot on sixteen millimeter by the Quaker Friends' Relief Service, and *While Germany Waits* (1946), useful for its coverage of the plight of the Germans after the war and the work of the relief services. *India Strikes* (1946, Bishu Sen) recorded India's contribution to the war, with her army of 2.5 million volunteers spread over every battlefront from North Africa to Burma, as well as volunteers serving in the RAF and the British Merchant Navy. One unusual film not strictly related to the war, but emerging from it, was *Personnel Selection in the British Army 1944—Officers* (Geoffrey Bell, given specialized release in 1946), the third in a series recording the use of psychological method in the British army; it included much unrehearsed interview material. In *Land of Promise* (1946), Paul Rotha redeveloped the technique of the "argument" film, *The World of Plenty,* for a film of postwar problems of housing and slum clearance in Britain, while in *Man—One Family* (1946, Ivor Montagu and Julian Huxley), Ealing Studios produced a vigorous short film destroying the Nazi legend of a *herrenvolk,* the so-called Aryan master race, by demonstrating that the peoples of Europe in particular are of very mixed stock. This exposure of the fallacies of Hitler's racial myth was produced for the Ministry of Information; it was translated into sixteen languages for distribution in liberated Europe.

Cooperating with the Netherlands Government, the British enabled the distinguished Dutch documentary cameraman and director, John Ferno, to make *Broken Dykes* (1945) and *The Last Shot* (1945–46). *Broken Dykes* (fifteen minutes) showed the fortitude of Dutch families on the island of Walcheren, whose lands and homes had to be sacrificed to the sea when a German battery commanding the approach to the harbor could only be forced to evacuate by flooding the island; the film was made with deep sympathy for and understanding of these stoic people, whose faces appear in Ferno's living portraiture. *The Last Shot* was an impressive camera record contrasting dramatically the near-hysterical joy of the people in Amsterdam on the day of their liberation with the appalling devastation of their country, the near-famine conditions, the orphaned children ("The little old men and women in Europe"), the smashed dykes, the fields washed out by

School for Danger (Now It Can Be Told (1946). Direction, Edward Baird for R.A.F.

The Last Shot (1946), directed by John Ferno.

salt and sand. The commentary, written by Arthur Calder-Marshall, reminded those better placed than the Dutch of their humane duty to help them restore themselves and their despoiled land.[2] Similarly, Hans Nieter made *Stricken Peninsula* (1945; fifteen minutes), using army-shot material to reveal the plight of the Italians as the war had left them—he showed scenes of mass-delousing and the food queues, followed by the initial attempts to restore the war-devastated earth. A twenty-minute film, *The Nine-Hundred* (1945), photographed by the combined Combat Camera Units of the Mediterranean Allied Air Forces, RAF, and British Army Film Units, showed how nine hundred wounded of the Yugoslav army were evacuated to Italy by air lift when their corps was cut off and surrounded by German forces in the mountains. The rescue operation was filmed by Lt. Francis Burgess who flew with the transports. The resistance struggle of the Yugoslavs excited the special admiration of the British, many of whom served with the partisans. *Star in the Sand* (1945; Gilbert Gunn, with commentary by Arthur Calder-Marshall) covered the story of UNRAA Camp Settlement for young, aged, or infirm Yugoslav refugees established in Egypt in 1944; here, in the face of wartime deprivation, but

The Nine Hundred (1945).

with UNRAA help, the refugees used every ingenuity to create a new community and educate the children. It was a wonderful story of rehabilitation. A third Yugoslav film, again written by Calder-Marshall, was *The Bridge* (1946; J. D. Chambers; thirty-nine minutes); this was a specially shot, but overlong record of reconstruction of an essential bridge by the villagers themselves in a remote area. In 1945 the Canadian Film Board made a thirty-minute study of UNRAA's relief work in Greece—*Out of the Ruins*—entertaining hopes for the rehabilitation and betterment of a people soon to be subject to new suffering through civil war.[3]

British feature films on the whole left war alone until sufficient time had lapsed to make the subject acceptable again in the light of reflection. In 1946, however, Ealing made *The Captive Heart* (Basil Dearden, with Michael Redgrave and Mervyn Johns) and, in Australia, *The Overlanders* (Harry Watt with Chips Rafferty). *The Captive Heart* was largely shot on location in the Marlag Milag Nord prisoner-of-war camp sited in the British Zone of Germany, and dealt with the experiences of a number of individual British prisoners; great trouble was taken to achieve authenticity by involving the screenwriter,

The Captive Heart (1946), directed by Basil Dearden.

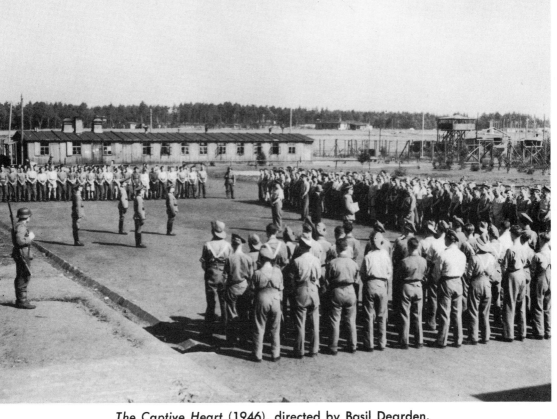

The Captive Heart (1946), directed by Basil Dearden.

Guy Morgan, in scripting. Morgan had been a wartime prisoner in the camp, and the emphasis was on the very special kind of community prolonged imprisonment of this kind creates. *The Overlanders*, on the other hand, offered a new kind of subject and environment; it reconstructed the true story of a two-thousand-mile desert trek undertaken in 1942 to save one thousand head of cattle when Japanese invasion of North Australia appeared imminent, and a scorched-earth policy was being adopted. At its best as the sheer record of a considerable feat, the film became weak only when it turned to individual relationships among the small party of drovers and the single girl who accompanied them. Other war films in the documentary style were Terence Young's *They Were Not Divided* (1950), celebrating the Guards' Armoured Division, and *Theirs Is the Glory* (1946, Brian Desmond Hurst), a reconstruction of the Arnhem operation of September 1944, when some ten thousand parachute troops were landed behind enemy lines. The film was a bold attempt to reenact the operation in the ruins of Arnhem, introducing some of the actual troops who had taken part. Two of the correspondents who had accompanied them—Alan Wood and Stanley Maxted—appear to recall

Odette (1950), directed by Herbert Wilcox.

the story through which they had lived a year or so earlier. In 1950, Anna Neagle appeared in *Odette* (director, Herbert Wilcox), the story of the heroic Frenchwoman, Odette Churchill, married to an Englishman, Captain Peter Churchill, and her exploits as an agent in France who is captured and tortured by the Gestapo.

Only one British film attempted, like *Perfect Strangers* before it, to make a dramatic point out of changes in the personalities of those who had been temporarily separated through war service. This was *The Years Between* (1946, Compton Bennett, with Michael Redgrave, Valerie Hobson, Flora Robson), in which a marriage is severely threatened when a war hero of the underground and a prisoner-of-war camp, an army colonel who had once been an MP, returns to find his wife, who thought him dead, installed in his seat in Parliament and totally changed in character as a woman parliamentarian. In addition, she is in love with another man. Unfortunately, the film let her give way to her husband's prejudices in order to retrieve the marriage. *Frieda* (1947, Basil Dearden, with Mai Zetterling; based on a play by Ronald Miller) was another Ealing film, presenting a different problem—the attitude of the British to the Germans in the period of "nonfraternization". Frieda has helped Robert, an RAF officer who was a prisoner-of-war, to escape, and in order to save her life he finally marries her and brings her back to England. Here they have to endure every kind of postwar hostility, in spite of what the girl has done to prove her good faith. This is placed in further doubt when her brother, who is still a secret Nazi, visits England in Polish uniform. Exposed for what he is, he alleges his sister is as dedicated a Nazi as himself. Frieda, in her unhappiness, is only just restrained in time from committing suicide. In spite of its melodrama, this film was a timely reminder to the British that they should decide their attitude to the German people, and to the difficult problem, on the one hand of the survival of Nazism, and on the other, the genuine innocence of many Germans of direct involvement in Hitler's regime, since they had been its prisoners rather than its accomplices. Michael Balcon claims that when the search for a suitable German actress had failed, Mai Zetterling of Sweden, whose appearance in *Frenzy* had been highly praised recently, was invited to play Frieda. This was to be the start of her long association with Britain and British films.

The Small Back Room (1948), produced and directed by Michael Powell and Emeric Pressburger, with David Farrar and Anthony Bushell.

Ealing followed *Frieda* with *Against the Wind* (1948, Charles Crichton), a not very effective story of the Belgian resistance, notable only for an early appearance of Simone Signoret in a British picture. Another, but mediocre picture about prisoners of war was Vincent Sherman's *The Hasty Heart* (1949), set in an army hospital in Burma. It contained a good performance by Richard Todd and a notable appearance by Ronald Reagan in a British film.

A film of unusual interest was *The Small Back Room* (1948, Michael Powell and Emeric Pressburger, with David Farrar; adapted from a novel by Nigel Balchin). This was a study of innate cowardice in a war research scientist addicted to alcohol. His personal frustration and misery are at least temporarily set aside, and his secret fear definitely overcome, when he is forced by circumstances to dismantle an intricate, unexploded bomb discovered on a beach. This film turned the normal war action film inside out, by seeing it wholly from within the mind of the leading character. The prolonged episode on the beach while the bomb is dismantled remains an outstanding example of how to handle suspense on the screen. Michael Powell has said of the film, which he considers to be his best: "It is a story of a hunted man who discovers a reason for living."

Atom bomb test at Bikini (1947).

The United States

For the American film industry the war could not be over too quickly —the subject was virtually dropped cold, except for Wyler's *The Best Years of Our Lives* (1946). Some interest was shown, however, in trials of the Nazi war criminals, especially that of the Nazi leaders at Nuremberg, which received full-scale newsreel coverage.[4]

The March of Time, however, gave some consideration to postwar problems. *Justice Came to Germany* (XI, 4: March 1946) covered the trial of a Nazi accused of killing prisoners of war, emphasizing that the hearing is conducted according to the principles of justice that allow the defendant proper legal representation. A more ominously slanted film, *Hitler Lives?*, released by Warners only in 1946, warned audiences against any easy-going lapse into "forgiving" the Germans, now that so many claim to be "innocent" and anti-Nazi, by showing how as a nation they have always sought to dominate—instancing the age of Bismarck, Kaiser Wilhelm in 1914, and the period culminating in the sadistic cruelties of Hitler. "Remember," says the commentary, "that among these simple, friendly and pleasure-loving people there still exist those imbued with the Nazi creed, of whom the Hitler Youth may be regarded as the most dangerous." The reviewer in the BFI *Bulletin* applauds the sentiment heartily; the film should, he thinks, "be resuscitated at half-yearly intervals and shown not only in this country but in all those where there is a seen a tendency to 'forgive and forget' too readily and too rapidly."

In *Report on Greece* (XI, 6: May 1946), *The March of Time* showed the position of Greece early in 1946—the years of occupation from 1941 leaving ruined cities and wasted countryside. Inflation has rendered the paper currency useless, and the country dependent on UNRAA. The commentary points out that Greece can only recover properly through her own efforts. Turning to the Pacific area, *The March of Time* in *The Philippines* (XI, 3: February 1946) showed the need for rehabilitation by the United States of these islands following the Japanese occupation, though independence lay ahead.

In the later 1940s the war films began to creep back onto the American screen. Some represented a revival of the combat films, and showed that, having gotten safely back and settled in, the former soldiers wanted to recall the excitement of past days and the dangers they had survived. The film acted as a vivid form of vicarious memory.

The better of the postwar combat films turned on character and human relationships in war conditions. Such were three films of 1948–

49, *Jungle Patrol* (1948, Joe Newman, with Kristine Miller, Arthur Franz), *Sands of Iwo Jima* (Allan Dwan, with John Wayne), and *Twelve O'Clock High* (1949, Henry King, with Gregory Peck, Dean Jagger, Gary Merrill). *Jungle Patrol* is set on a lonely airfield in New Guinea where a small group of pilots are holding out. A girl singer, a frontline entertainer isolated from her company, arrives suddenly in a supply plane. The luck of the group changes, and all are killed but their captain and the girl; the film ends with the Japanese bombs raining down on them. This unusual film, without stars and without direct combat scenes, concentrated on the effect the presence of this beautiful girl had on the doomed men; it reminded audiences of the reverses with which the war had started, and the tragedy of men left unrelieved in isolated outposts.

Sands of Iwo Jima features a tough sergeant, Stryker (John Wayne), whose men conceive a hatred for him, though his training makes them battleworthy in two tough campaigns—Tarawa and Iwo Jima. Stryker undergoes some change of character while on leave owing to the influence of a woman he befriends and her child, an influence which modifies his attitude to life sufficiently to make his men, in their turn, recognize him to be a fine leader. Wayne takes over the picture, his command of the screen absolute since the rest appear to be little more than raw male dummies. The old, traditional point of harsh-seeming leadership, with its inner core of paternalism, is made, but nothing more. In *Twelve O'Clock High* the nature of combat leadership is examined closely from inside. A hard-pressed group of the 8th Air Force based on Britain is suffering from decline in morale; the commanding officer (Gary Merrill) is in fact the invisible cause of their feeling over-sorry for themselves. They are too fond of him and he of them; discipline has become lax and the daylight missions over Germany less effective than they should be. The commanding general sent to "stretch" them (Gregory Peck) is himself overstretched, and eventually cracks up, but the group, though deeply hostile to him at first, come to understand him and his make-or-break policy. He is the "born leader," but one who presses himself too far. The dialogue is tense and dynamic, the casting and acting admirable; only here and there does the touch of male box-office sentiment become apparent, though firmly handled by Peck who has to retain the sympathy of the audience while doing the unpopular thing by his men—even to the extent of "breaking" one of them, who has become specially self-indulgent and disruptive to the morale of the group. *Twelve O'Clock High* tells more of the American attitude to war than most films.

Other combat films included *Command Decision* (1949, Sam

12 *O'Clock High* (1949), directed by Henry King, with Robert Arthur and Gregory Peck.

Wood) and *Eight Iron Men* (1952, Edward Dmytryk), both set in the European sector, William Wellman's *Battleground*, with a script by Robert Pirosh dedicated to "the battered bastards of Bastogne" during the Battle of the Bulge in 1944, *Decision before Dawn* (1951, Anatole Litvak), which was shot on location in Germany, about the use of German prisoners of war to assist the work behind enemy lines in Germany, *The Frogmen* (1951, Lloyd Bacon) about an underwater demolition team in the Pacific war, *Halls of Montezuma* (1950, Lewis Milestone) about neurosis in a Marine unit landed on a Japanese-occupied island, with Richard Widmark as a drug-taking company commander, and the fiercely militaristic *Flying Leathernecks* (1951, Nicholas Ray), set in Guadalcanal.

One film looked at the war from a lesser known angle. *The Beginning or the End* (1947, Norman Taurog; with Brian Donlevy, and Godfrey Tearle as Roosevelt) used a semidocumentary style to tell a fictional, backroom story of the researches leading up to the manufacture of the atom bomb with the full backing of Roosevelt, and although the film is marred here and there by sentimentality, it deserves recognition for dealing very early with the problems of conscience involved in the development of nuclear weapons. The first atom-bomb explosions are shown, and there are reconstructions of the bombing of Hiroshima.

The other films of the period included *13 Rue Madeleine* (1946, Henry Hathaway, with James Cagney, Annabella, Richard Conte), the United States-Swiss film, *The Search*[5] (1948, Fred Zinnemann, with Montgomery Clift, Aline MacMahon), and Billy Wilder's film shot in Berlin, *A Foreign Affair* (1948, with Jean Arthur and Marlene Dietrich). The first is a secret service film about three intelligence agents, two men and a woman, who are parachuted into occupied Europe on a mission before D-Day. One of the men is a double agent, serving both the Nazis and Americans. The mission is successful, but both men die, one while in Gestapo hands. The film was effectively made in the semidocumentary style already familiar in *House on 92nd Street*. The other film moved ahead to the postwar situation in Europe. *The Search* dealt with the

13 Rue Madeleine (1946), directed by Henry Hathaway, with James Cagney and Richard Conte.

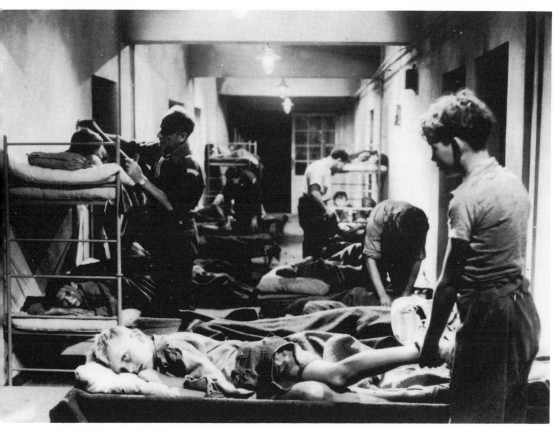

The Search (1948), directed by Fred Zinnemann.

The Search (1948), directed by Fred Zinnemann.

psychological problem of displaced children, and with one child in particular who has lost the capacity to speak; although in the care of UNRAA, the children burst out like escaping birds from the transport van sent for them because they believe it to be a gas chamber. The speechless child is found by an American soldier (Clift) who cares for him. He regains his speech—even learns baseball—and is finally reunited with his distracted Czech mother. The difficult part of the child was finely played by Ivan Jandl. The film did not hesitate to show the mental condition of these deeply disturbed children, though it might be accused of oversimplifying the process of their recovery. A *Foreign Affair* aimed solely at satirical comedy in a setting where most people saw little but gloom, the ruins of Berlin. A woman member (Jean Arthur) of a congressional committee visits Berlin to investigate the suspected low morale of the twelve thousand United States troops in the city only to become involved herself with an army captain and his German girlfriend (Dietrich). Wilder, however, does not gloss over the background of the black market, the problems of de-Nazification, or the low morale sometimes present among American forces based in Germany. Marlene Dietrich manages, before being ordered off to a de-Nazification center, to tell the Congresswoman (in the words of Axel Madsen) "what silly shrews American women are."[6] The situation is all the more ironic since the captain's duties are concerned with de-Nazification, though this does not stop him fraternizing with the singer until the congresswoman intervenes and cuts her out.

The American film that dominated the postwar years was *The Best Years of Our Lives*. It won Academy awards in both the United States and Britain; but it also attracted right-wing disapprobation (along with *Mission to Moscow* and *Song of Russia*) as "subversive" during the 1947 un-American Activities investigations into alleged Communist influences in Hollywood.[7] *The Best Years of Our Lives* was produced by Sam Goldwyn, directed by William Wyler, and adapted by Robert E. Sherwood from a novel by MacKinlay Kantor; it starred Fredric March, Myrna Loy, Dana Andrews, Virginia Mayo, and the armless war veteran, Harold Russell. The film presented the varied problems with which these men returning home after service abroad were faced—Fredric March (a former bank manager with a weakness for alcohol) to a maturing family with whom he feels out of touch, Dana Andrews to a failed marriage and inability to settle to work, and Harold Russell to the problem of keeping his fiancee and getting her used to his disability, all in the same American small-town setting. The film (which moved at a deliberate, leisurely pace so that every detail of behavior could be observed) was calculated to touch

The Best Years of Our Lives (1946), directed by William Wyler, with Hoagy Carmichael, Harold Russell and Fredric March.

The Best Years of Our Lives (1946), directed by William Wyler, with Dana Andrews.

every vein of sentiment with its restrained and skillful handling of the universal emotions involved—family life solidly shaking down in spite of the head of the family's drinking, marriage violently disrupting, the slow, awkward tenderness of Harold Russell and his girlfriend facing their new experience of each other. It is difficult to conceive how this film could ever have been thought subversive; it staunchly upholds the sacred stability of home and family, and even (through Fredric March) of free enterprize and the virtues of big business. Goldwyn as producer seldom failed to sense the box-office values in a serious subject, and *The Best Years of Our Lives* undoubtedly matched the American mood of the period. The comforting resolution of every difficulty raised made the kind of sense the American people wanted.

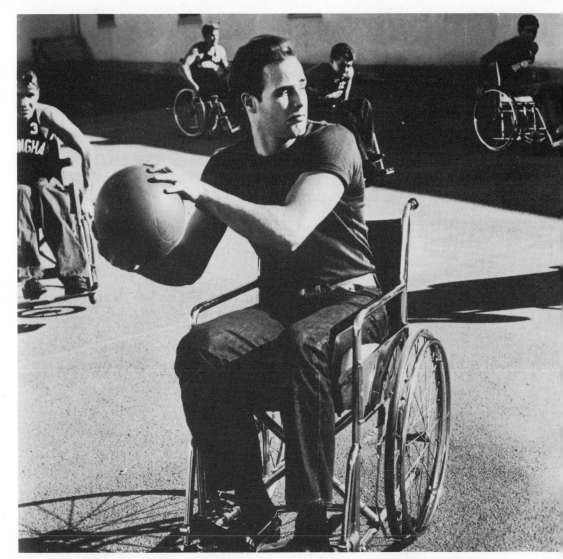

The Men (1950), directed by Fred Zinnemann, with Marlon Brando.

A more modestly budgeted film dealing with another aspect of the same problem, Fred Zinnemann's *The Men* (1950), offered Marlon Brando his first starring role as a paraplegic, an ex-soldier paralyzed by war wounds; he recovers from a state of despair through the help of the girl who successfully resists his self-pitying rejection of her and becomes his wife.

Italy

The Germans withdrew from Naples in October 1943, Rome in June 1944, and finally surrendered in the North in May 1945. For almost two years the more central parts of Italy and the North became a battleground between the Allied armies and Hitler's entrenched forces. After signing an armistice with the Allies, Marshal Badoglio had joined them, and the Italians found themselvs in the unenviable position of being suspect by the Germans and the Allies alike; they were divided between those who still supported Mussolini's discredited regime (the Italian Social, or Saló Republic) and those violently opposed to fascism, largely but not entirely men of the Left, some

The March of Time: Crisis in Italy (1948).

quarter million of whom became partisans of very mixed political and other motives directing guerrilla operations against the Germans and the Italian fascists in city and countryside. The most difficult period in Italy's recent history was to be reflected in many of the postwar Italian films, made alike by directors who adhered to the Left, such as Aldo Vergano, Giuseppe De Santis, or Carlo Lizzani, and to the Right, most notably Roberto Rossellini, a Catholic Christian Democrat. In fact, the war seen from the indigenous, Italian point of view was epitomized in Rossellini's two most celebrated films—*Rome, Open City* (shown late 1945) and *Paisa* (1946).

Rome, Open City went into production in 1944 only a few weeks after the Germans had left Rome, using scratch equipment and odd scraps of film, and drawing on the very varied talents of a notable team, including the writer Sergio Amidei and the actress Maria Michi (both Resistance workers), Aldo Fabrizi, a popular character actor and his sketch-writer, Federico Fellini (who was otherwise scraping a living drawing caricatures of the newly arrived GIs in Rome), the film star Anna Magnani, the photographer Ubaldo Arata, and Rossellini's brother, the composer Renzo Rossellini. It was a labor of absolute dedication, financed initially by some £10,000 from a wealthy Roman contessa who wanted a short film made to record the heroism of a priest, Don Morosini, who had been killed by the Germans; the film, however, was expanded to feature length when Sergio Amidei and Maria Michi (who plays Marina, the prostitute in the film) contributed their own direct experiences from the Resistance, and the character of the communist, Manfredi (based on the communist Resistance leader, Celeste Megarville) became as central to the film as that of the priest, called Don Pietro. The part of Manfredi was played by Marcello Pagliero, himself a film director. To achieve the closest authenticity, the film was shot as near to places where some real-life parallel to the events of the film had occurred; only a few interiors had to be studio reconstructions—but these too were based on real places, especially the Gestapo headquarters in the Via Tasso. The film was as deliberately realist as possible, its closest equivalent being Huston's *Battle of San Pietro*, the real action shot under fire.

The plot has all the complexities of the situation it reflects: Manfredi, who is continually on the run, and takes refuge with Francesco, a fellow communist; Pina (Anna Magnani), a practising Catholic due to marry Francesco, and already pregnant by him, who relies for help on a priest of the Resistance, Don Pietro; Manfredi's new mistress, Marina, a prostitute addicted to drugs, of whom he is already tiring. Marina betrays Manfredi, and through him Francesco,

Paisa (1946), directed by Roberto Rossellini.

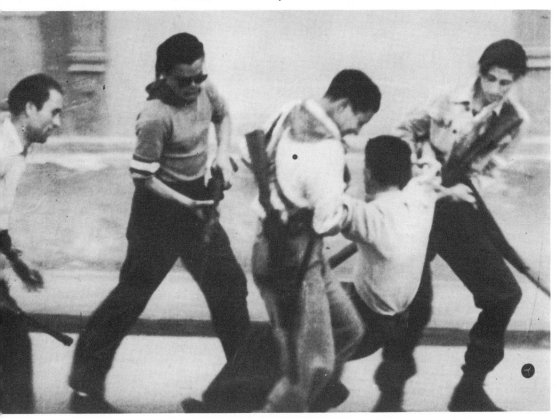

Paisa (1946), directed by Roberto Rossellini.

Rome, Open City (1945), directed by Roberto Rossellini, with Anna Magnani and Aldo Fabrizi.

Pina, and Don Pietro. Only Francesco among the protagonists is to survive. Manfredi is tortured to death by the Gestapo; Pina is shot; Don Pietro executed. Bergmann, head of the Gestapo, is no caricature, but a hard, cold, astute interrogator, while his aide Hartmann, in charge of Don Pietro's execution, uses alcohol continuously to allay his feelings. Ingrid, the woman Gestapo officer, is a lesbian who exploits the hold she has over Marina.

This marvelously realized film, with its wholly credible story and characterization, was only successful in Italy after the Italians learned of the shock-wave of excitement it caused elsewhere following the award of the Grand Prix at the 1946 Cannes Film Festival. Its success spread over Europe and the United States, where it earned half a million dollars in a year, a large sum at the time for a foreign-language film. Rossellini has said that it was born out of his own fear at the time of the German occupation of Rome, and the greatness of the film lies in its sheer truthfulness as well as the credibility of its Roman background—the priest trying to play football with the street-boys, the angry women led by Pina storming the bakery where they have been denied their rations. Many of the people seen in the film were nonprofessionals, "ordinary" people reliving experiences fresh in their minds. Rossellini's truthfulness lies especially in the characterization of his leading figures. Manfredi is by no means a wholly admirable character; he is human, and only shows "heroic" qualities when in the hands of the Gestapo. His mistress is a slut. Pina is full of doubts and worries. Don Pietro is fearful. How many war films were prepared to show that few people are by nature heroes, and that much of the undoubted heroism "ordinary" men and women reveal under the stress that war brings is a vein in their characters that certain circumstances bring out, rather than a noble imprint planted on their brows.

If *Rome, Open City* set entirely new standards for the war film— and introduced the approach and techniques of filmmaking that came to be called neo-realism—*Paisa* confirmed these standards, taking the Italian perspective of war as it moved up the body of Italy south to north from Sicily to the Marshlands of the Po, in a series of vignettes, short episodes that reflect the morale of the times through human contact, especially the contact of the newcomers, mainly American GIs, and the Italians they "liberate." No film of the period except Rossellini's own *Germania Anno Zero* more deeply reveals the corruption that war generates in its path, behind its lines, alongside its songs of victory. Most of the stories reveal misunderstanding through the inability of disparate people to make full human contact—the GIs in the Sicilian episode who quite unjustly blame their comrade's death at the hands of the Germans on the Italian girl he was guarding, the Negro GI in the Neapolitan episode whom the orphaned streetboys rob and who has to learn at first hand what utter deprivation means, the collapse in the Roman episode of a decent, warm-hearted girl into prostitution and the decline after a few months of the young GI she made love to on the day of the liberation into a drunken user of whores, the consternation of the simple Catholic monks in a remote monastery in the Appenines little touched by war when three burly American army chaplains arrive and they discover one is a Lutheran and the other a Jew—"lost souls" to be converted. In the Florentine episode the inter-Italian conflict (fascists hunted by partisans) is played out before the eyes of an American nurse seeking her prewar lover, a painter who has been killed as a Resistance worker. In the last episode the useless, inhuman chaos of the struggle is shown with extraordinary reticence and power—

Americans, British, Italian partisans, Popsky men, and the Germans shooting out the final months in the desolation of the marshlands until peace is suddenly declared and those still living can at least stay alive. The men we have seen, however, have been executed in cold blood by a youthful German officer.

Paisa is as near real war as postwar reconstruction could ever get, and it is acted out for us by people very few of whom were to be regarded as professionals. Rossellini recruited them as he found them. In his own words as quoted by Roy Armes:

> The American Negro claimed to have played some supporting roles but I realized that in reality he had lied to me to get the job. All the monks in the monastery scene were real, as were the Protestant and Jewish chaplains with whom they converse. It is the same with the peasants of the marshes around Ravenna who speak in the dialect of the region, just as the Sicilians at the beginning spoke their dialect. The English officers are as authentic as the German soldiers whom I chose from among the prisoners.[8]

Rossellini's third war film of the period took him to Germany itself, in March 1947, to make a film with French backing. Rossellini explained his approach in *Cahiers du Cinéma* again quoted by Roy Armes:

> The Germans were human beings like the rest; what could have brought them to this disaster? The false morality which is the very essence of Nazism, the abandonment of humility in favour of the cult of heroism, the exaltation of force rather than of weakness, pride against simplicity?

Here the immediate aftereffects of Nazism and defeat in war are seen through the experience of a thirteen-year-old boy, Edmund, in the desolate, corrupt surroundings of Berlin a year or so after the end of the fighting when it had become a center for human exploitation and the evils of black marketeering. Edmund's family—his bedridden, self-pitying father who had served in the First World War, his older brother still impregnated with and tormented by his Nazism after return from war service, his daughter resisting decline into prostitution as she works to keep the family in food. For Edmund himself, it is a matter of picking up what he can rather than receiving proper re-education; he is still being corrupted by his former Nazi schoolteacher, whose relations with him reveal homosexual inclinations. (In both *Rome, Open City* and this film Rossellini directly equates Nazism with moral perversion, which extends into the sexual area.) It is the influence of this teacher that leads Edmund to commit his crime—following the Nazi doctrine of his congenital illness. Then, consumed by a new-found sense of guilt, he becomes an almost infantile fugitive among the ruins of Berlin, finally killing himself when he feels there is no place for him in the family, or in society as a whole.

Rossellini's search for truth sprang from his sense that a Christian-inspired moral code is essential to society. He has said (*Sight and Sound*, April 1950):

> In *Rome Open City* and *Paisa*, all the acts of heroism or human kindness obviously spring from faith, and the brutalities of war from cynicism and absence of moral code. In the tragic emptiness of the postwar world shown in *Germania Anno Zero*, the struggle between faith and mere opportunism is still more accentuated. For the child standing unconsciously between the two extremes, it is a tightrope balancing act.

To effect this, his approach allowed no tampering with the human situation as he directly observed it—which is why he has preferred for the most part in his war films to avoid the use of professionals, except in *Rome, Open City*. His interest lies in seeing people as they really are, rather than as the actor sees and reenacts them. He prefers the people he has so carefully chosen to remain themselves before the camera.

Two feature films dealing with partisan activity were sponsored by ANPI, the ex-Partisans' Association (Associazione Nazionale Partigiani Italiani): *The Sun Also Rises* (*The Sun Rises Once More, Il Sole Sorge Ancora*, Aldo Vergano, 1945–46), and *Tragic Chase* (*Caccia Tragica*, made 1947; Giuseppe De Santis, with Carla del Poggio). These two films were closely integrated, coming from a closely knit, left-wing group. Vergano, aged fifyy-six, had had a long career behind him as an anti-fascist, and as a filmmaker going back to association with Alessandro Blasetti on the silent film *Sole* (1929); he had also served notably with the partisans, and said in 1947: "There is nobody in Italy or abroad who doubts the value of our partisans, but there are few, on the contrary, who know the reasons why these 'adventurers' fought on one side rather than on the other."[9] De Santis, aged thirty and so a generation younger than Vergano, had helped Visconti script *Ossessione* (1942) and also worked on Vergano's film, while the Marxist filmmaker, Carlo Lizzani, worked on the scripts of both partisan films, as well as playing the priest in *The Sun Also Rises*.

The central character in *The Sun Also Rises*—the signal-slogan for partisan uprising in the film—is a young soldier, Cesare from Lombardy, whose regiment is disbanded in 1943 at the time of the collapse of Mussolini's regime. As the Germans take over control of Italy, Cesare, totally

The Sun Also Rises (1946), directed by Aldo Vergano.

inexperienced in political thinking, has to face the acute divergencies
in Italy as they are reflected in the society of his own village of Villa-
vecchia in Lombardy; he is caught between the opposing streams of
being redrafted to serve the fascist cause alongside the Germans, or
taking to the hills to serve with the partisans. He finds himself involved with the latter, and their direct confrontation with the
brutal German occupation of the village, where the officers ca-
rouse in the house of Donna Matilde, the wealthy local representative of the fascist cause and collaboration with Nazism. The Germans succeed in capturing and executing the partisan leader alongside the village priest, but with the final flight of Mussolini in 1945
the partisans prevent the Germans razing the village and overpower
them. A love theme is worked in between Cesare (Vittorio Duse),
the ordinary Italian peasant-soldier who learns the complex political involvements of the time, and Laura (Lea Padovani), a refugee
already alert in these matters when Cesare finds her working in his
village.

The Tragic Chase, De Santis's first film as director, dealt with the
immediate, chaotic postwar situation. Michele and his bride Giovanna
are carrying money to a collective farm they intend to join when they

are ambushed by bandits. In the words of Vernon Jarratt written in Italy shortly after the film was made:

> . . . it is set in the north of Italy in that curious period immediately after peace was declared when straggling across the countryside were bands of Partisans, still armed, returning home, Republican Fascists seeking to evade capture, odd German and other deserters, and bandits posing as Partisans. . . . What gives the film its distinction is De Santis' success in capturing the atmosphere of that chaotic period when the countryside bore a strange resemblance to those periods in Italian history hundreds of years before when armed bands made life hazardous outside the big towns. . . .[10]

The bandits also kidnap Giovanna as a hostage, and the "tragic chase" is undertaken by Michele and the members of the collective farm, who need not only to rescue Giovanna but receive the money on which their livelihood depends. Meanwhile Alberto, a member of the bandit group (and once a prisoner in the same concentration camp as Michele), is obsessed with the bandit's woman leader, Daniela, a fascist and former collaborator with the Germans, a fatal, destructive relationship not unlike that in *Ossessione. The Tragic Chase* is a remarkable film in which human relationships—Giovanna and Michele, Alberto and Daniela, and even Giovanna and Daniela—are as important as the political contrasts that the film naturally emphasizes, not only in action but in speeches. De Santis also made another fine film on a similar theme, *No Peace among the Olives* (*Non c'e pace tra gli ulivi*, 1949, with Raf Vallone and Lucia Bosé), a passionate indictment of wrong done to a young farmer who returns from the war to find both his farm and the girl he loves stolen from him. It is based on a true story, and set in the Ciociara region in the West between Rome and Naples, where De Santis was brought up.

Italy was to make few war films, and indeed few enough about the social conflicts of the period. Involving the war period itself, three films made by Luigi Zampa are of importance for the way in which they managed to extract comedy and even farce out of serious social issues of the "difficult years." These were *Living in Peace* (*Vivere in Pace*, 1946; with Aldo Fabrizi), *L'Onorevole Angelina* (1947, with Anna Magnani), and *The Difficult Years* (*Anni Difficili*, 1948; with Umberto Spadaro). Zampa's prolific output aimed primarily at entertainment, but with these three films he exposed the comic absurdity to which the twists and turns of the situation had led without any real examination of the problems involved. They showed Italian ebullience in parts provided for robust character acting, as well as an innate affection for Italian resilience when in difficulty. In their way these films were "conformist" because

Living in Peace (1946), directed by Luigi Zampa, with Aldo Fabrizi (center).

their outlook was so comforting. They could therefore scarcely fail to be popular, though treating subjects that could still be embarrassing in the years 1946 to 1948. *Vivere in Pace* dealt with the German occupation as seen in the village of Rocca Ripesena, where a farmer unwillingly involved in his own humanitarianism agrees to hide two American soldiers, one white, one black, whom his daughter has found. The film has two climaxes—the comic climax when a German soldier, riotously drunk on the farmer's wine, is suddenly confronted by the American Negro, also riotously drunk. After a hot session of cornet playing, in which the Italian family are unwillingly forced to dance with their drunken guests, the two official enemies go off together through the night in the empty streets singing and shouting that the war is over. The second climax is tragic— Aldo Fabrizi done to death by the retreating Germans, the mood of the film unevenly transformed to melodrama.

L'Onorevole Angelina[11] is set on a badly built housing estate of the Mussolini era, which has degenerated postwar into a slum. Anna Magnani plays the role of the wife of an impoverished police official with six children to feed, and she becomes the local housewives' champion; she leads them in a demand for their proper pasta ration, and when their slum homes are flooded, she leads them in the occupation of a newly built block of flats elsewhere. Zampa, however, is more concerned with making a box-office comedy with "women's interest" than he is with facing the true nature of the social and political issues involved. His third film, *The Difficult Years*, also reduced to comic absurdity the attempts by an inoffensive "little man" and his family to keep on the right side of things during the various deviations involved in keeping up with the fascists.

If Zampa's way was to tread lightly through the "difficult years," past and present, other films dealt more solidly with social problems of the aftermath of war. These, like *Caccia Tragica* and *L'Onorevole Angelina*, are not properly war films and are therefore outside our scope except insofar as they reflect, directly and indirectly, social problems immediately resulting from the war. *Shoeshine Boys* (*Sciuscia*, 1946; Vittorio De Sica) was made with compassion and humanity and dealt with the moral condition of the Roman shoeshine boys, many of them orphans or living precariously with families indifferent to their welfare. It was the film that established the highly productive relationship between De Sica and the left-wing writer, Cesare Zavattini, in their studies of impoverished people in the immediate postwar years—*Bicycle Thieves* (1948), *Miracle in Milan* (1950, and *Umberto D* (1951). Other films dealt with the problem of youth and delinquency—Pietro Germi's *Lost Youth* (*Gioventu Perduta*, for example, and Renato Castellani's *Under the Roman Sun* (*Sotto il sole di Roma*), both released in 1947.

Germi also made a film about the Mafia, *In the Name of the Law* (*In Nome della Lege*, 1949), which had complicated relationships resulting from the war situation. The Mafia, starting initially as a kind of self-advancing brotherhood of the underprivileged in the lawless society of Sicily, and with a ruthless code of conduct, including the freedom to kill, soon became involved in the violences of the time, forming armed gangs that might or might not be engaged in "resistance" rather than banditry, and might or might not be regarded in a heroic light by the ordinary people, who at once feared to become identified with them or to betray them to the authorities, whoever these might be—the fascists, the Germans, the occupying armies bringing "liberation." The American army deliberately used the Mafia for partisan activity and left them to become a social scourge in the future. As we shall see, the young wartime Mafia "hero," Salvatore Giuliano, who was to be assassinated, became the central figure in a remarkable film by Francesco Rosi shown in 1962.

Fellini helped create the script for Pietro Germi's film, *In the Name of the Law*, in which Charles Vanel played a Mafia chief, Passalacqua, opposed to a young judge (Massimo Girotti) who attempts to bring conventional law to a village where the Mafia creates the rules. The ethics of the film are curious; Charles Vanel establishes the dignified authority of the Mafia chief throughout, though unnaturally bowing in the end to the rule of state law as represented (heroically) by Massimo Girotti. The Mafia killers appear in an almost idealistic light, which reflects, perhaps, the confusions of the time. Germi's other film with a Sicilian setting, *The Road of Hope* (*Il Cammino della Speranza*, 1950), showed the exploitation of impoverished laborers seeking work in France. Further films that projected the problems of postwar Italy were Alberto Lattuada's two subjects, *The Bandit* (*Il Bandito*, 1946, with Amadeo Nazzari, Anna Magnani, Carlo Del Poggio), a drama about the problems of a returned prisoner-of-war from Russia who finds himself drawn into a gang-ridden society in the area of Turin, and *Without Pity* (*Senza Pietà*, 1948, with Carlo Del Poggio and the Negro, John Kitzmiller, seen also in *Vivere in*

Il Cammino della Speranza (Road to Hope) (1950), directed by Pietro Germi.

Pace), another social melodrama that Fellini also helped to script, concerning two people with no place in society, the prostitute Angela and a Negro from the American army, both of whom become involved in crime.

These films appeared at the time to be sufficient to deal with the war and its outcome in Italy. Italian audiences, like others elsewhere, preferred their films to take them "out of themselves" rather than to deal with contemporary problems, and the neo-realist movement, primarily concerned with social issues, had lost both sponsorship and momentum by the end of the decade.

France

French filmmakers began work early as part of Resistance activity, producing collectively *Le Journal de la Résistance* (1944; thirty-four minutes), under the combined leadership of Jean Painlevé, Jean Grémillon, Louis Daquin, and the actor Pierre Blanchar, members of the Comité de la Liberation du Cinéma Français. The film, largely shot clandestinely, covered the six-day rising in Paris that led to the German retreat from the capital—it was shot in the deserted streets where men and women waited tensely under cover for the action that had to come, the sporadic outbursts of street fighting. The cameramen went into the heart of the action, producing records of historic importance—such as the scenes (snatched, in some instances, under fire) of German tanks nosing their way uncertainly down the streets, of Red Cross workers risking death to bring in wounded resistance fighters. There are shots, too, of murdered hostages, of Germans surrendering, of French collaborators taken into custody. The film ends with the wild rejoicing as de Gaulle moves around Paris jointly liberated by the Resistance and the Allied forces of General Leclerc. What matters most about this film is the intensity of feeling that image and commentary combine to produce.[12]

A remarkable Franco-American film, not released in Britain, appeared a year later, *Le Retour* (also known as *Reunion*, in a slightly reedited form), the result of the keen eye for editing shown by Henri Cartier-Bresson and Richard Banks, and, according to Jay Leyda, including material specially shot by Cartier-Bresson. The subject was the liberation of French prisoners from German concentration camps, and their arrival in France. Leyda agrees with the commentator of the Museum of Modern Art in regarding this film as "the greatest human document to come out of the war," and goes on to describe its emotional treatment:

It almost seems one cameraman's work, so single-purposed is Cartier-Bresson's attitude to the selection and arrangement of its material. It is almost impossible to make a distinction between what he photographed (though the powerful conclusion at the Gare de l'Est, from the waiting hands on the barrier, must have been his own work), and what he chose from the work of many other cameramen. It was his art throughout that directed a penetrating editorial spotlight on the significant detail that might easily be missed by anyone else—the "decisive moment"—and it was clearly he who determined the slow, tense cutting before the shocking slap of a collaborator. The film's opening has an effect of joyous confusion, using shots that a lesser artist would have discarded. The almost intolerable *holding* on a staring, incredulous, freed man is as painful as the tattooed arms of children.[13]

Another compilation film of importance was a sixteen-minute study of prison-camp atrocity, *Camps of the Dead*. Jean Grémillon's *Le Six Juin à l'Aube* (1945) was also an emotional film, a personal reflection of the effects of war, the D-Day landings on rural Normandy, Grémillon's native earth—he was born in Bayeux. Grémillon is more involved in the aftermath of war, the reestablishment of the destroyed farmlands, than in the landings themselves. The film is melancholy, elegiac, dark in mood; Grémillon composed his own music, and his fatalistic outlook colors the whole work, which suffered some recutting by the distributors before it was shown.

The number of feature films made on the occupation was small—the subject was too bitter and controversial, and the nation was divided over the issue of collaboration.[14] Those films which were made during the immediate postwar years tended to come from directors of the Left, notably Grémillon and René Clément with his first feature film, *La Bataille du Rail* (1945–46), in effect a documentary reconstructing true events from the record of the Resistance and using a cast of mixed professional and nonprofessional actors, the railwaymen who had conducted sabotage; the film was part-produced by the Coopérative Général du Cinéma Français for the Railway Resistance movement. The film used an incident showing how the sabotage of transport was carried out by a single, highly organized group of railwaymen intent on preventing a convoy bringing reinforcements to the front shortly after D-Day. There is an impressive scene when the drivers protest at the execution of members of the Resistance by a combined shrilling of their engine-whistles.[15] After helping the actor Noël-Noël make *Père Tranquille* (1946), in which Noël-Noël starred as an innocent-looking "little man" who is secretly a Resistance leader, Clément turned to an unusual but necessary subject in his *Les Maudits* (1947), which concerned a group of prominent

La Bataille du Rail (1945–46), directed by René Clément.

La Bataille du Rail (1945–46), directed by René Clément.

Nazis escaping by submarine to Latin America, ostensibly to carry on the fight after the German collapse, but in fact deeply divided among themselves. The film ended with a fight between those who want to escape and the fanatical Nazi SS leader, Forster, played as an intense study of villainy by Jo Dest. The French are represented in this closely incarcerated group by a doctor, played by Henri Vidal, who has been captured and is finally left alone to drift on the submarine, the rest of the party being already dead. The film becomes a study in deep hatred of the German occupier and all those who collaborated with him. But it also reveals Clément's fascination with their characters, whom the doctor closely observes.

Le Silence de la Mer (1947, Jean-Pierre Melville), made independently and based on a short story by Vercors, again reflects French fascination with the German character. Vercors' story was published clandestinely during the Occupation; an aristocratic German Officer, billetted on a French provincial household, charms the old man and his young niece and overcomes their hostility. The niece falls in love with him. The situation is resolved when the officer, appalled by Hitler's policy in France, leaves with the intention of seeking death on the Eastern front rather than continue to serve such a master. An episodic film, Retour à la Vie (1949) with contributions from several directors, has little in common with this kind of romantic fatalism. It deals with the common theme of the return of men and women after the war. Five short stories are told by four directors, H. G. Clouzot, Georges Lampin, André Cayatte, and Jean Dréville. Clouzot's episode, Le Retour de Jean, again reflects the fascination combined with hatred from which French filmmakers seemed to suffer in their attitude to the Germans. The great actor Louis Jouvet plays Jean, a soldier who has returned, wounded and disillusioned, only to find an escaped German prisoner hiding in the room where he lives alone. The German (Leo Bapara) proves to be one of the worst kind of Nazi sadists who tortured prisoners; Jean forces him to reveal the details of his crimes, and then sets upon him and finally poisons him. Violence breeds violence, and it would appear with the approval of Clouzot. Clouzot's own film of the same year, Manon, was an updating of Prévost's novel with a contemporary background—Robert, obsessed by his love for Manon, deserts from the Resistance, and becomes involved in black-market operations in Paris after the Liberation. He finally escapes with her on a ship taking illegal immigrants from Marseilles to Palestine, where he is left, still besotted even by her dead body, after she has been killed by Arabs. The film is more important for its revelation of Clouzot's attitude to his char-

acters than for its study of postwar conditions in France, though
Manon's initial appearance shows the lynch-law administered by
indignant French patriots to suspected collaborators and girls who
have consorted with the Germans.

Germany

The devastation of the great industrial cities of Germany made them
at first barely habitable. By the time the Allied forces had occupied their
various zones early in the summer of 1945, the production of films had
low priority as distinct from the production of food, housing, and transport, and the handling of the overwhelming problem of refugees and
displaced persons numbered in millions. Only a very small proportion of the original cinemas were open even by January 1946, though
Berlin on the whole fared better in the reconstruction of theaters
owing to political rivalry between the occupying powers—170 were
operating by January 1946, about one third in East Berlin and the
rest in the other three sectors of the West.

The policy of the occupation authorities was to impound all films in
circulation for strict censoring, and to import subtitled American, British, Soviet, and other films selected either as entertainment without
any political overtones, or as films that were considered to represent
established democratic values. Facilities for dubbing into German
were quickly set up, and old German films were rereleased once
they had been vetted and considered politically harmless.

Greater difficulties were faced when it came to licensing new production in Germany. Virtually a year passed before this happened.
Meanwhile certain directors and actors were brought before de-
Nazification tribunals, among them Werner Krauss, Heinrich George,
Emil Jannings, and the directors Karl Ritter (who had made,
among other films, *Stukas* and the anti-Soviet *GPU*), Veit Harlan
(who had made the anti-Semitic *Jew Süss*, and Goebbels's final spectacular, *Kolberg*), and Leni Riefenstahl, whose hearing was conducted by the French. All were allowed to work again, though in
some cases only after a lapse of time. The Russians, who controlled
the best of the former studio facilities in the East, founded DEFA
(Deutsche Film Aktiengesellschaft, the German Film Company)
as a state-sponsored enterprise in May 1946. The British followed by
licensing small individual companies in Berlin and Hamburg, while the
Americans brought back the prominent German producer, Erich
Pommer, to supervise German production in their zone.

DEFA's initial productions immediately began to take stock of the

The Murderers Are Among Us (1946), directed by Wolfgang Staudte.

The Murderers Are Among Us (1946), directed by Wolfgang Staudte.

The Murderers Are Among Us (1946), directed by Wolfgang Staudte.

moral and social position in Germany in 1946. Wolfgang Staudte's *The Murderers are among Us* (*Die Mörder sind unter Uns*) reflected the German reaction to the men with a criminal Nazi record who had managed to dodge the de-Nazification tribunals and create a new image for themselves as model citizens. Ironically, the worst of the Nazi murderers had often been good family men in their own homes. The businessman in Staudte's film had while in uniform conducted a massacre of the inhabitants of a Polish village. A witness to this war crime, now an alcoholic, is obsessed by the need to hound down the criminal as an act of private vengeance. He is deterred, however, by a German girl, who has survived imprisonment in a Nazi concentration camp; she saves the alcoholic from himself and persuades him that the proper thing to do is to report the murderer to the authorities. This film remains one of the best of the initial postwar German films of self-examination, and has a fine performance by Hildegard Knef (Neff) as the girl. A recurrent visual feature of the film is the ruined city of Berlin, and it became the first of a genre of German pictures to do this—the so-called rubble films.

Other DEFA films parallel those made in Italy, and deal with postwar social problems in a defeated and ruined country seeking a new

The Murderers Are Among Us (1946), directed by Wolfgang Staudte.

Irgendwo In Berlin (Somewhere in Berlin) (1946), directed by Gerhard Lamprecht.

Marriage in the Shadow (1947), directed by Kurt Maetzig.

Free Land (1946), directed by Milo Harbig.

social entity as well as moral, social, and political rehabilitation. Gerhard Lamprecht's *Somewhere in Berlin* (*Irgendwo in Berlin*, 1946) dealt with the problems of half-starved soldiers returning home, Werner Klinger's *Round-up* (*Razzia*, 1946–47) with the black market, while others took more specifically the communist line, such as Milo Harbig's *Free Land* (*Freies Land*, 1946) on the break-up of the old landed estates for resettlement by land-workers. Anti-Semitism in Nazi Germany was broached in Kurt Maetzig's *Marriage in the Shadow* (*Ehe im Schatten*, 1947), based on the true story of the actor Joachim Gottschalk and his Jewish wife, Meta Wolff, an actress, who had committed suicide rather than be forcibly parted, while anti-Jewish feeling in Germany of the 1920s appeared in Erich Engel's *The Blum Affair* (*Affaire Blum*, 1946), showing this racial antipathy to have been endemic in Germany before Hitler. Of the DEFA films, both *The Murderers Are among Us* and *Marriage in the Shadow* had considerable success when shown in Britain and the United States. They seemed to offer hope of a neorealist movement in Germany that might come to equal that in Italy.

All these films were realist in background, but dramatized in the treatment of character—professional actors' pictures. They and their counterparts in the other zones represented only a comparatively short-lived movement before German commercialism in the West revived in the 1950s and reduced the German cinema virtually to the level of artistic nonentity, while in the East the uniform level of "socialist realism" led to uninspired pedestrianism.

Meanwhile, the Western Zones, though more intent on entertainment, produced a few films that were equivalent to DEFA's films of "rehabilitation." Studio 45 made *Birds of Migration* (*Zugvögel*, 1946) about the problems of German postwar refugees seeking some place to settle, while Wolfgang Liebeneimer's *Love '47* (1947, with Hilde Krahl) turned on a woman's gradual disillusionment with Hitler and the rebirth of her faith in humanity when she falls in love with a man suffering from war wounds. A lighter approach to disillusionment with Nazism was Rudolph Jugert's *Film without Title* (*Film ohne Titel*, 1947) with Hildegard Knef—this was a "discussion" film about how to set about making a comedy for German audiences while they are still in a dire situation; the film which eventually emerges from the debates involves an interesting reversal of fortune. A young country girl working in the house of a wealthy man attracts his attention, but their social situation is disparate; after his house is destroyed and he himself becomes "displaced" he finds her again in the comparative luxury of her father's farmhouse, and considers himself fortunate when she accepts him in marriage. Another British-licensed film that drew on past experiences was Arthur Brauner's *Morituri* (1946), set in a concentration camp.

Arthur Elton, Film Adviser to Information Services Control in Germany, writing in *DNL* in January 1948, maintained that the best film made in the British Zone was Helmut Käutner's *In Those Days* (*In Jenen Tagen*, 1947), but adds a significant point of criticism:

> It is imaginative; simple effects, like the reflection of trees in the windscreen of the car, have been used brilliantly; the acting is vivid and sincere, and I shall long remember the old baroness being driven out of burning Berlin in a battered car, or the sergeant being shot as he is driving a German officer along a snowy road in mid-winter. The Hero of the film, by the way, is a motor-car which tells its own story to prove that, throughout the Nazi regime and the war, there were decent ordinary people in Germany. True enough, of course, but the film lacks something all the same. It lacks a kind of toughness. For its characters Fascism was a horrible background. None of them participated. None of them fought back. No. I'm afraid *In Jenen Tagen* falls finally into the class of films showing the German people as orphans of the storm. Then there are *Zug Vögel* (*Birds of Passage*) from the British Zone and *Ehr im Schatten* (*Marriage in the Shadows*) from the Russian. Both are finely made, but both suggest, or at least imply, that the only way out of difficulty is—suicide. Both I contend are dangerous. On the other hand, *Morder sind unter Uns* (*Murderers are Amongst Us*) from the Russian Zone avoids these dangers, and is besides a masterly piece of film-making worthy to be ranked beside any film made in Europe this year. . . . But if you ask me which will be the better box-office success in Germany, I shall reply the former. Not because it is the better film, but because people will pay more readily to see something that implies that non-participation is innocence, than to see something which does not evade the realities of the present situation. A vivid example of the dangers of taking the box-office point of view when determining a film policy for Germany.

The newsreels shown in German cinemas in the British and United States zones, *Welt im Film,* became a directly controlled Anglo-American operation, carried out almost entirely by German technical staff.

In the American Zone, under Pommer's supervision, production only began again in 1947. A result was the brilliant satiric film with music, Robert Stemmle's *The Ballad of Berlin* (*Berliner Ballade,* 1948) with Gert Frobe, which drew on the tradition of the Berlin cabaret, with its sharp, quick-witted lyrics on contemporary problems. It was not without a certain touch of self-pity in its rueful mockery of the fate of Otto (Frobe), the "little man" of Germany who is pushed around by everyone. After being imprisoned by Hitler, he finds

Ballad of Berlin (1948), directed by Robert Stemmle.

a black marketeer has taken possession of his flat and he is torn apart by the postwar political strife that is dividing Berlin. H. B. Fredersdorf and M. Goldstein's *Long is the Road* (*Lang ist der Weg*, 1947) was more specifically a war film; it exposed in a rather heavy-handed way the sufferings inflicted on the Jews in the Warsaw Ghetto of 1939, including deportation and extermination. This was the first feature film deliberately to show German audiences the ultimate barbarity of Nazi treatment of the Jews. Audiences showed varied reactions—from indifference by those who still disbelieved or did not care, to active signs of remorse. The truth about the concentration and extermination camps had been shown already in the cinemas by means of a special newsreel compilation produced by the Western occupying Powers, *The Mill of Death* (*Die Todesmühle*)—again the reactions to this had been mixed, silence or weeping, even hysterical laughter. But whereas *The Mill of Death* had been imposed on the Germans by the authorities, *Long Is the Road* had been made by Germans, with a Jewish cast many of whom had known the sufferings they recreated on the screen. Reflecting the postwar period, Josef von Baky's *The Challenge* (*Der Ruf;* 1949, with Fritz Kortner) shows the disillusionment suffered by a Jewish professor who, after exile in the United States, insists on trying to work again in Germany. *The Sons of Herr Gaspary* (*Die Söhne des Herrn Gaspary;* 1948, Rolf Meyer) introduced a rather more dubious implication than most of these "rehabilitating" films; it contrasted two brothers one of whom, an anti-Nazi, grows rich in exile in Switzerland, while the other, who stays to serve the Fatherland in the Luftwaffe, remains poor. The rich exile, however, comes back after the war to work alongside his brother in order to help rebuild the new Germany.

Parallel with the feature film, the authorities in all the zones either produced documentaries themselves or encouraged the Germans to do so. Some of these dealt with the significance of Hitler's regime in German history, notably *It's Up To You* (*Es Liegt in Dir*), concerned with the reconstruction of Germany.[16]

By 1949 the German film industry was on its feet again, and the mood was all for entertainment. The rubble was fast disappearing. The new Germany was being born out of hard work and economic reconstruction with massive help, especially from the United States. German audiences were tired of the name of Hitler, and tired of being required to display remorse for the past. But films up to that year had shown a commendable capacity to analyse the past in provocative terms, to work the past to some degree out of the national system. A summary was made mid-1949 by H. H. Wollenberg on the record up to that date, based on a report made at the time:

> The total of German films released or completed but not yet shown or in production was seventy at the beginning of this year. Of this total, thirteen subjects have a distinctly political flavour, including two which present their story in a humourous or satirical manner. They deal with such provocative themes as war-guilt, racial persecution, pacifism, land-reform, and so on. Another thirty-one films (including fifteen of the light, humourous type) deal with a variety of contemporary problems, but without political implications; matrimonial problems, caused by the war for instance, postwar youth, readjustment of returning servicemen, black-market, bureaucracy—and so on. The third category is entertainment pure and simple. It comprises romance, musicals, crime thrillers, escapist material of all kinds, and its total is thirty-seven, including fifteen comedies. Finally, there are four period and biographical pictures. The conclusion to be drawn is that of the seventy films made, no less than forty-four (or more than half) are films with a present-day background and with a contemporary message of some kind. [*Sight and Sound,* Summer 1949, p. 64]

Soviet Union

After their long series of documentary campaign films, the Russians turned to making a series of features that reconstructed the principal campaigns in such a way as to glorify Stalin's leadership and strategy. In such films as *The [Great] Turning Point* (January 1946, Friedrich Ermler), which centred on the evolution of strategy by the generals under Stalin's guidance, and *The Vow* (July 1946, Mikhail Chiaureli), a historical survey of Soviet history emphasizing the fulfillment of the vow Stalin made when Lenin died in 1924 to continue his work, the Sphinx-like father-figure of Stalin (interpreted in *The Vow* by M. Gelovani) either appears with due mystique as the heart and head of the Soviet Union and its peoples, as in *The Vow*, or transmits his strategy from above, as in *The Turning Point*. The aim of *The Turning Point*, as explained by its makers, was to reveal the mentality of generals; he and his screenwriter, Boris Chirskov, researched their subject on the battlefields while the war was still being fought—"at the front we came to understand that we were not planning a battle film but a psychological film," one reflecting the strain and tension at headquarters. The central character, a fictional general Muravyov (played by Mikhail Derzavin) was a man compounded out of many they had met. The ruins of Leningrad were used as a stage for the battle scenes.

The Vow was a finely made film revealing the full force of the "cult of the personality" which was to be condemned so absolutely in public by Nikita Khrushchev in 1956, three years after Stalin's death. In *The Vow* the development of Russia under successive five-year plans is shown from the point of view of a "typical" family in Stalingrad, the central character being a widow whose husband had been killed in the early 1920s. The film was in its own way as rich in "lyrical" propaganda as *Trumph of the Will*; it links Stalin and his satellite leaders with the people in a film that is really a celebration of his long career as leader, a triumph of *his* will, culminating in *his* strategy that won the war with the devoted help of *his* people. The old lady, at the concluding ceremony, bows in loving reverence over the hand of the deliverer of her family and her country. In another film there is a sequence directly reminiscent of the opening of *Triumph of the Will*, in which the leader descends from the sky to stand, isolated but welcomed by the crowds drawn up to greet him. The reaction is near hysterical in its purposeful admiration of Stalin. The film, however, is also a celebration of the Soviet people themselves, and its propaganda has a positive side because it presents them with so much warmth.

The Turning Point (1946), directed by Friedrich Ermler.

The Vow (1946), directed by Mikhail Chiaureli, with Mikhail Gelovani as Stalin.

The Vow (1946), directed by Mikhail Chiaureli, with Mikhail Gelovani as Stalin.

The Turning Point (1946), directed by Friedrich Ermler.

The Third Blow (1947), directed by Igor Savchenko.

The Story of a Real Man (1948), directed by Alexander Stolpev.

Battle of Stalingrad (1950), directed by Vladimir Petrov.

Battle of Stalingrad (1950), directed by Vladimir Petrov, with Alexei Diki as Stalin.

The enforced emphasis on Stalin and the stultification caused by censorship was to bring the film industry almost to a halt in the early 1950s. But the glorification of Stalin's role in the war was to be seen, for example, in Vladimir Petrov's two-part *Battle of Stalingrad* (1950) with Alexei Diki as Stalin, while in the same period Mikhail Chiaureli made the two-part film, *The Fall of Berlin* (1949) with Mikhail Gelovani as Stalin. Both films suffered from being elaborate studio reconstructions of combat. Earlier films of 1947 drew on war themes seen from the regional standpoint of the Baltic—Vera Stroyevna's *Marite*, about a Lithuanian girl killed during the occupation, and Herbert Rappoport's film of an Estonian play, *Life in the Citadel*. Boris Barnet's *The Scout's Exploit* (1947) was made at Kiev. Sergei Gerasimov's film of Komsomol resistance in Krasnodin, *Young Guard* (1947), is condemned by Jay Leyda in *Kino* as "grandiose, inflated, mock heroics."

As a further unhappy symptom of the times, the Russians accepted the American challenge to play at cold-war politics, first seen emerging in Mikhail Romm's *The Russian Question* (1948) and Grigori Alexandrov's *Meeting on the Elbe* (1949).[17]

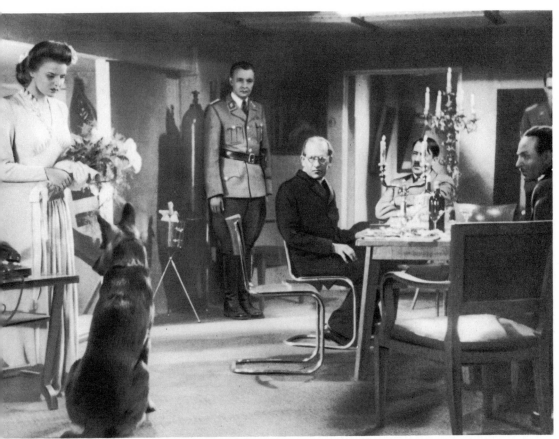

Fall of Berlin (1949), directed by Mikhail Chiaureli, with Savelyov as Hitler.

Fall of Berlin (1949), directed by Mikhail Chiaureli, with Mikhail Gelovani as Stalin.

Fall of Berlin (1949), directed by Mikhail Chiaureli, with Mikhail Gelovani as Stalin.

The Russian "Katiushas" in *Alexander Matrosov* (c. 1949), directed by L. Lukov.

Meeting on the Elbe (1949), directed by Grigori Alexandrov.

Meeting on the Elbe (1949), directed by Grigori Alexandrov.

Czechoslovakia, Poland, Hungary, Yugoslavia

The Nazi hold on Czechoslovakia ended in May 1945, and the Soviet army entered Prague on May 9.[18] Prague had a long tradition of prewar filmmaking, and this to some extent continued during the German occupation. The film industry was formally nationalized in August 1945, and a Film Faculty was founded at the Academy of Dramatic Arts. Czech and Slovak filmmakers, many of whom had been linked to the underground and had made film records of the last days of Nazi terrorism and street fighting, were anxious to produce films about the years of occupation. These films celebrated the work of the Resistance—*Men without Wings* (1946, František Cáp, a prize-winning film at the 1940 Cannes Film Festival), concerning a group of Czechs working at the Prague airfield during the occupation, *The Heroes are Silent* (1946, Miroslav Cikán), *Supermen* (1946, Václav Wasserman), *The Mountains are Rumbling* (1946, Václav Kubásek), films made under the general supervision of Martin Frič and Otakar Vávra who were concerned in the administration of the new, small, nationalized industry. Jirí Weiss (who had been in exile in England, where he was part of the team of documentary filmmakers attached to the Crown Film Unit) returned to Prague to make *Stolen Frontiers* (1947), which dealt with the Munich crisis and the German seizure of the Sudetenland. In Slovakia where a new film industry was being set up, František Cáp, with Soviet help, made *White Darkness* in 1948, a film about joint action by Soviet and Slovak partisans in the mountains; this was followed in 1948 by *Wolves Lairs* (Palo Bielik), another account of partisan warfare.

In February 1948 the Communist Party coup within the government led to the establishment of a fully socialist state following the resignation of President Benes, and the films produced thereafter were subject to strict ideological pressures that did not ease until after the death of Stalin. However, further films of the Resistance appeared—*The Silent Barricade* (1949, Otakar Vávra), on the May 1945 rising in Prague, and *The Trap* (1950, Martin Frič). A single film was made about the fate of the Jews of the Teresín concentration camp, *The Long Journey* (1949, Alfréd Radok).

Stolen Frontiers (1947), directed by Jirí Weiss.

In Poland, the prewar studios and equipment had been virtually all destroyed or confiscated by the Germans. Some clandestine filmmaking took place—especially coverage of the Warsaw uprising of 1944. While some Poles, such as Eugeniusz Cekalski, worked in New York on Polish Information films, others grouped under Aleksander Ford formed a Polish Army Film Unit in the USSR (including Jerzy Bossak, Adolf and Wladyslaw Forbert, Ludwig Perski, and Stanislaw Wohl), covering the liberation of Poland by the Soviet armies. From this latter group sprang the beginnings of the new, postwar Polish film industry, together with prewar members of an experimental film society, START (Society of the Devotees of the Artistic Film), which included, in addition to Ford and Cekalski, Wanda Jacubowska and Jerzy Toeplitz, who had spent the war years in Britain, but returned to Poland and became head of the most progressive film school in Eastern Europe at Lodz.

Out of the political morass of 1945, after Poland had been liberated by forces that included Polish divisions fighting alongside the Russians, and its frontiers, east and west, had been decided, the provisional government, set up in June 1945, moved during the later 1940s nearer to alignment with the USSR. Few films were made during these years, but among them were Wanda Jacobowska's film about the extermination camp at Auschwitz, *The Last Stage* (1948), with Aleksandra Slaska; it was based on the personal experiences of Wanda Jacubowska and a German companion, Gerda Schneider, who scripted the film with her. It is a quiet, restrained study of life in the women's section of the camp, presenting what it was felt could be presented on the screen at the time to reveal the appalling conditions in which the women had lived and died, and the manner in which they were treated. It was shot on the site of Auschwitz. Other films among the small output of the early period covered the years of occupation—*Forbidden Songs* (1947, Leonard Buczkowski), the first postwar feature to be produced, *House of the Wastelands* (1950, Jan Rybkowski), a film of the partisans who visit a house outside Warsaw, *Unvanquished City* (1950, Jerzy Zarzycki), a film of the Warsaw Uprising, *Others will Follow* (1949, Antoni Bohdziewicz), showing a cross-section of Polish people during the Occupation and their varied political outlook.

Hungary had a considerable film industry prewar, even briefly experimenting with nationalization in 1919 until private enterprise was restored by the Horthy regime, whose severity led to the exodus of many Hungarian filmmakers to Western Europe or the United States, including Alexander Korda. After the Hitler war, the industry had to recover from bomb damage and the need for complete reorganization

The Last Stage (1948), directed by Wanda Jacubowska.

after the dislocation of the war years and the damage done by Nazi German influence. The industry was formally nationalized in March 1948, the year in which it became clear that Hungary would join the chain of socialist-satellite states, which it did formally the following year.

Hungarian feature production existed on a very small scale during this period, nine features only prior to nationalization, mostly under the sponsorship of the various political parties. Of these films, only two were of any significance—István Szöts's *Song of the Cornfields* (1947), an exposure of the depressed condition of the peasants before the Liberation, and Géza Radványi's *Somewhere in Europe* (1947), scripted by Hungary's leading writer and film theorist, Béla Balázs, and produced by the Communist Party. The last was about a group of boys bombed out of reform school. They form a gang, wandering uncontrolled and stealing for a living until they are taken in hand by a recluse, a musician (Artúr Somlay) who set up a community with them in an empty castle, teaching them social discipline, which in turn fits them to support the socialized society to come.

Somewhere in Europe (1947), directed by Géza Radvány.

After nationalization, Hungary immediately set about the production of films dealing with social problems from the socialist standpoint, particularly that of the oppressed peasantry who looked forward now to better times. The first of these was Frigyes Bán's *The Soil under Your Feet* (1948). Postwar conditions in Budapest were shown in Imre Jeney's *A Woman Makes a New Start* (1949), the story of a middle-class woman who works in a factory while waiting for her husband's return from war service; the second part of the film concerned the husband. But the subject of the war itself, as distinct from stories reflecting adjustment to new social conditions and attitudes was virtually excluded. Indeed, the subsequent films of 1950–52 were concerned almost entirely with propaganda, presenting an idealized picture of the new age.

Yugoslavia, unlike the other countries that adopted socialist regimes, had little tradition of filmmaking; in fact it was conceived as a quite new undertaking among the partisans fighting for the liberation of their territory, and took the form initially of news records of their activities. Partisans held most of the mountainous regions from 1944, and the Russian Red Army liberated Belgrade in October.

The provisional government, with Tito as prime minister, held elections in November 1945, which returned an overwhelming vote in favor of Tito and communist rule. The open break with the Soviet Union was revealed in 1948, when Yugoslavia was expelled from the Cominform and became isolated from the other socialist states, turning to the West for economic help.

The film industry had been nationalized in 1945, with production in the six constituent republics, but the number of features made prior to 1950 was minimal. In 1947 there were only three hundred cinemas in the whole country. Yugoslav filmmakers had to be virtually self-taught. When they eventually found their feet, they were to turn to war themes for many of their films. Partisan subjects soon appeared in the roughly made, early films—for example, *On Our Own Soil* (France Štiglic) and *The Prisoners* (Gustav Gavrin, 1949).

In the other socialist countries, Bulgaria and Romania, with little or (in the case of Albania) no filmmaking experience to draw upon, production emerged more slowly, usually with strongly antifascist films such as *Dawn over the Homeland* (Bulgaria, 1951; Anton Marinovitch).

Slavica (1947), directed by V. Afric.

Japan

Over half of Japan's cinemas were destroyed or out of action by the time of the surrender, and the rest closed for a week after the emperor's announcement at midday on 15 August 1945—"the enemy has begun to employ a new and most cruel bomb, the power of which to do damage is indeed incalculable, taking the toll of many innocent lives. Should we continue to fight, it would not only result in an ultimate collapse and obliteration of the Japanese nation, but it would also lead to the total extinction of human civilization. . . .We are keenly aware of the innermost feelings of all of you, Our subjects. However, it is according to the dictate of time and fate that We have resolved to pave the way for a grand peace for all the generations to come by enduring the unendurable and suffering what is insufferable."[19] It was the first national defeat the Japanese people had ever sustained.

Stunned and apprehensive of savage treatment, the Japanese waited for the touch-down near Tokyo of the first occupation troops. The Americans drove in convoy to Yokohama, the chosen headquarters, passing through the ruins their bombs had caused, with Japanese soldiers spaced along the route, back to them, to forestall demonstrations. There were none; few people were in sight. The succeeding troops landed by sea and air, behaved with strict discipline, and so immediately relieved Japanese anxieties of universal reprisals and rape. As for the Japanese themselves, the Emperor's command to lay down arms was all but universally obeyed. The formal surrender was signed in September 1945 in the presence of General MacArthur, who remained in Japan as Supreme commander for the Allied powers until his dismissal by President Truman in April 1951. MacArthur was to live in Japan in almost Olympian majesty for over six years, controller of SCAP, the supreme command of the Allied powers, the occupation authority. It had been recognized that war trials would be held; over five thousand were tried for crimes against prisoners of war, and over nine hundred were executed, while the political "purges" involved for a while some two hundred thousand Japanese.

Film production virtually ceased until its revival in 1946, although the studios and their overworn equipment had mostly escaped the bombing. Slowly a policy for the future was evolved; existant films were reviewed and any showing militaristic, nationalistic, feudal, or racist tendencies, action involving indulgence in cruelty, the subjection of women or children to exploitation, or other antisocial attitudes, were prohibited—in fact half of the currently available product was viewed, banned, and the prints (technically) destroyed. Producers were required to make films showing peaceful occupations, the rehabilitation of soldiers as civilians, the emancipation of women, the development of a new democratic way of life in which all were to share in the process of government. Japan had to be shown to be "democratized." At the same time, the film industry was "unionized" on the American pattern.

In these circumstances, films dealing with the war itself or with the immediate past (as in the case of the better films in Germany) were not to find expression until later years. The Occupation authorities viewed each film due for release, and it could not be shown without their seal of approval. They were opposed to some forms of production in which the Japanese were at their best—for example, the period and historical films, which were accused of being dangerously feudal. The problem of "war criminals" in the film industry had also to be faced—many heads of wartime companies were dismissed from the industry permanently; others were dismissed temporarily or ordered to rehabilitate themselves, including the directors Kajiro Yamamoto, Kimisaburo Yoshimura, Koji Shima, Yasushi Sasaki, and Kunio Watanabe.

The only films touching on war experience were Kinoshita's *A Morning with the Osone Family* (1946), about a family dispersed during the war years—some being arrested, others in the services, but brought together again once peace was restored, the dawn of a new morning for them, and Kurosawa's *No Regrets for My Youth* (1946), about a girl whose pacifist lover dies in prison during the war years, while her democratic-minded father is oppressed by the militarist regime. She leaves to work on a farm, and decides to stay on the land after the war. Other films, such as Gosho's *Once More* (1947), which showed the changes taking place in postwar intellectual thought, reflected the "New Japan," while Mizoguchi's *Women of the Night* (1948) and Ozu's *A Hen in the Wind* (1948) attacked prostitution. Kurosawa's *Drunken Angel* (1948, with Toshiro Mifune) had for its background the postwar problem of the Black market. Some communist-inspired films managed to escape censorship. Tadashi Imai's *An Enemy of the People* (1946) attacked the concept of the Japanese emperor's position which no doubt encouraged the authorities, as yet inexperienced, to let it through. Satsuo Yamamoto and Jumio Kamei's *War and Peace* (1947) was also left-wing, dealing with the problems of two soldiers returning to civilian life.

The Japanese, like the West Germans, with the vast economic aid given them by their conquerors, set themselves vigorously to work in order to rebuild their shattered economy, both nations making themselves in the two decades following the war formidable powers in the world's economy. Both reestablished extensive, highly

Senso To Heiwa (War and Peace) (1947), directed by Satsuo Yamamoto and Fumio Kamei.

commercialized film industries, while Japan in particular was to become a leading manufacturing nation for film and television equipment.[20]

One of the more unusual stories of wartime filming is that told by Erik Barnouw, until 1973 professor at the Center for Mass Communication at Columbia University, concerning his "rediscovery" of the substantial material shot by Japanese cameramen in Hiroshima and Nagasaki shortly after the dropping of the atom bombs on these cities. A team from the Japanese Documentary Unit, Nippon Eiga Sha, was instructed to undertake this coverage by the Japanese Education Ministry, and was already at work when the American Army of Occupation arrived. The producer in charge of this operation was Akira Iwasaki, and Professor Barnouw has quoted Iwasaki's account of what happened:

> In the middle of the shooting one of my cameramen was arrested in Nagasaki by American military police. . . . I was summoned to GHQ and told to discontinue the shooting. . . . Then came the group of the

Strategic Bombing Survey from Washington and they wanted to have a film of Hiroshima and Nagasaki. Therefore the US Army wanted to utilize my film for the purpose, and changed its mind. Now they allowed or better ordered me to continue and complete the film.

Iwasaki finished the film under American supervision. The final footage was edited into a compilation form some three hours long, entitled *Effects of the Atom Bomb*, with parts showing the effects on concrete, wood, vegetation, and finally (in a section some half-hour long), its human effects. The film was declared top security, and taken to Washington.

Early in 1968, twenty-three years later, a copy of the original print was donated by the American government to the Education Ministry in Japan, the original sponsors. Meanwhile, the material was also released at his request to Professor Barnouw at Columbia. The Center for Mass Communications produced from the footage showing the human effects a sixteen-minute short documentary, *August 1945*, very quiet and factual in style, with a commentary written by Paul Ronder, and spoken by him and by Kazuko Oshima. Within five months of its initial screening at the Museum of Modern Art in February 1970, some five hundred copies of the print had been sold. The film was televized in many countries, including Japan. Iwasaki, the original producer, came forward with statements about the work (such as that quoted above). In 1970, the Japanese themselves made a half-hour film (with an English-language version), *Hiroshima—A Document of the Atomic Bombing*, produced in cooperation with the Hiroshima local authorities and local press agencies, as well as private citizens from this city whose name is permanently written on the human conscience.

The film from Columbia University ends its tragic, horrifying record with the statement that the present nuclear bombs under test are twenty-five hundred times more powerful than the one that killed, burned, maimed, and irradiated some two hundred thousand people in one single moment's holocaust in Hiroshima alone. The Japanese film ends with an appeal for a ban to be imposed internationally on the manufacture and testing of all nuclear bombs. These appeals to reason need the reinforcement of the images themselves. Nothing from the battlefields equals these stark, silent records of silhouettes of the dead burned by radiation onto the concrete surfaces of roads and walls, of a woman with the pattern of her dress outlined upon her naked flesh, of maimed people with their skin reduced to distorted weals or with their hair dropping away in skeins from their skulls. Their eyes stare in helpless, bewildered appeal toward the camera. It was to this that the great technological and scientific advances of the Second World War had led us. A few selected shots from the Japanese material were released to the newsreel companies at the same time as certain shots of the Bikini atomic-bomb tests in 1946, but for near a quarter of a century we hid away these images from Hiroshima and Nagasaki as if in shame behind the thick screen of security.

6
Retrospect: 1950–70

The postwar period following 1950 was one of gradual, complex dis-
engagement by the Western Allies from German and Japanese affairs.
The war crime trials conducted in the British, American, and French
zones had led to only 5,025 Germans being convicted of serious crimes,
with 806 death sentences imposed but only 486 finally executed. The
new German constitution of 1949 had abolished the death penalty,
and in 1952 a Clemency Board was established by the British and
American authorities along with the Germans to review war crime
sentences. Commutation became the rule in order to free the prisons
of the hundreds still held; by 1954 only some three hundred remained
in custody. Prosecutions in the East, including Eastern Germany (the
DDR, the German Democratic Republic) had been much more numerous, involving an estimated eighty-seven thousand receiving sentence. At the same time, the German courts of the Federal Republic (West Germany) began their investigations into the war
crimes of over thirty thousand individuals; between 1955 and 1962,
charges were brought against 12,846, of whom 5,426 were sentenced,
often (in the opinion of some) too lightly. It became increasingly
difficult to assemble sufficient evidence that would stand up in
the courts, and at times impossible to bring in witnesses now dispersed over many countries and often unwilling or unable to testify.
The ages of the guilty and potentially guilty began to rise; many sus-
pects died of old age or ill health without ever being brought to trial.
Investigation in the courts of grim cases of mass murder have dragged
on into the 1970s, involving an extension of the traditional German
Statute of Limitations, which normally puts a limitation of twenty
years on the initiation of proceedings in trial for murder. An official
Central Co-ordinating Agency for investigating Nazi Crime was
set up in 1958.

293

An outburst of underground anti-Semitism in West Germany around 1960 reminded the authorities that this aspect of Nazism had not been entirely eliminated in German society; indeed surviving right-wing, Nazi, or semi-Nazi enclaves showed signs of activity on a relatively small scale, while one of the standard aspects of the cold war between East and West Germany was the constant accusation by the East that the Federal Republic permitted former Nazi officers and officials to retain positions of authority in business, administration, and the new German army. The West German government has made reasonable financial reparation to surviving Jews driven into exile by the Third Reich and living now abroad, and has supported financially the establishment of the International Red Cross Tracing Centre at Arolsen, with its large staff of linguists involved in the ceaseless search for lost individuals caused by the mass movement of peoples and the genocide of millions by the SS administration between 1940 and 1945.

In Japan, the official period of Occupation ended in 1952. Meanwhile Japan had been reconstituted as an Asian capitalist counterpart of the United States, and later as a "bulwark" against Communist China, strong, economically resilient, and even rearmed. The original disarmament clause in the new constitution fathered by MacArthur's supreme command, SCAP, was increasingly disregarded, to the dismay of Japanese with a progressive outlook that excluded resort to war. The new constitution asserted that all should enjoy basic human rights. Ironically, Japan's economic recovery was speeded by American involvement in the Korean war. The bombed cities were rebuilt, and Japanese industry was well on the way to recovery by 1951, the year in which a peace treaty was signed with the agreement notably of Britain and Australia.

Later Film Studies of Hitler and the Third Reich

During the 1950s and 1960s a number of films were made in various countries that attempted, through the use of newsreel and other actuality material, to survey Hitler's career and character, or the nature of the regime he established. Of these the principal were :

Night and Fog (*Nuit et Brouillard;* France, 1955; Alain Resnais).
The German Story (*Du und mancher Kamerad, You and other Comrades;* E. Germany, 1956; Annelie and Andrew Thorndike).
Nazi Crimes and Punishment (*Der Nurnberger Prozess, The Nuremberg Trial;* also known as *The Executioners;* W. Germany, 1958; Felix von Podmanitsky).

Reason vrs. Insanity (USSR, 1960; Alexander Medvedkin).

Mein Kampf (*Den Blodiga Tiden, The Bloody Years;* Sweden, 1960; Erwin Leiser).

Eichmann and the Third Reich (*Eichmann und das Dritte Reich;* Switzerland, 1961; Erwin Leiser). Also known as *Murder by Signature.*

The Life of Adolph Hitler (*Das Leben Adolf Hitler;* W. Germany, 1961; Paul Rotha).

The Black Fox (USA, 1961; Louis Clyde Stoumen).

Evidence (*Svědestvi,* Parts I and II; also known as *The Czechoslovak Story;* Pavel Háša and Roman Hlaváč; Czechoslovakia, 1961).

Le Temps du Ghetto (France, 1961; Frédéric Rossif).

The Struggle for Peace (USSR, 1961; Nikolai Shpikovsky).

Requiem for 500 Thousand (Poland, 1962; Jerzy Bossak and Waclav Zaźmierczak).[1]

Ordinary Fascism (USSR, 1965; Mikhail Romm).

1973:   *The Double-headed Eagle* (Lutz Becker, with Philippe Mora) and *Swastika* (Philippe Mora, with Lutz Becker).

Two impressive, feature-length compilation films assembled from archive material (including Eva Braun's "home movies"). The first covers the period of the Nazis' rise to power 1918–33, and the second the history of the regime from 1933. Authentic period material (some in color) is presented without commentary, but with music scores selected by the directors, recorded voices (for example, for Hitler), and some dubbed dialogue based on lip-reading of silent film. Lutz Becker, a young German historian working in Britain, claims these films to be "anthropological documents," and not a political analysis.

DEFA's films aiming at compromising men prominent in postwar West Germany included:

Operation Teutonic Sword (1958; Annelie and Andrew Thorndike). Directed against Hans Speidel.

Holiday on Sylt (1959; Annelie and Andrew Thorndike). Directed against Heinz Reinefarth.

So Macht Man Kanzler (*That's How Chancellors are Made;* 1961; Joachim Hellwig). Draws a parallel between Hitler and Adenauer.

Aktion J. (1961). Directed against Hans Globke.

Resnais's *Nuit et Brouillard* was one of the earliest, if not the earliest films to attempt to give at once historical perspective and a poetic depth to the universal tragedy of genocide. Scripted in close association with the novelist, Jean Cayrol (who had been deported by the Nazis, and whose brother had died in Oranienburg concentration camp), the film is a meditation on the significance of Auschwitz; the remains of the Nazi center for genocide in Poland are filmed in

Night and Fog (1955), directed by Alain Resnais.

color, while the memory of what had happened there little more than a decade earlier is recalled by the records in black and white—films, documents, photographs—the two elements developed together in a slowly cumulative rhythm. The film has an almost stately beauty, which lifts the unimaginable suffering it recalls beyond the ugly reach of sensationalism; Hanns Eisler's music is now gentle and melodic, now sharp and high-pitched, reinforcing the contemplative mood of the whole film. The last words of Cayrol's deeply moving commentary stand as a universal comment on those years:

> Nine million dead haunt this landscape. Who is on the lookout from this strange tower to warn us of the coming new executioners? Are their faces really different from our own? Somewhere among us, there are lucky Kapos, reinstated officers, and unknown informers. There are those who refused to believe this, or believed it only from time to time. And there are those of us who sincerely look upon the ruins today, as if the old concentration camp monster were dead and buried beneath them. Those who pretend to take hope again as the image fades, as though there were a cure for the plague of these camps. Those

of us who pretend to believe that all this happened only once, at a certain time and in a certain place, and those who refuse to see, who do not hear the cry to the end of time.[2]

"Who then is responsible?" is the sombre, melancholy, open question at the end of this film.

Few of the compilation films that followed equal the effect of Resnais's brief, half-hour film on its special subject, though *Le Temps du Ghetto* and the somewhat sentimentalized *Requiem for 500 Thousand* are powerful and dedicated films. Any account of the Third Reich and its leaders carries with it a dark temptation toward melodrama and sensationalism. The events are therefore best treated with sober objectivity by those who cannot bring the genius of epic poetry or dramatic tragedy to bear on events that even after a quarter century have still not been fully absorbed by those who attempt to evaluate their significance in the psychology or social history of our species. Sobriety of treatment was attempted in Paul Rotha's feature-length compilation, made for the West German company, Real Film, and selected from some two and a half million feet of archive material originating from twelve countries. Rotha's supreme editorial skill is manifest in this film. It included rare, little-seen shots from Hitler's early career, and traced his rise and fall thematically rather than merely chronologically. Rotha estimated about one third of his archive material had not been seen in any previous compilations before. At its best in the first, prewar section, the film loses some of its objectivity, and consequently historical authority, as it loses direct touch with the character of the man Hitler during the crowded events of the war years; the voice of propaganda creeps into the commentary. Hitler virtually disappeared from public life during the height of the war, and this presents difficulty in the search for significant visual coverage in these climactic years. Rotha's film must be matched with the exiled German journalist Erwin Leiser's earlier compilation, *Mein Kampf*, which achieves objectivity by leaving the spectator to draw his own conclusions from the images selected. These two films, taken together, are the most valuable studies of Hitler so far to have appeared on the screen. A further, lesser film, *Nazi Crime and Punishment*, intercut scenes from the Nuremberg trial of the Nazi leaders with archive material of Nazi persecution; while *Black Fox* (with a commentary spoken by Marlene Dietrich) added to the familiar archive material of Hitler's career illustrations to Goethe's adaptation of *Reynard the Fox* in order to afford a fanciful parallel in the rise of Hitler, the Fox, through deceit in the court of the Lion (Hindenburg), an allegorical treatment that only served to weaken the actual significance of contemporary history.

Erwin Leiser, having suffered directly from fascism, dedicated himself at this stage to its exposure; his second, feature-length film on Eichmann and genocide was produced in Switzerland at the time of the Eichmann trial in Israel. Made somewhat hurriedly from the archive material about Nazi persecution and genocide, it intercuts this with scenes from the trial and interviews with victims from the camps shot in Israel. The film lacked the historical objectivity of *Mein Kampf* and became in consequence more journalistic in treatment. Later Leiser was to make a third film, *Wählt das Leben* (*Choose Life;* Switzerland, 1963), an impassioned plea against a drift to further war, introducing remarkable material from Japan showing the aftereffects of the bombing of Hiroshima and Nagasaki.

The compilation films made in the socialist countries naturally reinterpreted the rise of fascism from a Marxist standpoint. Annelie and Andrew Thorndike's *The German Story* outlined the history of Germany from 1896 to 1956, drawing on some six million meters of film held by the East German State Archive as well as material from elsewhere, supplementing the impact of this archive material with other pictorial records, as well as interviews, their dramatic effect sharpened by means of music by Paul Dessau. The three-hour Czech film *Evidence,* according to Jay Leyda made in the same style as the Thorndikes' work, traces in two parts the history of the republic from 1929 to the Red Army's entrance into Prague in 1945. Of the Russian films made in 1961, Leyda regards Medvedkin's as the more technically scientific; while *The Struggle for Peace* concentrates more soberly on the events of the Second World War, Medvedkin widens his theme to cover both world wars and what he holds to be the preparation for a third confrontation. Using animation techniques, he manipulates this newsreel material mercilessly to provide satiric effects—freezing, speeding up, reduplicating, or reversing the image. I would hold this to be a misuse of actuality material in the context of a historical film, however effective it may be in avant-garde or experimental film satire; I found Cavalcanti's celebrated compilation, *Yellow Caesar* (1940), using similar techniques to mock Mussolini equally distastefully. The bombast of dictators, the megalomania of marching represented by the goosestep, are horrific manifestations of human behaviour, and to reduce them to some kind of absurd ballet is to evade the danger they represent.

Ordinary Fascism, coming later, was more concerned with the analysis of the nature of fascism than with going over the ground again chronologically. Parallels are drawn (the murder of Alexander of Yugoslavia with that of President Kennedy), and the little-known, "private" material introduced, such as a still of Hitler practicing speech-making before a mirror. (One wonders if this could be genuine.) While the tone of the English-language commentary becomes oversarcastic, the visuals are rarely overstrained in their attempt to trace the origin of fascism in Germany and elsewhere.

Fiction films dealing directly with historical events during the Third Reich include G. W. Pabst's two studies of Hitler, *Ten Days to Die (Der Letzte Akt, The Last Act,* Austria, 1954) and *The Jackboot Mutiny (Es geschah am 20 Juli, It took place on 20 July;* West Germany, 1955). Both films—the first dealing with the events leading up to the suicide of Hitler, and the second with the abortive officers' plot to assassinate him on 20 July 1944—suffer from the inevitable failing that actors cannot successfully impersonate such volatile and over familiar public figures as Hitler, Goebbels, and Göring. Some gap in time will have to elapse before they can be interpreted in terms at once fully acceptable both as art and psychology.[4] The image of the monolithic, immobile Stalin was far easier for an actor to assume on the screen. Hitler's extraordinary amalgam of shabby lower middle class ordinariness with electrifying, hyp-

Ten Days to Die (1954), directed by G. W. Pabst.

Ten Days to Die (1954), directed by G. W. Pabst, with Albin Skoda as Hitler.

notic power over men and women of every class and status is extremely difficult to realize through acting with credibility especially since so much of his more extreme behavior reflected a conscious, calculated, theatrical pose. The conscientious actors of Pabst's films (Hitler was played as well as possible on this level by Albin Skoda in *The Last Act*) cannot match up to the psychology of the personalities they had to assume, nor could Pabst, however conscientious himself in getting the outward facts right, penetrate the "mystery" of Hitler's all-powerful hold over his people. The young, fictional officer played by Oskar Werner, and purporting to represent the dawning German conscience, is a gross oversimplification, as is the idea that, in some symbolic way, the officers involved in the attempt on Hitler's life in 1944 were motivated by a single, united idea. The motivation of the plot was in fact extremely complex. Both films oversimplify the situation dangerously by appearing to represent Hitler, and Hitler alone, as responsible for Germany's moral and military catastrophe. The vast numbers of people who acted

Ten Days to Die (1954), directed by G. W. Pabst, with Albin Skoda as Hitler.

as his willing, enthusiastic agents must bear their measure of the great guilt involved.

The few West German films that risked death at the box office by recalling events that the vast majority of Germans wanted to forget were mostly concerned to show German resistance to Hitler— for example, *Canaris* (1954, Alfred Wiedenmann), a study of the head of German Military Intelligence who was for many years a leader of resistance to Hitler's policies, Helmut Käutner's two films, *The Last Bridge* (1954), about a German woman doctor who helps Yugoslav partisans, and *The Devil's General* (1955), about a general in the Luftwaffe who, disillusioned, eventually takes his life. This incident was based on the wartime suicide of the air ace, Ernst Udet. Other antifascist films were Wolfgang Staudte's *Roses for the Prosecutor* (1959), an ironic story of a Nazi prosecutor who survives in office in postwar Germany, and Bernhard Wicki's antiwar film, *The Bridge* (1959). East Germany's *Duped till Doomsday* (Kurt Jung-Alsen, 1957) was a stern indictment of the duplicity of Nazi

The Bridge (1959), directed by Bernhard Wicki.

The Devil's General (1955), directed by Helmut Käutner, with Curd Jürgens.

Roses for the Prosecutor (1959), directed by Wolfgang Staudte, with Martin Held.

militarism. A cool, ironic exposure of Nazi-influenced militarism in postwar Germany appeared in Jean-Marie Straub's two-reel short, *Machorka-Muff* (1963). More ambitious, and more significant, was Straub's second film, *Not Reconciled* (German title, *Nicht Versöhnt oder Es hilft nur Gewalt, wo Gewalt herrscht* 1965, fifty-three minutes), of which Straub has said: "by putting the past (1910, 1914, 1934) on the same level as the present, I have made a film which is a reflection on the continuity of Nazism both with what preceded it (first anti-Communism, then anti-Semitism) and what followed it."[5] Time is merged in order to stress the recurrent nature of what has come to be called Nazism. Both films were adapted from stories by Heinrich Böll.

More recently, in 1973, a British film, *Hitler—the Last Ten Days* (directed by Ennio De Concini) offered a portrait of Hitler in decline played almost to the point of sympathy by Alec Guinness, a performance conceived with great restraint. Hitler passes to his final extinction through suicide after attempting to browbeat the remnants of his General Staff in the seclusion of the Bunker, and defend Berlin with non-existant forces. Much is made of his relation-

Hitler: The Last Ten Days (1973), directed by Ennio De Concini, with Alec Guinness, John Bennett, and Mark Kingston.

Hitler: The Last Ten Days (1973), directed by Ennio De Concini, with Alec Guinness and John Bennett.

ship with Eva Braun, for whom at this stage he appears to have more contempt than affection.

Among the British and American films that have attempted to deal with the immediate aftermath of war, the following were of special interest:

The Divided Heart (GB, 1954; Charles Crichton, with Yvonne Mitchell).
The Gentle Sergeant (USA, 1955; Richard Murphy); also known as *Three Stripes in the Sun*.
Verboten (USA, 1958; Samuel Fuller).
Judgment at Nuremberg (USA, 1961; Stanley Kramer, with Spencer Tracy, Richard Widmark, Maximilian Schell, Marlene Dietrich, Burt Lancaster, Judy Garland, Montgomery Clift).

The Divided Heart is the story (only too frequently repeated, as the records of the International Red Cross Tracing Service at Arolsen in Germany reveal) of a child deliberately stolen from occupied

The Divided Heart (1954), directed by Charles Crichton, with Yvonne Mitchell.

territory by the Germans to be reared as German by foster parents. In this case, a Yugoslav mother (Yvonne Mitchell) claims her son, aged ten, from the only parents he has known and loved, Franz and Inga Hartl (Armin Dahlen and Cornell Borchers); the film's location scenes were shot in Yugoslavia. The case is heard before the United States Court of the Allied High Commission. Mother and child cannot even speak the same language, and everyone—the officials of the International Refugee Organization, the judges in the court, the German foster parents do their best to respond to the needs of the child and his distracted mother, whose difficulties of communication in this foreign land are heart-rendingly conveyed by Yvonne Mitchell, speaking wholly in a specially assumed foreign tongue. "This is a case where justice cannot be done," remarks one of the judges.

The Gentle Sergeant also employed a mixed cast—American and Japanese—in a story that was also derived from a real event about an American sergeant (Aldo Ray) who, against all his anti-Japanese prejudice, finds himself in love with a Japanese girl who interprets at an orphanage in Japan run by Catholic nuns. Somewhat sentimentalized, this film tries to emphasize the mending of relations between the American and Japanese people, and the goodwill of the occupying forces at least when it comes to helping orphans or falling in love with Japanese girls.

Judgment at Nuremberg, with its all-star cast, works on an altogether larger canvas. It is set in Germany in 1948, and involves the trial of four German judges of the Nazi period for war crimes, before a team of judges led by an elderly American, Dan Hayward (Spencer Tracy). Again, a mixed American and German cast rake over the impossible problem of resolving German national guilt for Nazi atrocities. The trial is being conducted at the same time as the Russian blockade of Berlin and the Allied airlift, which introduces an element of pressure toward clemency and suspension of judgment against German war criminals in the face of newer antipathies. One man in the dock, however, Ernst Jannings (Burt Lancaster), responds to Hayward's desire to maintain justice in spite of corrupting outside influences to take a new, expedient line.

No one could deny that *Judgment at Nuremberg*, adapted from a television play, is dealing with live, serious issues of the period it recalls, although in a film coming well over a decade late, in 1961. Unhappily, it is too often sentimental, sensational, and overplayed at the very points where restraint is most called for—for example, the scene of evidence on his sterilization given by the witness interpreted by Montgomery Clift in his most studied neurotic manner. Given re-

Judgment at Nuremberg (1961), directed by Stanley Kramer, with **Spencer Tracy** (center).

straint, *Judgment at Nuremberg* could have been one of the most important films to have been made about the war and its aftermath. As it is, it has constantly to be rescued by the viewer from its excesses in order to be appraised adequately for the values it is trying to assert.

Samuel Fuller's *Verboten* is almost isolated in dealing with postwar conditions in Germany. Samuel Fuller had served in the war as an infantryman, serving in North Africa and Europe in the division known as "The Big Red One," and had been decorated with a Purple Heart. War, says Fuller, is "organized lunacy"; most of his war films have dealt with the wars that came afterward, in Korea and elsewhere. But *Verboten* (1958), celebrated for its technique of long takes (two of over five minutes, and one of three and a half minutes), deals primarily with postwar Germany and the hangover of Nazism in the Werewolf youth organization. Corruption comes with hunger, a corruption that, the film shows, can only be cured by understanding applied by those who are not corrupted through physical need.[6]

The Revival of Combat Films: Britain and the United States

The greater number of films produced during the 1950s and 1960s and looking back toward the Second World War were combat films demonstrating specific actions (such as *The Dam Busters, Battle of the River Plate, Dunkirk,* or *Battle of the Bulge*), or exploiting unusual stories that had come to light, usually in books about espionage, resistance, or psychological warfare (such as *I was Monty's Double* or *The Man who Never Was*). They were seldom concerned with anything more than war action, though many were given a fictional form in which invented characters became prominent as distinct from the "characterized" representation of real persons by actors, as in *The Dam-Busters,* in which Richard Todd gave as close an impersonation of Wing-Commander Guy Gibson as he could reconstruct, while Michael Redgrave impersonated Barnes Wallis in a freely characterized version of his own development.

The Dam Busters (1953), directed by Michael Anderson, with Richard Todd and Michael Redgrave.

Dunkirk (1958), directed by Leslie Norman.

The following gives examples of these many action or combat films made by American and British directors, together with their subjects:

Angels One Five (GB, 1952; George More O'Ferrall, with Jack Hawkins). The Battle of Britain.

The Cruel Sea (GB, 1952; Charles Frend, with Jack Hawkins). Psychological effect of battle of the Atlantic and convoy work.

Stalag 17 (USA, 1953; Billy Wilder, with William Holden). Informing in a German prisoner-of-war camp.

The Desert Rats (USA, 1953; Robert Wise, with Richard Burton, James Mason). The siege of Tobruk.

Malta Story (GB, 1953; Brian Desmond Hurst, with Alec Guinness). The defense of Malta.

The Red Beret (GB, 1953; Terence Young, with Alan Ladd). Parachute unit in combat.

The Sea Shall Not Have Them (GB, 1954; Lewis Gilbert, with Michael Redgrave). Air-sea rescue.

The Colditz Story (GB, 1954; Guy Hamilton with John Mills, Eric Portman). Escape strategy from a top-security German prisoner-of-war camp.

The Cruel Sea (1952), directed by Charles Frend, with Jack Hawkins.

The Colditz Story (1955), directed by Guy Hamilton.

The Purple Plain (GB, 1954; Robert Parrish, with Gregory Peck). An RAF outpost in Burma.

The Dam Busters (GB, 1954; Michael Anderson, with Michael Redgrave, Richard Todd). The destruction of the Ruhr dams using Barnes Wallis's special bombs.

Battle Cry (USA, 1954; Raoul Walsh, with Van Heflin). US marines in the Pacific war.

Cockleshell Heroes (GB, 1955; Jose Ferrer, starring himself). Marine commandos.

The Man Who Never Was (GB, 1955; Ronald Neame, with Clifton Webb). Decoy devised by British Naval Intelligence to deceive Germans concerning the location of S. European landings in 1943, by using a body planted with false papers.

The Battle of the River Plate (GB, 1956; Michael Powell and Emeric Pressburger, with Peter Finch). The action leading up to the scuttling of the *Graf Spee*.

A Town Like Alice (GB, 1956; Jack Lee with Virginia McKenna, Peter Finch). The sufferings of a group of British women in Malaya during the Japanese occupation.

Reach for the Sky (GB, 1956; Lewis Gilbert, with Kenneth More). The career of Douglas Bader, the legless pilot of the Battle of Britain.

Attack! (USA, 1956; Robert Aldrich, with Eddie Albert, Jack Palance). An American infantry company in Belgium, 1944.

Ill Met by Moonlight (GB, 1956; Michael Powell and Emeric Pressburger, with Dirk Bogarde, Marius Goring). Capture of a German general by British agents and local partisans in German-occupied Crete.

The Enemy Below (USA, 1957; Dick Powell, with Robert Mitchum, Curt Jurgens). The mutual dedication to their respective Services of a German U-boat commander and the American captain of a destroyer.

Bridge on the River Kwai (GB, 1957; David Lean, with William Holden, Alec Guinness, Jack Hawkins, Sessue Hayakawa). Ambivalent study of a British officer's misplaced concept of morale for himself and his men while they are prisoners-of-war in the hands of the Japanese.

Sea of Sand (GB, 1958; Guy Green, with Richard Attenborough, John Gregson, Michael Craig). Desert commando unit in action just before El Alamein.

I Was Monty's Double (GB, 1958; John Guillermin, with John Mills). Clifton Parker, an actor who actually impersonated Montgomery, is employed by MI5 to deceive Germans over exact location for D-Day landings.

The Silent Enemy (GB, 1958; William Fairchild, with Laurence Harvey). Attempts by Italian frogmen to attach mines to British ships in Gibraltar waters in 1941, frustrated by British divers led by Lieu. Crabb RNVR.

Carve Her Name with Pride (GB, 1958; Lewis Gilbert, with Virginia

The Bridge on the River Kwai (1957), directed by David Lean, with Sessue Hayakawa and Alec Guinness.

McKenna, Paul Scofield). The career of Violette Szabo as underground agent in France, caught and shot by the Gestapo.

Orders to Kill (GB, 1958; Anthony Asquith, with Paul Massie, Leslie French). Fictional story of the mutual attraction between an underground agent in France and the man he is ordered to kill.

Dunkirk (GB, 1958; Leslie Norman, with John Mills, Bernard Lee, Richard Attenborough). A comprehensive attempt, with representative individual characters, to compass the rescue of British troops from Dunkirk.

The Naked and the Dead (USA, 1958; Raoul Walsh, with Aldo Ray, Cliff Robertson, Raymond Massey). Dissension among a unit in action on a Japanese-held Pacific island.

The Young Lions (USA, 1958; Edward Dmytryk, with Marlon Brando, Montgomery Clift, Dean Martin). Anti-war "epic" concerned with exposing alike sadism and disillusion on both sides.

Battle of the V1 (GB, 1958; Vernon Sewell, with Michael Rennie). Polish underground workers reveal the V1 researchers at Peenemunde.

Orders to Kill (1958), directed by Anthony Asquith, with Paul Massie.

Orders to Kill (1958), directed by Anthony Asquith, with Paul Massie and Leslie French.

Dunkirk (1958), directed by Leslie Norman.

Run Silent, Run Deep (USA, 1958; Robert Wise, with Clark Gable, Burt Lancaster). Submarine warfare off Japan.

The Camp on Blood Island (GB, 1958; Val Guest, with André Morell). The blood-letting occasioned by organized resistance in a Japanese prisoner-of-war camp commanded by a sadistic officer.

The Gallant Hours (USA, 1959; Robert Montgomery, with James Cagney). War in the Pacific area seen through the personality of a Commander, Admiral William F. Halsey.

Yesterday's Enemy (GB, 1959; Val Guest, with Stanley Baker, Leo McKern). A British officer in the Burmese jungle who commits a war crime in order to obtain information becomes himself a prisoner-of-war and has in turn to give his own life in withholding information.

Sink the Bismarck! (GB, 1960; Lewis Gilbert, with Kenneth More). The sea battles leading up to the sinking of the *Bismarck*.

The Long and the Short and the Tall (GB, 1960; Leslie Norman, with Laurence Harvey, Richard Harris, Richard Todd). From a play by Willis Hall. Poison of suspicion in an isolated British unit in the Far Eastern jungle when a Japanese scout is captured.

The Valiant (GB/Italy, 1961; Roy Baker, with John Mills, Robert Shaw, Ettore Manni, Roberto Risso). On the ethics of treating prisoners—two frogmen captured after mining the *Valiant*.

Guns of Navarone (GB, 1961; J. Lee Thompson, with Gregory Peck, David Niven, Anthony Quinn, Stanley Baker, Irene Papas). Commando expedition in 1943 to sabotage two massive German guns that hinder evacuation of British forces from an island off Turkey.

Merrill's Marauders (USA, 1962; Samuel Fuller, with Jeff Chandler). US Army unit in Burma in 1942 under "tough-guy" Commander Brig. Gen. Frank Merrill.

The Longest Day (USA, 1962; Ken Annakin, Andrew Martin, Bernard Wicki, Darryl F. Zanuck, with all-star, multinational cast). D-Day 1944, seen from the British, American, German, and French collective viewpoints.

Hell is for Heroes (USA, 1962; Don Siegel, with Steve McQueen). Suicidal tough-guy who resists discipline in the course of duty near the Siegfried Line, 1944.

The Great Escape (USA/West Germany, 1962; John Sturges, with Steve McQueen, Richard Attenborough). The mass escape of RAF prisoners-of-war from Stalag Luft North, and their mass execution on their recapture.

The Victors (GB, 1963; Carl Foreman, with all-star, multinational cast). The Allied invasion of Europe as experienced by a group of American soldiers, showing them not in periods of action but in their life and contacts meantime.

Captain Newman MD (USA, 1963; David Miller, with Gregory Peck). Worthy-style tribute to the fight for recognition of treatment of war psychotics.

The Train (USA/France/Italy, 1964; John Frankenheimer, with Burt Lancaster, Paul Scofield, Jeanne Moreau, Michel Simon). Resistance sabotage in 1944 to the fanatic efforts of a German colonel to evacuate a trainload of works of art to Germany.

The Secret Invasion (USA, 1964; Roger Corman, with Stewart Granger, Raf Vallone, Henry Silver, Mickey Rooney). Coup brought off by a group of criminals in Yugoslavia when they rescue an Italian general, and ending in a macabre general massacre.

Operation Crossbow (GB/Italy, 1965; Michael Anderson, with George Peppard, Jeremy Kemp). A sabotage operation against the V1 weapon at Peenemunde.

The Battle of the Bulge (USA, 1965; Ken Annakin, with Henry Fonda, Robert Shaw, Robert Ryan). The German attempt at a breakthrough in December 1944.

In Harm's Way (USA, 1965; Otto Preminger, with John Wayne, Kirk Douglas). Demoralization in service life in the American Navy after Pearl Harbor.

The Heroes of Telemark (GB, 1965; Anthony Mann, with Kirk Douglas, Richard Harris). The Norwegian Resistance, after discovering developments at the Norsk Hydro Heavy Water Plant at Vermork, conduct a successful sabotage raid on the plant.

King Rat (USA, 1965; Bryan Forbes, with George Segal, Tom Courtenay, James Fox). Study of survival in a prisoner-of-war camp in Singapore, and the effect of corrupt dealing by an American corporal.

The Victors (1963), directed by Carl Foreman, with Vincent Edwards.

The Hill (GB, 1965; Sidney Lumet, with Sean Connery, Harry Andrews, Ian Bannen, Alfred Lynch). Sadistic punishment and its outcome in a British military detention camp in N. Africa during the Second World War.

The Night of the Generals (GB/France, 1966; Anatole Litvak, with Peter O'Toole, Omar Sharif, Tom Courtenay, Philippe Noiret). Large-scale melodrama of a sadistic German general set mainly in Paris at the time of the abortive attempt on Hitler's life, and his final exposure postwar by a French inspector of police.

The Dirty Dozen (USA/GB, 1967; Robert Aldrich, with Lee Marvin). US major detailed to lead a commando of GI prisoners under sentence for execution or life imprisonment in a desperate attempt to blow up a French chateau that is a rest center for high-ranking German officers.

The Battle for Anzio (Italy, 1968; Edward Dmytryk, with Robert Mitchum). A sermon on war as observed ironically by an American war correspondent, and presenting a reconstruction of the Anzio beachhead.

The Bridge at Remagen (USA, 1968; John Guillermin, with George Segal, Robert Vaughn). Spectacular study of the Remagen operation seen from the dual viewpoint, American and German, and with a cynical philosophy of war.

Hell in the Pacific (USA, 1968; John Boorman, with Lee Marvin, Toshiro Mifune). Attempt to examine the nature of enmity when an American pilot and a Japanese naval officer are stranded together on an atoll.

The Long Day's Dying (GB, 1968; Peter Collinson, with David Hemmings, Tony Beckley, Tom Bell and Alan Dobie). A psychological study of the effect of war service on three "amateur" conscript soldiers, and their German prisoner, a professional soldier, who are all fighting in isolation.

The Battle of Britain (GB, 1969; Guy Hamilton, with all-star cast). An all-round, calm, perspective view of the Battle of Britain 1940–41, seen from the point of view of both sides.

Patton: Lust for Glory (USA, 1969; Franklin J. Schaffner, with George C. Scott, Karl Malden, Michael Bates). Character study of Patton, the fanatic general and disciplinarian, in his relations with Bradley and Montgomery.

Castle Keep (USA, 1969; Sydney Pollack, with Burt Lancaster). Allegory of War, destruction, and individual fantasy.

Too Late the Hero (USA, 1969; Robert Aldrich, with Michael Caine, Cliff Robertson). High cynicism among a British unit opposed to the Japanese on a Pacific island.

Catch 22 (USA, 1970; Mike Nichols, with Alan Arkin). A fifteen-million-dollar "black" satire in the "absurd" style about the disintegration of a US Air Force Unit based on the Mediterranean in 1944.

Tora! Tora! Tora! (USA/Japan, 1970; Richard Fleischer). A dual production from the relative points of view of Japan and the United States showing events leading up to Pearl Harbor, as well as the attack itself.

The Battle of Britain (1969), directed by Guy Hamilton.

Patton: Lust for Glory (1969), directed by Franklin J. Schaffner, with George C. Scott as General Patton.

Tora! Tora! Tora! (1970), directed by Richard Fleischer.

Figures in a Landscape (GB, 1970; Joseph Losey, with Robert Shaw, Malcolm McDowell). The nightmare pursuit by helicopter of two fugitives in unidentified "enemy" country.

Murphy's War (GB, 1971; Peter Yates, with Peter O'Toole). A side-action of war, set in Venezuela—a private and ultimately suicidal war between Murphy, sole survivor of a British merchantman, and the U-boat that had torpedoed him.

Too many of the British films lessened understanding of the worst features of war by intrusive, or virtually intrusive, love stories, such as the subplots in *Malta Story, The Man Who Never Was, A Town like Alice,* and *Carve Her Name with Pride,* or turned extremely hazardous exploits into occasions for melodrama, such as *The Silent Enemy.*

As the years pass, the antagonisms between the former enemies become relaxed into a form of mutual respect for prowess and dedication in war, as in the British, *Ill Met by Moonlight* and *The Battle of Britain,* or in the American, *The Enemy Below* and *Tora!*

Murphy's War (1971), directed by Peter Yates.

Tora! Tora! The latter proved a curious, mutual recognition by Japan and the United States of diplomatic incompetence, with additional incompetence at high level in the United States Navy, with incredible disregard for all warnings of the Japanese threat to Pearl Harbor. Occasional films have emphasized a mutual disillusion with the sadism of war or its ideological hypocrisies, as in *The Young Lions.* On the other hand, deep conflict among the men serving in American or British units is exposed in many fictional war films—for example, in the American *Attack!* and *The Naked and the Dead* and the British *Sea of Sand, The Hill,* and *Guns of Navarone. Attack!,* which it would appear received no cooperation from the War Department, was a savage, aggressively made exposure of virtually pathological cowardice in the commander of an American infantry unit (Captain Cooney, played by Eddie Albert), as well as corruption in his superior officer, whose postwar political career would be at stake if he revealed his knowledge of Cooney's grave inadequacy as an officer. Cooney is shot when near insane with fear by one of his own officers. In the case of *The Naked and the Dead* the reactionary sergeant Croft (Aldo Ray) is probably shot by his own men (the matter is left open) after deliberately causing the wounding of his lieutenant (Cliff Robertson), of whose liberal views he disapproves, while the orders of the authoritarian commanding general (Raymond Massey) are exposed as inadequate and costly in life. Even so, *The Naked and the Dead* is a palely censored-down version of Norman Mailer's outspoken book, though scripted by Denis and Terry Sanders, who made the notable antiwar period short, *Time Out of War. The Guns of Navarone* also attempted to debate the loyalties of men (and in this case women also) involved in war but faced with conflicting values—the nature of courage in action, the problems involved in leadership, the summary execution of a woman found to be a traitor. When Mallory, the leader of the expedition (Gregory Peck) flinches from shooting this woman, she is shot out of hand by a woman partisan who cannot understand the reason for such false chivalry.

Failure to achieve a sounder understanding of the fundamental weakness of warfare as a solution to human ills frustrated the good intentions of *The Young Lions,* with its clumsily integrated story of Christian, a young German officer (Marlon Brando), and his disillusionment with the Nazism he had once admired, dovetailed with the persecution of a Jewish recruit Noah (Montgomery Clift) by a sadistic officer in the American army, and the attempted exposure of this by the liberal Michael (Dean Martin). The film ends with Michael and Noah, American soldiers, shooting down Christian out

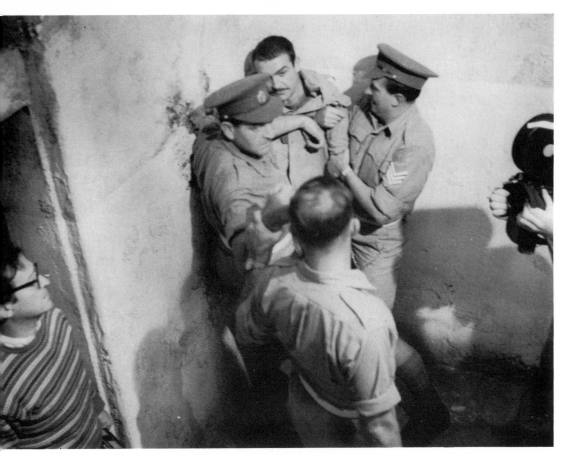

The Hill (1965), directed by Sidney Lumet.

The Hill (1965), directed by Sidney Lumet.

of hand during the liberation of a concentration camp, where in fact he is as horrified as they at the conditions revealed.

A strange ambivalence shrouded the "message" of David Lean's film *Bridge on the River Kwai*—Alec Guinness's dumb-minded martinet of a colonel who maintains the morale of his men, fellow-prisoners of the Japanese, by inducing them to take pride in the bridge they are building for their captors, who need it as a supply line. The camp commandant, Saito (Sessue Hayakawa) is of the same mettle as his prisoner, who withstands torture in order successfully to maintain the Geneva Convention that officers should not undertake manual work. But the delicate, ironic balance between a misplaced, heroic stance and its ultimate absurdity (which excites at once admiration and pity) is not maintained at a sufficiently sophisticated level, while the significance of the situation is again side-stepped at the end when the colonel's body falling in death is allowed to detonate the bridge of which he is so proud. The medical officer's single choric comment, "Madness, madness," reiterated at the end of the film is, after all, an insufficient analysis of a situation the inhumanity and inconsistency of which extend far wider than the colonel's "misdemeanor." It could even be claimed that he is saner than those who invented the rigid book of rules that he inadvertently betrays, to his own ultimate consternation, a consternation that (for me) is out of character. A similar ambivalence informed *Yesterday's Enemy*, in which a war crime committed by a British officer in order to obtain information is matched by that committed against him subsequently when he is captured by the Japanese—nevertheless, both the British and the Japanese commanders are made into "sympathetic" characters in order to up-point the irony of the murders their position "forces" them to commit. In the same director's *The Camp on Blood Island*, however, the Japanese are shown as uniformly sadistic; the old wartime message of hate is still being maintained thirteen years afterward, on the grounds, no doubt, that the Japanese were notorious for their contempt for and consequent ill-treatment of men who allowed themselves to become prisoners.

Gradually, however, the war films began to slip back into their national clichés, epitomized in the long, meandering epics—*Dunkirk*, with its balance of stock characters reacting to type, *The Longest Day*, taking in four clichés at once (a reductio ad absurdum of British "phlegm," American man-boy camaraderie, French behaviour performed in italics, and Germans rasping in the Prussian style), *The Victors*, which demonstrated to the point of fictionalized overstatement how war corrupts both soldier and civilian (made as a kind of personal

The Victors (1963), directed by Carl Foreman.

statement by Carl Foreman), and *The Battle of the Bulge,* a ruthless exposé of tank warfare in which human life counts for nothing.

The war films, indeed, became increasingly sadistic as the censorship relinquished in part much of its restraint on violence in the
1960s. The nadir of violent war films should surely include *The
Dirty Dozen,* which tries to get the best of both worlds, indulging
in horrific thuggery committed by thugs in the name of honorable
war service. They commit a war crime the like of which only the
Gestapo could have devized. The same theme is handled with far
greater finesse and sense of the macabre in Roger Corman's *The
Secret Invasion,* but ending with its own peculiar sense of horror
without any false heroics. It is difficult, too, to see a more violent
contrast than the films presenting wartime heroics and that severest
of black satires against war, *Catch 22.*

France

The comparatively rare examination of the war years in French feature films and the impact of occupation was developed largely in terms of fiction. Clément, who had made *La Bataille du Rail* on Resistance activity, made in 1948 *Forbidden Games (Jeux Interdits)*, reflecting the war through the combined experience of two small children, one a girl from Paris whose parents were killed in 1940 in one of the refugee columns on the French roads, the other the son of the peasant family who adopt her. Their understanding of the situation is revealed in a necrophilic graveyard for dead animals that they create and tend with obsessive care. In the same year André Cayatte, the lawyer turned filmmaker, produced *Are We All Murderers?* (*Nous Sommes Tous des Assassins*, the interrogation significantly nonexistant in the French title), a study of a young, subnormal killer whose instincts are encouraged by enlistment in the Resistance; he kills his own commander during the battle for Paris. The film develops into a passionate case against capital punishment as

Jeux Interdits (Forbidden Games) (1952), directed by René Clément.

The Vanishing Corporal (1961), directed by Jean Renoir.

this youth, reared in destitution and without any social conscience or understanding, lies in the condemned cell awaiting the sudden, unannounced arrival in the night of his executioners—a technique that no doubt quite unconsciously echoes that of the Gestapo.

On a deeper, more personal level Robert Bresson made *A Man Condemned to Death Escapes* (*Un Condamné à Mort s'est Echappé,* 1956), a film that might be termed an act of religious thanksgiving for survival from imprisonment by the Gestapo, an event celebrated by the use of Mozart's Mass in C Minor to accompany the film, and especially the final moments of escape. Derived from a true story of escape and recreated here in the completely restrained, unstressed, and "unacted" manner familiar in Bresson's films, it shows life in its timeless continuity and detail until the two prisoners, working together, achieve victory over their captors because, as Bresson would stress, it is the will of God they should do so. This film, with Resnais's *Nuit et Brouillard* (already noted) and also his first feature film, *Hiroshima, Mon Amour,* emerge as the great records of war experience to come from France.

Hiroshima, Mon Amour (1959) was written by the novelist Marguerite Duras in close association with Resnais, who asked her initially for a "love story set in Hiroshima." The result, opening with a brief documentary study of the effects of the atom bomb in the Japanese target city that parallels *Nuit et Brouillard*, preludes the brief love affair of a French actress making a peace film in Hiroshima, and a Japanese whose family had been involved in the holocaust. The Frenchwoman as a girl had lost her lover, a soldier in the German army of occupation, and had temporarily lost her reason following his death at the hands of the French Resistance, and the subsequent persecution she had to endure from her fellow countrymen. The Japanese, who appears to have come to terms with the tragedy in his past life, is now in a position to help her resolve her own kindred, but deeper trauma, the disturbing memories that still haunt her. This profound study of the workings of a very special, though brief love relationship is wholly poetic, and must stand among the first in any list of films dealing with the war and its aftermath.

The French virtually continue to ignore the unhappy period of the war and the occupation, and this can be understood considering the problems that faced the recent film, *Grief and Pity* (*Le Chagrin et la Pitie*, 1971), made by Marcel Ophuls (son of Max Ophuls) and André Harris, and playing four hours, twenty minutes. It is a film that shocked the old in its frank revelation of the depth to which collaboration went in occupied France; rejected by French television, on which it was due to be shown, it eventually reached the cinema and played to packed houses largely made up of young people who wanted to understand more clearly the nature of the previous generation's "resistance" and "collaboration," its considerable support for Pétain in 1940, and rejection of the appeals coming from De Gaulle in Britain. The film brought together many representative stories, both from the side of the Resistance and from that of the collaborators. It contained many remarkable statements, including that by the biologist, Dr. Claude Lévy:

> France collaborated. It is the only European country which collaborated. The others signed armistices, capitulated. This is the only country in Europe which had a government which adopted laws which on a racialist level went even further than the Nuremberg laws, since the French racialist criteria were even more strict than the Germans. France was covered with concentration camps: Lurs, Avgelès Rivesaites, Drancy.[7]

Finland

An outstanding film from Finland, *The Unknown Soldier* (1955,

Edvin Laine), reconstructs almost in the style of newsreel episodes
the adventures of a Finnish detachment that in 1941 pushes into
Soviet-held territory in Karelia, only to be pushed back in 1944. The
film is primarily concerned with creating the illusion of actuality; the
soldiers talk (as the subtitles more than hint) with unfettered blunt-
ness, and are characterized with a lively reality, and both the locations and the war action have an often horrifying authenticity.

Italy

Italy has produced four films in more recent years that look back
to the war period. The first is Rossellini's *Il Generale della Rovere*
(1959, with Vittorio De Sica); adapted from a true story, it shows
how a two-faced and cowardly agent, who works for the Germans
as well as Italian patriots in Genoa in 1943, is caught by the Germans. In prison, he assumes the identity of an Italian general, a celebrated patriot who has been killed; in this guise, he finds himself

Il Generale Della Rovere (1959), directed by Roberto Rossellini, with Vittorio De Sica.

adopting the point of view of the general even to the point of allowing himself to be shot rather than betray those he has come to respect after witnessing the brutalities of prison life. Rossellini is said to regret having made this film. A second film, *Night in Rome* (*Era Notte a Roma*, 1960), goes back to the setting and period of Rome in the last months of occupation, tracing the movements of an English major (Leo Genn), an American pilot, and a Russian sergeant (Sergei Bondarchuk), all escaped from a prison camp, and the help given them by Esperia (Giovanna Ralli), a young Roman girl, whom the Englishman in turn helps when she escapes following arrest by the Germans. The film acts, in fact, as a further comment by Rossellini on the period, now some fifteen years back, which began with *Rome, Open City*. The emphasis now is on the internationality that the war in Italy developed.

Rossellini's films were followed by Luchino Visconti's *The Damned* (*La Caduta degli Dei*, 1969), a joint Italian-West German production, the German title of which was *Götterdammerung*. The cast was multinational, led by Dirk Bogarde and Ingrid Thulin, and the story concerns the miniature Nazi coup d'état that takes place inside a wealthy German industrial family, the Essenbecks. The events of 1933 are reflected in the violent takeover of the family's steel works by the Nazi enclave among the Essenbecks, which in its turn is finally overthrown by the SS themselves, collapsing through its own decadence, symbolized by the Nazi transvestite Martin (Helmuth Berger). Martin represents the homosexual decadence that Hitler used to bring about the downfall of the SA leaders during the Night of the Long Knives in 1934. This film has an atmosphere of ornate claustrophobia, which culminates in the internecine struggles of the Essenbecks (including Martin's rape of his evil mother), which symbolize events in Germany outside the enclosed walls of this horrific, baronial household. The effect, however, is more that of an operatic melodrama with political overtones than a full comment on the nature of Nazism, but possibly this was its sole intention.

De Sica followed with a somewhat comparable film, *The Garden of the Finzi-Continis* (*Il Giardino dei Finzi-Contini*, 1970), another study of an upper-class enclave in the Nazi-fascist period, in this case an aristocratic Jewish family living in patrician splendor on a landed estate behind locked gates in Ferrara. Confined to the years 1938 to 1943, these status Jews and their less wealthy friends find themselves gradually frozen out of the anti-Semitic fascist society that (the film slightly implies) their self-centred bourgeois indulgence has helped to bring into existence. Adapted from a perceptive nove'

The Damned (1969), directed by Luchino Visconti.

The Garden of the Finzi-Continis (1970), directed by Vittorio De Sica, with Dominique Sanda.

by Giorgio Bassani, the film ends with the dispersion of the family following the round-up of Jews for deportation; nevertheless, De Sica concentrates on the enclosed luxury of the family with a romantic, almost lyrical emphasis on their withdrawn world, with its private drives, tennis courts, elegant trees, and frustrated love affairs. The author of the original story, apparently, withdrew his name from any form of association with the film, which he felt had been overmuch twisted or softened.

A further comment on the nature of fascism came from the young director, Bernardo Bertolucci, in a co-production sponsored by Italy, France and West Germany, *The Conformist* (*Il Conformista*, 1969), based on a novel by Alberto Moravia. Once again, we are shown the kind of social decadence out of which fascism can be nurtured in a wealthy and depraved household, and in particular the sexual trauma (a homosexual assault in youth) which in this case motivates Marcello Clerici (Jean-Louis Trintignant), a civil servant of the fascist era, to involve himself in fascist espionage to compensate for his innate weakness of character. What the film exposes is indeed the very fallacy of conformism, the pursuit of a social and political mirage at the expense of the individual. Marcello's father is confined

The Conformist (1969), directed by Bernardo Bertolucci.

in a mental institution, but this escape from conformism makes him capable of saying what most needs to be said, indeed lies at the root of this film, "unless the State conforms to the will of the individual, how can the individual conform to the will of the State?"

Japan

Some of the more remarkable postwar films were to come from Japan. One which should have been significant was *Children of Hiroshima* (*Children of the Atom Bomb*, 1952), directed by Kaneto Shindo; adapted from a best-selling novel, and made in association with the Japan Teachers' Union, it sentimentalized to some extent the suffering resulting from the bomb. There is no recrimination against the United States, no real bitterness, and the film avoided the very issues the Teachers' Union had in mind in supporting its production. The story involves the return in 1952 of a young woman teacher to Hiroshima to visit the grave of her parents; during the visit she encounters cases of long-term suffering caused by the aftereffects of the bomb, and there is a remarkable, if somewhat formalized, "study" of the bomb's detonation, with tracking shots of stricken people accompanied by emotive music. The Teachers' Union rejected this over-conventional film, and supported the production of another that would, in their view, help more effectively the "fight to preserve peace." The result was *Hiroshima* (1953), directed by Hideo Sekigawa; it was conceived with strong left-wing, anti-American feeling, and reconstructed the explosion and its aftermath with spectacular effect. The film accused the Americans of treating the Japanese people as if they were mere animals in a mass laboratory experiment.

These films formed part of a strong antiwar movement in the Japanese cinema, partly (according to Anderson and Richie) inspired by the American action in Korea, in which the Japanese were most anxious not to become involved. These films exposed the sufferings of soldiers in war, including Sekigawa's *Listen to the Roar of the Ocean* (1950), which shows a unit made up of students who are all killed, and Senkichi Taniguchi's *Escape at Dawn* (1950), in which an officer shoots down a deserter when his fellows refuse to do so. More virulent in its attacks on Japanese militarism, with left-wing political overtones, were Yamamoto's *Vacuum Zone* and Sekigawa's *Dawn, 15 August*. A rare film that sought to investigate responsibility for war crimes was Masaki Kobayashi's *The Thick-walled Room* (1953–56), based on diaries of Japanese war criminals. This film, though dealing with admitted war crimes, also suggests that many

Children of Hiroshima (1952), directed by Kaneto Shindo.

of those imprisoned by the Occupation authorities were innocent, while
the guilty often escaped. Some films, however, (Anderson and Richie
cite *Mothers in a Storm* and *A Mother Calls Tearfully*, among other
titles) attempted to advance sentimental arguments for the release
of men held in prison for war crimes, while others attempted to white-
wash the army, notably Kiyoshi Saeki's *Tomoyuki Yamashita*, with
Sessue Hayakawa as the "hero" general "framed" for war atrocities,
and Inoshiro Honda's *Eagle of the Pacific*, made in honor of Admiral
Isoroku Yamamoto; this film went so far as to suggest he was seeking
peace throughout his war career.

The anti-American *Hiroshima* led to further films seeking to expose the Americans, notably as whore lovers in the notorious *Red-
Light Bases* (1953) and in Sekigawa's *Orgy* (1954). Others attacked
the Americans for leaving behind thousands of orphans of mixed
blood—again it was Sekigawa who made *Mixed-Blood Children*
(1952)—or committing the equivalent of war crimes, as in Tadashi
Imai's film, *The Tower of Lilies* (1953), in which the pupils in a
girls' high school, all enrolled as combat nurses, lose their lives in
an American preinvasion attack. Since most of the anti-American, or
so-called anti-American, films were made by adherents of the Left,
there were far fewer anti-Soviet films. However, Kunio Watanabe's

Repatriation (1949) was an attack on the Soviet Union for mistreatment of Japanese prisoners-of-war and their slow repatriation while the horrors of imprisonment were shown in *I Was a Siberian POW* (1952).

The culmination of anti-militarism in Japanese film was Kon Ichikawa's *The Burmese Harp* (1956) and *Fires on the Plain* (1959), as well as the celebrated trilogy by Masaki Kobayashi (who had been a prisoner-of-war himself), *No Greater Love* (1959), *Road to Eternity* (1959), and *A Soldier's Prayer* (1961). *The Burmese Harp* is permeated by the Buddhist spirit; a private in a Japanese unit in Burma has a harp that is his delight. After his capture by the British he volunteers to try to induce a Japanese garrison to surrender. He is unsuccessful; they reject him with contempt. He escapes their fate (which is annihilation) and is cared for by a Buddhist monk. He then wanders the countryside burying the corpses of his countrymen; this becomes a vocation after he sees a British group of soldiers and nurses holding a memorial service for the "unknown Japanese soldier." He is now dressed as a monk, and although he comes upon his old unit, he refuses repatriation with them, preferring to dedicate himself to the ritual burial of the dead. The British are shown in

The Burmese Harp (1956), directed by Kon Ichikawa.

this film as sharing with the Japanese a nostalgic desire to return home, but this simple Japanese soldier asserts his spiritual leadership by sublimating his despair in reverence for human life and respect for those who have died. Again, this film works on the poetic level. It is a strange, symbolic film, flowing back and forth in time, one of the rare films to resolve the emotions of war through an assertion of idealism.

Fires on the Plain goes further than most films in its picture of brutalization through war. The action is set on Leyte in the Philippines in 1945 during the last weeks of war; a private suffering from tuberculosis loses contact with his unit, kills a Filipino girl who screams at the sight of him, joins with other starving soldiers, and is finally faced with cannibalism; he shoots a man in the act of eating the flesh of his comrade before he is himself shot. The film, photographed with wonderful chiaroscuro by the cinematographer Setsuo Kobayashi, is one of the most uncompromising and fatalistic statements against war. Masaki Kobayashi's trilogy (based on a six-volume novel by Jumpei Gomikawa) concerns Kaji, a humane and pacifist labor overseer sent from Japan with his bride to supervise oppressed labor in a South Manchurian steelworks. He is persecuted by the authorities and police alike for his clemency to the labor force and to a desperate contingent of prisoners-of-war who revolt; his weakness brands him as a "Red." He is imprisoned, tortured, released only to be drafted into the army. His unit suffers defeat in the North from Soviet forces in 1945, and he joins other wanderers in an effort to reach home in South Manchuria. But he falls into Soviet hands, escapes, and finally reaches his beloved wife in a state of utter exhaustion, his socialist idealism shattered, his outlook disillusioned. The whole nine-hour study presents the gradual, wearing disintegration of a man of high ideals at the hands alike of his fellow countrymen and his enemies. This ambitious series of films is magnificently conceived and executed, though the fulfillment of the role by Tatsuya Nakadai is held by some to fall short in greatness commensurable with the character he is playing. Kaji is a kind of saint suffering prolonged persecution for his humanity.

The Japanese continue to make more conventional feature films dealing with war. Among those released more recently have been:

> 1970. *The Militarists* (director, Hiromichi Horikawa). The struggle between the "hawks" and the "doves" among the Japanese during the whole span of the war under the war-minded leadership of Tojo.

1971. *Battle of Okinawa* (director, Kihachi Okamoto). The costly defense of Okinawa, and its final downfall in 1945.

1972. *Men and War* (director, Satsuo Yamamoto). A two-part epic set in Manchuria during the period of Japanese occupation, and events leading up to and following after the assassination of Chang Tso-lin.

The Socialist Countries

It is, however, the socialist countries that have produced collectively the most massive survey of the war years. The flow of war films went on throughout the 1950s and 1960s, the more obvious reaffirmations of the political implication of the war and its aftermath, the more penetrating (notably the films of Andrzej Wajda) reevaluations of the significance of what happened. The list of all these later war films would prove interminable; a selection follows:

USSR. *Soldiers* (1956; A. Ivanov).

The Cranes are Flying (1957, Mikhail Kalatozov, with Tatiana Samoilova, Alexei Batalov). Lovers separated by war and eventually by his death.

Destiny of a Man (1959; Sergei Bondarchuk, featuring himself). A prisoner-of-war returns to find his family destroyed; he adopts an orphaned child.

Ballad of a Soldier (1960; Grigori Chukrai, with Vladimir Ivashov). A war hero's adventures returning to his mother while on short leave.

The Flaming Years (1961; Yulia Solntseva; script by the late Alexander Dovzhenko). Heroic projection in 70mm of the indestructible spirit of the Russian people in the person of the soldier-hero, Ivan Orlyuk.

Peace to the Newcomer (1961; Aleksander Alov and Vladimir Naumov). The adventures of three Russian soldiers who in the last days of war drive a pregnant German girl to a field hospital in Kvikau.

The Longest Months (1963; Alexander Stolpev).

Two in the Steppe (1964; Nikolai Efros).

The Great Patriotic War (1965; Roman Karmen)

A Soldier's Father (1965; Revaz Chkheidze). War from the Georgian viewpoint.

Liberation, a four-part film: *The Flaming Bulge, The Breakthrough, The Direction of the Main Blow, The Battle for Berlin* (1969–; a coproduction with Poland, Yugoslavia, East Germany, Italy; director, Yuri Ozerov). The last two years of war in Eastern Europe, 1943–45; the liberation of Byelorussia and

The Cranes Are Flying (1957), directed by Mikhail Kalatozov.

Destiny of a Man (1959), directed by Sergei Bondarchuk.

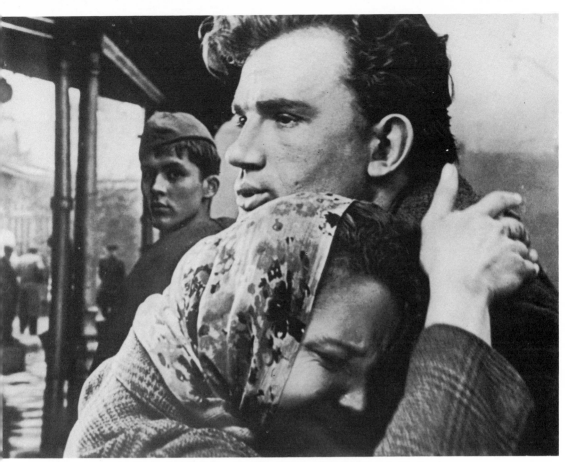

Ballad of a Soldier (1960), directed by Grigori Chukrai.

Ballad of a Soldier (1960), directed by Grigori Chukrai.

the push that brought the Russian armies into Germany. A shortened version of the first two parts as a single film dubbed in English as *The Great Battle* (1971).

Poland. *Five from Barska Street* (1954; Aleksander Ford). Postwar problems of wartime juvenile delinquents.

Hours of Hope (1955; Jan Rybkowski). A group of prisoners of various nationalities released from Nazi prison camps.

A Generation (1954), *Kanal* (1956), *Ashes and Diamonds* (1958) Andrzej Wajda's trilogy dealing with wartime and postwar Poland.

Eroica (1958; Andrzej Munk). A varied group in a war camp for Polish prisoners.

Lotna (1959; Andrzej Wajda). Symbolistic story of the Polish cavalry.

Farewells (1958; Wojciech Has).

The Passenger (1961–63; Andrzej Munk, completed by Witold Lesiewicz). Intimate study of the jealous relationship of two women, an SS overseer and her prisoner-assistant, while living in Auschwitz concentration camp.

Samson (1961; Andrzej Wajda). A Jew who escapes from a ghetto, becoming a hunted alien during the Occupation.

Kanal (1956), directed by Andrzej Wajda.

Ashes and Diamonds (1958), directed by Andrzej Wajda.

Ashes and Diamonds (1958), directed by Andrzej Wajda.

Eroica (1958), directed by Andrzej Wajda.

The Passenger (1961–63), directed by Andrzej Munk and Witold Lesiewicz.

The Passenger (1961), directed by Andrzej Munk.

Landscape after the Battle (1970; Andrzej Wajda). As described by Wajda: "This is my most difficult film. Many films showing how people suffered from German cruelty in concentration camps have been made before. But here we are rather concerned with the marks left by Nazi crimes on the minds of their victims . . . , the mental rehabilitation of a young boy, liberated from a concentration camp and staying temporarily in a DP camp."

Czecho-
slovakia.

It Is not Always Cloudy (1950; Vojtěch Jasný and Karel Kachyna). Resettlement of the border region after expulsion of German settlers.

Life was at Stake (1956; Jirí Weiss). A wife helps the Resistance without her husband's knowledge.

Romeo, Juliet and Darkness (1960, Jirí Weiss). A student hides his Jewish girlfriend from the Nazis.

A Higher Principle (1960; Jirí Krejčík). The period of terror after the assassination of Heydrich in 1942.

Midnight Mass (1962; Jirí Krejčík). Problems of the bourgeois during the war.

The Boxer and Death (1962; Petr Solán). Slovakian film set in a concentration camp.

Transport from Paradise (1962; Zbynek Brynych). Conditions in Terezín concentration camp for Jews.

Death is called Engelchin (1963; Ján Kadár and Elmer Klos) The struggle for independence during the final days of Nazi occupation.

—And the Fifth Rider is Fear (1964; Zbynek Brynych). Persecution as experienced by a Jewish physician.

Diamonds of the Night (1964; Jan Nemec). Experiences of two young fugitives from a concentration camp.

Assassination (1964; Jirí Sequens). Assassination of Heydrich by Czech patriots.

Long Live the Republic! (1965; Karel Kachyna). The last days of World War II as experienced in May 1945 by a 12-year-old boy in a Bohemian village.

The Shop on Main Street (1965; Ján Kadár and Elmer Klos). The round-up and dispossession of Jews in

Diamonds of the Night (1964), directed by Jan Nemec.

Assassination (1964), directed by Jirí Sequens.

a small Slovakian town, and the relationship between a well-meaning artisan and the Jewish woman of advanced age whose shop is allocated to him.

Requiem for Friend and Foe (1965; Jirí Sequens). Episode from the period of Nazi occupation in Greece.

Closely Observed Trains (1966; Jirí Menzel). Ironic
sexual comedy set in the final years of the occupation.

Carriage to Vienna (1966; Karel Kachyna). A Czech
girl falls in love with a young German soldier.

Hungary. *Spring Comes to Budapest* (1955; Félix Máriássy). The
siege of Budapest in 1944.

A Strange Mark of Identity (1955; Zoltán Várkonyi). The
wartime struggle of the communists.

The Bells Have Gone to Rome (1958; Miklós Jancsó).
Jancsó's first feature film, about a teacher and his
students who evade Nazi orders to help oppose
Soviet advances.

The Shop on Main Street (1965), directed by Elmar Klos and Ján Kadár.

The Shop on Main Street (1965), directed by Elmar Klos and Ján Kadár.

Half-Time in Hell (1961; Zoltán Fabri). A grotesquely tragic football match between the Germans and their prisoners in a prison-camp toward the end of the war.

20 Hours (1964; Zoltán Fabri). Aftermath of the war in Hungary seen through the experiences of four friends.

My Way Home (1964; Miklós Jancsó). A group of adolescents at the time of the Russian liberation of Hungary.

Father (1966; István Szabó). The gradual disillusion of a child about the wartime reputation of his father.

Cold Days (1966; András Kovács). A Hungarian atrocity committed during the war years under Horthy.

Love Film (1970; István Szabó). A panorama of Hungary during and after the war.

East Germany. *Stars* (1959; Konrad Wolf). Co-production with Bulgaria; a study of anti-Nazism.

Professor Mamlock (1961; Konrad Wolf). A remake of the story of the persecution of a German Jewish professor.

The Divided Sky (1964; Gerhard Klein) and *Stories of That Night* (1967; Gerhard Klein and others). Stories set in a divided Berlin.

Yugoslavia. *The Sun Is Far Away* (1953; Radoš Novakovič) and *Two Peasants* (1954; Zorž Skrigin). Films dealing with partisan warfare.

Many of these films reconstruct events of the war in terms that bring out the humanity of the characters, sentimentally perhaps in *The Cranes Are Flying*, one of the first films in the Soviet Union to swing over from heroic, ideologically correct characterization to genuine studies of individuality. *The Cranes Are Flying* is full of sympathy for its heroine Veronica in her difficult and torturing separation, her marriage to her lover's cousin when she thinks him to be dead, the unhappiness of this substitute marriage spent in Siberia. The film emphasizes its unhappy end. *Ballad of a Soldier* also has great charm and humanity. An altogether stronger film is *Destiny of a Man*, made with feeling but no taint of sentimentality. It was a debut for Bondarchuk as a director, and the film was based on a novel by Mikhail Sholokhov.

The dictum in Bertolucci's film *The Conformist*—"Unless the State conforms to the will of the individual, how can the individual conform to the will of the State"—becomes in a variety of ways the theme of the more enlightened films of the 1950s and 1960s produced in the socialist countries and looking back on the struggles arising

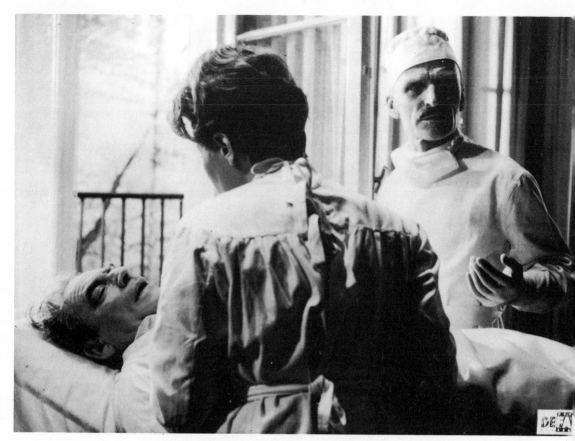

Professor Mamlock (1961), directed by Konrad Wolf.

from the war years—films such as the Czechoslovakian *The Shop on Main Street,* or the films of Munk and Wajda in Poland. *The Shop on Main Street* is a tragicomic portrait of a man in a small Slovakian town who attempts to conform to the new, fascist society and take over the Jewish-owned shop he has been allocated, only to become like a devoted son to the old Jewess who has run it for decades in her own way and does not begin to comprehend the situation that he is there to dispossess her and not to help her in her old age. When at last she sees the Jews being rounded up for deportation, the age-old fear of racial persecution finds expression in her as she shrinks back in terror into the darkest corner, muttering "Pogrom, pogrom." She dies of shock, and with this the humane man who had become her friend and so through sheer humanity a nonconformist, kills himself in utter shame.

The Polish films have gone furthest among the films produced in the socialist countries in their examination of the difficulties the Polish people had to face during the worst decade in their history, the period 1939 to 1949: conquest and occupation, division of their country initially between German and Russian invaders, total occupation by Germany in 1941, the presence on Polish soil of the principal Nazi genocide camps, the death of six million people, one fifth of the population, the postwar division of the country between elements of Left and Right. Andrzej Munk, whose film *Eroica* showed how even a cheat and a crook might get caught up in the heroic impetus of the 1944 Warsaw uprising, made one of the ultimate comments on the death camps in *The Passenger*, though he died before the film was completed.

In *The Passenger*, Lisa, a German girl formerly an SS overseer in Auschwitz but married now and living in the United States, is brought momentarily on an ocean liner face to face with Marta (or her double), a Polish girl whom she had known as a prisoner and whom she had thought to be dead. Lisa had lied to her husband about her exact position in the camp, and her jealous relationship with Marta, her prisoner-assistant. This film, made with an absolute reticence that reminds one of Bresson's work, avoids any taint of sensationalism and turns, like the work of Resnais, on the nature of recollection. It is enhanced (rather than the reverse) by the use of stills from the uncompleted film to recreate links in Lisa's memory, with its supressions and falsifications, of the persecution (born of jealous love) that she had imposed on Marta and the man Marta loved, another prisoner at Auschwitz. This film, with its deep almost subliminal recollections of Auschwitz, is all the more profound and poetic in selecting women for its protagonists.

It is perhaps in the films of Andrzej Wajda that the profoundest resolution of the war years in terms of individual experience has so far taken place. The only comparable filmmaker is Resnais. Son of a Polish army officer, Wajda at the age of only sixteen in 1942 joined the home army, the Resistance force directed by the Polish government in exile. In 1945, when the war was over, he was nineteen. During the difficult postwar years he was a student at the Cracow Academy of Fine Arts; from 1950 a student at the film school at Lodz. After working with Ford on *Five Boys from Barska Street*, he made his first feature, *A Generation* (1954), which in relatively simple terms reflects the experiences of Stach, a working-class boy in Warsaw who in 1942 joins the Polish left-wing underground and falls in love with a girl leader in the movement who instructs him. After her arrest, he is mature enough to take over her duties as head of the Youth Fighter Group. Stach and the others are portrayed as normal human beings, suffering and feeling fear; there are no heroics, only hard work in the adverse circumstances of life as it had been ten years previously. In his second film, *Kanal* (1956),

Wajda's portrait of Polish youth in the Resistance becomes more diverse and complex, while in *Ashes and Diamonds* (1958), he studies the motivations of a disoriented young man (played by Zbigniew Cybulski), who, in 1945 at the time of the German surrender, after opposing them as a member of the home army, now works, with some doubts, as an assassin for the Right. With this film, Wajda began to show the strife in postwar Poland that led finally to the establishment of a government of the Left. Wajda is deeply conscious of Poland's long and troubled national history, and the need to remain responsive to tradition while feeling loyalty to the new, completely reoriented society of the 1950s. This response to tradition is also shown in his beautiful film, *Lotna* (1959), which in its own particular way lays to rest the old, romantic image of death and self-sacrifice associated with the Polish cavalry detachments who had thrown themselves against the German tanks in September 1939.

The war has brought fundamental changes to the Eastern European border countries, lying between the Soviet Union and the present Germany, divided but highly conscious of its powerful national identity. These new, socialist countries need filmmakers of the high sensitivity of Wajda to assist them to understand the adjustments (alike of government and people) necessary to make these changes tolerable and fruitful. The tendency is still too great, after a full generation, to interpret recent history in set terms with prescribed human values blindly based on prejudice. As for countries such as the United States, France, and Britain, the more they change, the more they remain the same. The experiences of the war are largely forgotten or, for men and women aged less now than forty to forty-five, virtually unknown. The majority of the films that have appeared so far do little to bring new, contemporary understanding of the significance of what happened, except in a purely factual, historical context.

The Second World War was unparalleled in extent, and in its devastation, its cruelty in war crimes, and its death toll throughout the world of some fifty-five million people, soldiers and civilians. It has left the Earth dismembered by ideological conflict and in the hands of a barely civilized species possessing new, immeasurable powers for self destruction. Through trying to understand the implications that lie on and beneath the surface of the great collection of films the war years have produced it may be possible to draw somewhat nearer to establishing prospects for lasting peace, circumventing the many dangers that could lead to yet another, and more terrible universal war. The sufferings of the immediate past have been put on living record as never before, and we have the means in both the cinema and television to make these sufferings and their consequences known to audiences of a size unimaginable even half a century ago.

The traditional appeal of war from generation to generation has been largely based on ignorance. War's atavistic appeal lies deep in the less civilized areas of human nature; men and women have been led to cry out for it because it represents for them the final test of strength in circumstances that their leaders always claim to have become unendurable. But what is really unendurable is war itself. The cinema's great gallery of pictures of the Second World War, so much of it seen at first hand and culminating in the horrifying climax of genocide and death from nuclear devastation, show what armed conflict in the twentieth century has come to mean for both soldiers and civilians. The new generation can study these portraits of human disintegration and suffering at first hand. This vicarious experience projected constantly on the cinema and television screens should in all conscience be sufficient to prevent any further resort in man's future history to universal war.

Notes

Chapter 1
Prelude to War

1. *The March of Time* was sponsored by the Time/Life Board, Chairman and President, Henry R. Luce. Roy Larsen, a member of the board, became Chairman of *The March of Time,* with Louis de Rochemont as overall producer, and his brother, Dick de Rochemont, as principal administrator, initially based on London. Louis de Rochemont's principal assistant and associate producer was Tom Orchard. The head of production in London from late 1936 to early 1939 was Edgar Anstey, with Maurice Lancaster as unit manager. Peter Hopkinson directed international subjects for *The March of Time* from 1946 to 1954.

In 1936 de Rochemont placed the technical management of *The March of Time* under a skillful film editor, Jack Bradford, who was succeeded later by another editor, Lothar Wolff, who subsequently became associate producer. The principal writer for the series was initially Tom Everitt, who was later succeeded by James Shute.

In *Films beget Films* Jay Leyda, writing from a leftist standpoint, is naturally opposed to any right-wing tendencies he can discover in *The March of Time;* he expresses concern over the "possibilities for distortion" that rose from the series' mixture of archive and specially shot material, and the reenactment of scenes otherwise unobtainable. Leyda claims (p. 43) that "a gullible audience would regard all this as equally 'real.'" An informed answer to Leyda's criticism appears in a letter by Peter Hopkinson in *Sight and Sound,* Autumn 1971, p. 229.

2. After seeing the first issue of *The March of Time,* Alastair Cooke contrasted this new form of documentary with the work of the British documentarians. Writing in *Sight and Sound* (Autumn 1935) he said: "My first vivid impression . . . is that men whose first and acute interest is the growth of fact into news have at every turn triumphed over men whose first interest is the technique of cinema. . . . The aloofness, intelligence and apt irony, which for the past ten years have made 'Time' so pathetically superior to any other newspaper or magazine in English, here make *The March of Time,* the first adult newsreel. . . . The filmed *Time* is admirable by the amount of concealed research, chasing, cabling, digested history its slickness represents."

3. Among left-wing directors interested in the Jews in Palestine was the Polish Aleksander Ford who, at the age of twenty-five made a film there, *Sabra.* Later he directed the documentary, *The Road of Youth* (1936), about Jewish orphans, which was banned in Poland but shown abroad. Ford spent the war years in the USSR, but returned to become a leading figure in postwar Polish filmmaking.

4. According to *Documentary News Letter* (Sept. 1940, p. 2) the German Embassy threatened *The March of Time* with "bluster and threats of a lawsuit." This intervention from Washington, however, helped the film gain "world-wide publicity and distribution." Note might also be taken here of an earlier British compilation film made by J. N. Williams, *Whither Germany?* (1934), which Paul Rotha in his book *Documentary Film* refers to as a "curious compilation of actual events."

The British Board of Film Censors (president, Lord Tyrrell; secretary, Brooks Wilkinson) made cuts now and then for political reasons in *The March of Time.* (See *Sight and Sound,* Summer 1936, p. 20.) Lord Tyrrell was against "the creeping of politics into films." He went on, "From my past experience I consider this dangerous.

Nothing would be more calculated to arouse the passions of the British public than the introduction, on the screen, of subjects dealing either with religious or political controversy. . . . So far we have had no film dealing with current burning political questions, but the thin end of the wedge is being inserted."

Issue 8, Year I was among *The March of Time* films to be cut by the British censor: *Inside Nazi Germany* remained uncut, however.

5. The pro-Franco supporters in the United States made *Fury over Spain* using, according to Jay Leyda, staged "incidents" and "atrocities." See *Films beget Films*, p. 39.

6. An early attempt in France to forecast the future struggle in terms of the threat to peace which the Polish Corridor represented was made in *Ombres sur l'Europe* (*The Polish Corridor*, 1934), made by Robert Alexandre. It made use of purposefully edited newsreel material. Note should also be taken of the following French short films: *The Pacific Problem* (3 mins.) a history of Japanese expansion told in cine-diagram, and *War Debts* (4 mins.), a history of German reparations and the problems of their repayment as seen from the French standpoint. (Both these were made by Atlantic Films.) Another French short, *All Quiet in the East* (P. Bianchi) offered a satiric study of the Sino-Japanese conflict told by means of cartoon and model animation, concentrating on the invasion of Manchuria.

7. *French Film*, Falcon Press, London, 1953, p. 88.

8. American films took little account of the war in other centers of the world. While the Spanish Civil War was active, a paltry melodrama, *The Last Train from Madrid* (James Hogan, 1937), with Dorothy Lamour and Anthony Quinn, was produced by Paramount; it concerned the desperate struggles of an assorted group of people to get out of Madrid. Similar use was made of the situation in Shanghai in a short feature directed by D. Ross Lederman, with James Craig and Betty Furness, *North of Shanghai* (1939). In this an American woman journalist and a newsreel cameraman combine to frustrate an attempt by the Japanese to bomb the Shanghai arsenal; its aim was to lend authenticity to its excitement by incorporating genuine actuality footage.

9. It is perhaps ironic that the Bund's activities were to some extent frowned upon by the Nazi authorities in Germany. The Bund stood for "Friends of the New Germany in the USA." Control of the Bund lay with Rudolf Hess, the Führer's deputy head of the National Socialist Party. See Manvell and Fraenkel, *Hess* (1971), p. 73.

10. *Cinema Journal, Winter* 1967–68, p. 2.

11. Lewis Jacobs, op. cit., points out that in addition there were certain films dealing with American service life and training. These included *Flight Command* (1940), showing fighter air squadrons and their training. *I Wanted Wings* (1941), about the training of army pilots, *Dive Bomber* (1941), with its study of the causes of "blackout," *Navy Blues* (1941) on gunnery practice. There were also many service comedies following the introduction of the Selective Service Act in 1941, from *Buck Privates* to *Caught in the Act*. *A Yank in the RAF* and *International Squadron* featured American pilots flying bombers to Britain; *Parachute Battalion, Flying Fortress,* and *Submarine Patrol* (all 1941) added to the increasing number of service subjects. Lewis Jacobs also claims that Howard Hawks's *Sergeant York* (1941), the true story of a conscientious objector of World War I who felt he was "converted" by God to go to war, and became America's number-one hero, helped to overcome prejudice against drafting.

12. Phyllis Bottome, an Anglo-American authoress of high reputation, with an interest in psychology derived from studies under Alfred Adler, was also the author of *Private Worlds*. She was living in Germany at the time of Hitler's rise to power. *The Mortal Storm* was published in 1938 as a paperback Penguin Special soon after its initial appearance in hardback. It is typical of the attitude of people remote from

the realities of Nazi Germany that the novel, a serious study, was reviewed in the *Atlantic Journal* as "the first significant novel torn out of the bleeding soul of modern Europe."

13. According to George Perry in *The Films of Alfred Hitchcock*, p. 74, this method of assassination was employed in actuality in Teheran the following year.

14. There is an interesting discussion of the psychology of this moment in the film in Peter Bogdanovitch's *Fritz Lang in America*, pp. 59–60. Bogdanovitch suggested to Lang that he was subconsciously drawing a parallel between Thorndike's failure to shoot Hitler in time with Britain's failure to oppose him before 1939.

15. Chaplin in his *Autobiography* (p. 424) says that Alexander Korda had suggested the basic idea to him as early as 1937 of doing "a Hitler story based on mistaken identity, Hitler having the same moustache as the tramp." As Chaplin puts it: "As Hitler I could harangue the crowds in jargon and talk all I wanted to. And as the tramp I could remain more or less silent. A Hitler story was an opportunity for burlesque and pantomime." Chaplin claims the story took two years to develop.

16. A very full outline of the film is given in Theodor Huff's *Charlie Chaplin*, pp. 241–43. See also Lewis Jacob, op. cit., pp. 6–7.

17. According to Huff, Chaplin's father came of Anglicized French-Jewish stock, while his mother was of combined Spanish-Irish origin.

18. The text of the speech is given in full in Chaplin's autobiography, p. 432.

19. Eisenstein, who was not given to making public statements apart from matters connected with film, twice went out of his way to attack Goebbels and the repressive policies of the Nazis. The first time was in an "Open Letter to Joseph Goebbels," published in *Film Art* and elsewhere in 1934, and again in an article entitled "My Subject is Patriotism" after completing *Alexander Nevsky* in 1938. See Marie Seton, *Sergei M. Eisenstein*, pp. 326, 397.

20. Russian documentary had to a limited extent dealt with the conflicts in Europe and the Far East. Esther Schub, Russia's pioneer director of compilation films from archive sources, produced *Spain* (1939); Jay Leyda in *Films beget Films* claims that this was her "last great demonstration of her analytical method"; just as Hemingway had written and spoken the commentary for *Spanish Earth*, the playwright Vsevolod Vishnevsky, after visiting Spain, wrote and spoke the commentary for *Spain*. Much of the material was shot in Spain itself by Roman Karmen and Boris Makaseyev. Karmen then went to China to film the struggle on the communist front. (See Jay Leyda, op. cit., pp. 39–41.) Roman Karmen, however, writing in 1948 on "Soviet Documentary" for my book, *Experiment in the Film* (1949), mentions none of these films. Karmen also made a film, *Abyssinia* (1936). A documentary of about an hour's duration, it offered a description of the country and its people as a prelude to preparations for the coming of war with Italy. Italy's assault from the air is shown from the point of view of those on the ground. An horrific picture is given of the results of a gas attack on an Ethiopian community, men, women, and children who are being treated by the Red Cross, and a raid on a British Red Cross center is covered with further terrible scenes of suffering.

21. In 1939 Eisenstein (rehabilitated in the eyes of authority) had been appointed artistic controller of Mosfilm, though he was relieved of this responsibility when he began work on *Ivan the Terrible*. Friedrich Ermler held a similar position at Lenfilm, Dovzhenko at the Kiev Studio, and Sergei Yutkevitch at Soyuzdetfilm.

22. The London Film Society tried the experiment of screening in juxtaposition sequences from this film and Roman Karmen's *Abyssinia* (see note 20 above), which, according to Arthur Vesselo, reporting in the BFI's *Monthly Film Bulletin* (December 1937, p. 264), made its strongest impact at the end, with Karmen's studies of the injured Ethiopians set against Mussolini's booming oratory and the rejoicings of the crowds in Rome. While the Russian film referred to imperialist aggression, the Italian

film refers to its "civilising mission" against these "savages" making "cowardly attacks" on Italian units, and Italy's right to a "place in the sun." The dignity of the Abyssinians, including the emperor, Haile Selassie, is emphasized in the Russian film.

23. See José Luis Guarner, *Roberto Rossellini*, p. 6.

24. Mizoguchi had made a nationalist film, *The Dawn of the Founding of Manchukuo and Mongolia* in 1931.

25. After Japan and Germany had signed the Anti-Communist Pact, limited co-production followed. Mansaku Itami collaborated with the Nazi-influenced director of mountaineering films, Arnold Fanck, in making a German-Japanese co-production, *The New Earth* (also known as *Daughters of the Samurai*), completed in the mid-1930s. The aim of this film is given in Anderson and Richie, *The Japanese Film* as "unity of the Nazi group-spirit and the racial spirit of the Japanese as opposed to the weak spirit of the democracies." The theme of *The New Earth*, scripted initially by Fanck in Japan, was intended to show the conversion of a Japanese "democrat" to the "Japanese family system." The directors failed to agree, since Itami realized Fanck's understanding of Japan was so limited he was falsifying many elements in the story. Two versions of the film resulted, and one critic said it was "no more than an attempt to form essentially alien [to Japan] Nazi propaganda out of Japanese raw materials." A second co-production, made with Wolfgang Berger, *The Oath of the People,* was also a failure. Co-production developed thereafter within Asia, especially with Korea, then a colony of Japan.

26. Hitler had made some previous use of short propaganda films as part of his election campaigns.

Chapter 2
The War: I. Single Combat—The British Commonwealth versus Germany,
1939–41

1. According to a report in *DNL*, the only two cameramen attached to the army in 1940 (Harry Rignold and Walter Tennyson D'Eyncourt) were summarily sent home when France was overrun, having had little opportunity to achieve coverage of the war in France. Only a single newsreel operator working with the Navy managed to secure film of the Dunkirk evacuation.

2. The Americans retitled the film, *Voices of the Night*. Asquith also at this period made two short films, *Channel Incident,* the Dunkirk evacuation reconstructed from a single woman's experience, and *Rush Hour,* on wartime transport. In collaboration with Burgess Meredith he made *Welcome to Britain* (1943), an hour-long film introducing American forces to British social life, and *Two Fathers* (1944) on Anglo-French relations.

3. See *Secrets of Crewe House: the Story of a Famous Campaign* (1920) by Campbell Stuart, which tells the whole story of the success of British propaganda during the First World War. See also *DNL,* July 1940, p. 3. Hitler also praised British propaganda. See *Mein Kampf* (translation Hurst and Blackett, 1939) pp. 163–64. "In England propaganda was regarded as a weapon of the first order. . . . In 1915 the enemy started his propaganda among our soldiers. . . . Gradually our soldiers began to think just in the way the enemy wished them to think."

4. Film Centre was set up in 1937 by Grierson, Arthur Elton, and others primarily to act as a consultative center for documentary, useful not only to filmmakers but to potential sponsors. It came to represent the movement as a whole in Britain.

5. In 1940 Grierson was also in Australia and New Zealand helping them establish a wartime film policy.

6. A full account of the MOI scheme for distribution and use of films, as well

as of its production roster, can be found in the PEP (Political and Economic Planning) publication, *The Factual Film* (1947), pp. 63–104. See also Manvell, *Film* (Pelican: revised edition 1950), p. 108 et seq.

7. In terms of direction, *The First Days* was a composite work, involving Cavalcanti, Harry Watt, Humphrey Jennings, Pat Jackson, and others.

8. Crown remained at first in the hands of Cavalcanti, who was later succeeded in August 1940 by Ian Dalrymple. When he left in 1943, J. B. Holmes took charge, to be followed by Basil Wright in January 1945.

9. The text of the commentary is given in full in *DNL,* Nov. 1940, p. 6.

10. Lewis Jacobs, op. cit., p. 5 says *"The March of Time* believed 'that the war shadow darkens America in 1940 just as ominously as it did in 1914.' A foreword read, 'The war we so thankfully consigned to history—the World War we wrapped in old newspapers and laid away for posterity to look back on—has suddenly become very much alive.' "

11. *Baptism of Fire,* Kracauer notes in *From Caligari to Hitler* (p. 275), is a version of a film *Campaign in Poland* shown in Berlin in February 1940; its 6,560 feet were edited from some 230,000 feet of newsreel material. The German version, *Campaign in Poland,* is said to have contained anti-Semitic material not carried in *Baptism of Fire,* which was intended for audiences outside Germany.

12. Nazi propaganda films had constantly to be revised to suit current policy. Kracauer gives examples, op. cit, pp. 280–81. For example, a Russian-German conference on the division of Poland in *Baptism of Fire* was cut from versions shown after June 1941. Also various services were more favored in some films than in others: for example, the proportion of Luftwaffe material in *Baptism of Fire* is virtually double the ratio in *Victory in the West.*

13. For some account of this film, which was set in an English school for the sons of political prisoners, see D. S. Hull's *Film in the Third Reich,* pp. 180–81. Another minor film with an Irish setting was *The Fox of Glenarvon* (1940), also directed by Max Kimmich.

14. According to D. S. Hull, op. cit., p. 172, Hippler was working as a travel agent in 1963. He was head of the Films Division of Goebbels's Propaganda Ministry from 1939 to 1943, when he moved over to the military film unit. He was a British prisoner of war for three years, and "de-Nazified" in 1951. Hippler supervised the production of *Campaign in Poland* (see note 11 above) and *Victory in the West,* as well as directing a documentary, *Legion Condor* (1943).

What appears to have been the first strongly anti-Semitic film issued on the eve of war, *Robert and Bertram* (July 1939), was directed by Hans Heinz Zerlett. It was a period film.

Chapter 3
The War: II. The Middle Phase—The War until Hitler's Defeat at Stalingrad,
January 1943

1. *DNL,* May 1942, p. 67.

2. Balcon, *Michael Balcon Presents,* p. 134.

3. *DNL,* May 1942, p. 67.

4. For the extraordinary story of Thorold Dickinson being regarded for a period as a security risk because he had been to Spain to make films in behalf of the republican cause, see Balcon, op. cit., p. 136. Dickinson was later commissioned in the army and rose to the rank of major.

5. *Twenty Years of British Film,* edited by Roger Manvell, pp. 84–85.

6. For the background to this unique venture, see Ralph Bond's article in *DNL,* April 1942, p. 63.

7. *DNL*, Nov.–Dec. 1942, p. 1.

8. *Cinema Journal*, Winter 1967–68, p. 10. Prof. Richard Dyer MacCann in *The People's Films* claims a tenuous link was kept with the abortive pre-war governmental US Film Service, which had been created in 1938 with Pare Lorentz and Arch Mercey as Director and Assistant Director. The Film Service had been closed down after making the impressive but controversial film, *The Fight for Life,* Joris Iven's *Power and the Land,* and Robert Flaherty's unfinished documentary, *The Land.* Arch Mercey, who had meantime produced *Power for Defence* (1941) on the Tennessee Valley Authority for the National Defence Advisory Council, became Lowell Mellett's deputy in December 1941.

9. The published script of *Mrs. Miniver* appears in *Twenty Best Film Plays.* For the quotation see pp. 831–32.

10. *Agee on Film*, p. 23.

11. *Portrait of a Flying Yorkshireman,* edited by Paul Rotha, p. 178.

12. *Cinema Journal,* Winter 1967–68, p. 12.

13. The published script of *Casablanca* appears in *Twenty Best Film Plays.*

14. *The Proceedings of the Conference held in October 1943 under the Sponsorship of the Hollywood Writers' Mobilization and the University of California,* pp. 22–26. Later referred to as *Writers' Conference.*

15. For a full description of the National Film Board organization at this stage, see *DNL*, September 1942, p. 129.

16. *DNL,* January 1943, p. 167.

17. The principal facts in this section are derived from Jay Leyda's *Kino, Soviet Cinema,* by Thorold Dickinson and Catherine de la Roche, and Georges Sadoul, *Le Cinéma pendant la Guerre.*

18. Leyda, op. cit., p. 367.

19. This film, using the same title, was adapted for British audiences by Ivor Montagu, the commentary being spoken by Wilfred Pickles.

20. In June 1942 the British MOI was distributing a seven-minute Russian short, *Five Men of Velish,* showing Nazi executions of Russian patriots, and the vengeance exacted by Russian guerrillas.

21. *Experiment in the Film,* edited by Roger Manvell, pp. 183–84. See also Sadoul, op. cit., pp. 125 et seq.

22. See Roy Armes, *Patterns of Realism,* pp. 53–60; also Geoffrey Noel-Smith, *Luchino Visconti,* pp. 14–32.

23. According to José Luis Guarner, *Roberto Rossellini,* p. 10, the only surviving print of *Un Pilota Ritorna* is preserved in Czechoslovakia. The negative is now lost, and there are no prints in Italy.

24. Guarner, op. cit., p. 11.

25. I am grateful in this section for facts recorded in Jay Leyda's *Films beget Films,* p. 61, and to Joseph L. Anderson and Donald Richie, *The Japanese Film,* p. 131 et seq.

26. Reprinted as a pamphlet from the December 1942 issue of the *Journal of the Society of Motion Picture Engineers,* pp. 341–47.

Chapter 4
The War: III. Victory in Europe and Asia, 1943–45

1. Leslie Fenton's half-hour featurette, *There's a Future in It* (1944), with Ann Dvorak and Barry Morse, had a parallel theme, that men serving in the bombers are helping to secure the future at the daily risk of their lives and have a full right to love. The story was by Flight-Lieutenant H. E. Bates; the score by William Alwyn.

2. Harry Watt wrote about the casting of *Nine Men* in *DNL,* Feb. 1943. Jack

Lambert was a Scottish stage professional with little screen experience; he was a major in the Royal Scots Fusiliers. Other professionals were Jock Scot, who had played the preacher in Michael Powell's *Edge of the World;* he was now a captain in the army. The lorry driver was a real soldier who helped train the civilian wing of the cast—Gordon Jackson, Bill Blewett (postmaster of Mousehole in Cornwall), Fred Piper, who plays the Cockney, and Eric Micklewood, the "Bookie."

3. The information in this and succeeding paragraphs is derived from a *DNL* survey in issue 5, 1943.

4. According to *DNL* (No. 2, 1944, p. 20) there had to be some reconstruction of the action in this film—the assault on Wadi Zig Zaou shot in England, and the United States attack on Hill 60 shot in Arizona. Nevertheless there was some brilliant coverage of real combat. The United States version of the film had its own sound track.

5. The British and Canadian Army Film Units released toward the end of 1944 their initial record of the D-Day landings, the half-hour *Left of the Line*, carrying the action into France and Belgium.

6. The original version (*I Was a Fireman*, eighty mins.), which was intended in part as a training film, was reduced to sixty-three minutes for the theatrical version, *Fires were Started*, omitting some of the fire-fighting drill.

7. A curiosity in Humphrey Jennings's films made during the war is *The Story of Lilli Marlene* (1944), the strange episode in the war of the universal adoption of the sentimental German song sung by men on both sides, German and Allied.

8. Charles Frend also made the short feature-documentary, *The Return of the Vikings* (1944), for the Norwegian government in exile, the cast being free Norwegians in Britain. It shows a group of Norwegian seamen in their wartime role, some still at sea, while one of their number becomes a paratrooper.

9. Korda had left Britain to work in the United States in the summer of 1940. He could raise no further money to work in Britain during this period, whereas he had offers in Hollywood. There was some bitterness, ill-will, and genuine misunderstanding about his wartime "desertion" of Britain, and he was openly attacked. He returned to Britain in March 1943 as head of production at British MGM-London Films. Meantime he had directed *Lady Hamilton*. Korda was a close friend of Winston Churchill and of Brendan Bracken, Churchill's Minister of Information; he was knighted on the personal recommendation of Churchill in 1942 during one of his regular visits to Britain. His company in the United States, Alexander Korda Productions, was accused by the isolationist Senators Nye and Vandenburg of being a center for British espionage and propaganda, and a Congressional Committee was due to hear the case when Pearl Harbor came and led to its abandonment. Korda had crossed and recrossed the Atlantic many times during the period of his "exile," sometimes crouched on a parachute with other official passengers in the bomb-bay of an RAF Liberator. See Paul Tabori, *Alexander Korda*, for a full account of this period in his career.

10. *DNL*, No. 5 1943, p. 219.

11. A form of dramatic or documentary-style revue on matters of topical social and political interest, first used during the 1930s as part of the American Federal Theatre project. It was so successful as a means of popularizing information and propaganda that it was also used during the war. The script of *World of Plenty*, by Eric Knight and Paul Rotha, was published in 1945.

12. See Rotha's note in *Portrait of a Flying Yorkshireman*, p. 198.

13. Frank Capra, in his autobiography *The Name above the Title*, explains first of all that in spite of his inexperience in documentary film, he was determined to keep the work free from the Signals Corps mentality. He had to acquire over the heads of the Signal Corps enemy footage from the Alien Property custodian. He was enormously encouraged by his recruitment of Eric Knight to his staff. It was, he says, a

case of "love at first sight"; Knight had "wit, compassion, sensitiveness." Both General Marshall and Churchill went out of their way to express appreciation of *Prelude to War*. Prior to Capra's appointment, Army training films had been made by Hollywood on a non-profit basis from 1940, largely under the supervision of Darryl Zanuck, then vice-president in charge of production at Twentieth Century-Fox. Afterwards, training films were produced in quantity by the Signal Corps at the former Paramount Studios at Astoria, Long Island, and came under Capra's supervision. See MacCann, op. cit., page 153 et seq.

14. In *Documentary Film* by Paul Rotha in collaboration with Sinclair Road and Richard Griffith (1952), p. 349.

15. See Paul Rotha, *The Film Till Now*, edition 1949, p. 462.

16. See Rotha's *Documentary Film*, p. 351; the quotation immediately below comes from p. 311.

17. See Leyda, *Films beget Films*, p. 59. The material available did not produce a satisfactory result.

18. Having worked closely on two compilation films—the CBS documentary in their "Twentieth Century" series, *Minister of Hate*, an ill-titled study of Goebbels, and the issue of the BBC-TV's series "The Lost Peace" dealing with propaganda, I am certain this is the more fruitful approach—footage first, comment after—provided the broad line of approach is predetermined to guide the researchers locating film.

19. Walt Disney produced a number of war films using animation. Some were instructionals for the Navy, which remained under security restriction; others were for the defense plants. Still others were for public propaganda, such as selling Canadian Defense Bonds. In 1943 he produced a sixty-five-minute feature, *Victory Through Air Power*, based on a controversial book by Alexander de Seversky demonstrating the importance of the long-range bomber with mobile maps and diagrams reminiscent of those designed for the *Why We Fight* series, though more extravagant in their attempts to make the movements of arrows and the like dramatically dynamic. It was, in effect, a brilliantly realized film lecture by Seversky.

20. Ford's unofficial productions began with *Sex Hygiene* (1941, for the United States Army), a thirty-minute "training" film on the dangers of venereal disease and how to avoid contamination. *The Battle of Midway* ran into some distribution difficulties. See MacCann, op. cit., pp. 131–2. Roosevelt, who saw the film at the White House, was enthusiastic; Mellett did not like it. Ford originally came into production for the Navy through Colonel William Donovan's Office of Strategic Services (OSS). Louis de Rochemont, and his associate from the *March of Time*, Thomas Orchard, were responsible for the programme of naval training films for the Photographic Division, their work produced from Washington. OSS remained responsible for such overall Service combat films as *The Battle for the Marianas* and *Brought into Action*, a study of the Seventh Fleet in action on the high seas.

21. For the problems of shooting this film, see *DNL* No. 4, 1944, p. 51.

22. When he left the army late in 1945, Capra was awarded the Distinguished Service Medal and the Legion of Merit.

23. Rotha, *Documentary Film*, p. 356.

24. *Grierson on Documentary*, edited by Forsyth Hardy, p. 28; the quotation immediately following from Grierson is on p. 248.

25. Production in wartime Australia was on nothing like the same scale as Canadian documentary. Only two features were made, both by Charles Chauvel. The first was *40,000 Horsemen*, a story of the Australian Light Horse in Palestine in the First World War, and *Rats of Tobruk* (1944), a semidocumentary feature, dealing with Anzac fighting at Tobruk; it incorporated material shot by the Army Film Unit, and is of interest because it includes early appearances by Chips Rafferty and Peter Finch. One of the better of the war documentaries was Tom Gurr's *Jungle Patrol*,

made in New Guinea, and Ralph Smart's record films for the Royal Australian Air Force are also notable.

26. Robin Wood, *Howard Hawks*, p. 92 et seq.

27. The script of *The Purple Heart* appears in *Best Film Plays of 1943–44*. The ensuing quotations are taken from this.

28. *Cinema Journal*, Winter 1967–68, p. 19.

29. *They Were Expendable* is very fully discussed in *The Cinema of John Ford*, by John Baxter, pp. 120–37.

30. Hollywood continued to pay equally sentimental tribute to Britain in the composite film *Forever and a Day* (1943, René Clair, Edmund Goulding, Cedric Hardwicke, Frank Lloyd, Victor Saville, Robert Stevenson, Herbert Wilcox), the history of an English family from 1804 to 1943, made as a contribution to war charities. Directors and stars gave their services free. Another sentimental goodwill film was *The White Cliffs of Dover* (1943, Clarence Brown, with Irene Dunne) set back in the First World War.

31. The script of *Watch on the Rhine* was published in *Best Film Plays of 1943–44*.

32. A sole attempt was made in *Dragon Seed* (1944, Jack Conway and Harold S. Bucquet, with Katharine Hepburn, Walter Huston, Akim Tamiroff, Turhan Bey; adapted from Pearl S. Buck's novel) to show something of China suffering Japanese aggression. The story looks at the situation from the point of view of a remote peasant family who come to learn through bitter experience that a scorched earth policy is the only way to resist the Japanese, but the film, elaborate and crowd-laden, remains firmly a Hollywood studio production.

33. The dialogue descended to the level of such interchanges as, Nazi Soldier: "Heil Hitler"; MacMurray: "Nuts to you, dope." See *Hollywood in the Forties*, by Charles Higham and Joel Greenberg, p. 92, where the film is discussed at greater length.

34. For a detailed critique of *Hangmen also Die*, see Paul M. Jensen's *The Cinema of Fritz Lang*, p. 141 et seq, and Lang's own account in Peter Bogdanovich's *Fritz Lang in America*, p. 60 et seq.

35. The script of *This Land Is Mine* appears in *Twenty Best Film Plays*. It is by Dudley Nichols.

36. *Cinema Journal*, Winter 1967–68, pp. 17–18. Curtiz also directed the army musical, *This Is the Army* (1943) with music and lyrics by Irving Berlin, and based on an army stage revue. The profits of over seventeen million dollars went to army relief. Other musicals with a service setting include George Sidney's *Thousands Cheer* (1943) with Kathryn Grayson, Gene Kelly, Frank Morgan, and *Anchors Away* (1945), with Frank Sinatra, Gene Kelly, Kathryn Grayson. In general the musical was kept as far away from "war" as possible. It existed to entertain, and entertain only.

37. François Truffaut, *Hitchcock*, p. 129.

38. Robin Wood, *Hitchcock's Films*, p. 32.

39. The script of *Hail the Conquering Hero* appears in *Best Film Plays of 1943–44*.

40. Jay Leyda, *Kino*, p. 375.

41. The film was considerably cut in the sixty-one-minute English-language version to save the eyes of the squeamish. The English commentary was written by Alexander Werth.

42. Quoted by Jay Leyda in *Films beget Films*, p. 69.

43. Roger Manvell in *Monthly Film Bulletin*, 1946, p. 23.

44. Jay Leyda, *Kino*, p. 379.

45. This section is derived from Anderson and Richie, *The Japanese Film*, pp. 130, 134–45.

46. Ruth Benedict, *The Chrysanthemum and the Sword*, pp. 193–94.

47. Quoted by Roy Armes, *Patterns of Realism*, p. 66. The quotation from De Sica immediately below is on pp. 65–66.

48. For further background to *Kolberg* see David Stewart Hull, *Film in the Third Reich*, p. 262. The budget was RM 8½m, and whole army units were used to provide the battle scenes.

Chapter 5
Aftermath: The First Postwar Years

1. *Monthly Film Bulletin*, BFI, 1946, p. 41.

2. *Walcheren* (1946) was a notable thirty-seven-minute documentary made by Ronald Harries on the fertile island on the Scheldt which had to be flooded. The film shows the laborious, even heroic task of rebuilding the dykes and gradual draining of the land. Ronald Harries also made *On Which They Depend* (1947), a parallel film on the rebuilding of Rotterdam, which was to be the subject of a later documentary of real distinction, *Houen Zo* (1953), made by Herman Van Der Horst.

3. A comparatively weak attempt to handle the subject of displaced people in a fiction film was *The Lost People* (1949, Bernard Knowles), and an anomalous form of Anglo-Italian co-production, Luigi Zampa's British film, *Children of Chance*, dealt with the problems arising from a home on Ischia for the illegitimate daughters of Allied soldiers! In 1950 a remarkable documentary, *Report on the Refugee Situation*, made for British Information Services put on record the sufferings of the displaced in Germany.

4. According to Peter Bogdanovich in *John Ford*, p. 135, Ford was involved for a period in the assembly of a seven- to eight-hour record film for use as evidence for the Prosecution at the Nuremberg trial of the major war criminals. This project, initially

Report on the Refugee Situation (1950).

under the supervision of General Donovan, was, however, abandoned. The trial itself, organized by the United States authorities, and lasting from November 1945 until judgment was given in October 1946, was fully covered by newsreel cameras, and the records of it have been drawn on for innumerable compilation films ever since. See, for example, Jay Leyda, *Films Beget Films*, pp. 88–89.

The Americans issued their record film of the trial for the Germans in their zone—*Nürnberg* (1946). It was sponsored by the American Film Section under the supervision of Pare Lorentz, produced by Stuart Schulberg, and edited by Jo Zigman. It gave a calm, unemotional account of the trial, with the greater part of its footage coming from the trial procedure, accompanied by German-shot scenes of pogrom, extermination, and so forth. It also had a montage of rhetorical questions put by Hitler in various speeches cut against excerpts from Roosevelt's statements. (See *DNL*, January 1949, p. 7; *Films Beget Films*, p. 73.)

The Russian version of the trial was directed by Roman Karmen, assisted by Yelizaveta Svilova—*Trial of the People* (also known as *Judgment of the Nations*, USSR, 1946). Karmen was in charge of the Russian film services at Nuremberg. See *Films Beget Films*, p. 74. The Polish version of the trial was known as *The Last Parteitag at Nuremberg* (1946; Antoni Bohdziewicz and Waclav Kaźmierszak).

Later films involving the trial included the West German *Nazi Crimes and Punishment* (1958, German title *Der Nürnberger Prozess;* also known as *The Executioners;* Felix Podmanitsky).

5. This film was made for MGM by Lazar Wechsler's Swiss Company, Praesens of Zürich. The company had also made *The Last Chance* (1945–46, Leopold Lindtberg), a fine film about the escape from Italy to Switzerland of a group of civilian refugees of many nationalities, men, women, and a child, led on a hazardous trek across the mountains infested with German patrols by three escaped prisoners-of-war, two English and one American. It was a story of courage and self-sacrifice, with dialogue in nine languages; the cast was largely nonprofessional, refugees and former prisoners-of-war reenacting an experience with which they were basically familiar.

6. For the tragic farce of de-Nazification in Germany, see Manvell and Fraenkel, *The Incomparable Crime*, pp. 245–49, 307–8. For Axel Madsen's comments on the film, see his book *Billy Wilder*, p. 74 et seq.

7. See Gordon Kahn, *Hollywood on Trial*, p. 135.

8. See Roy Armes, *Patterns of Realism*, p. 76, and for the quotation immediately below p. 82. Throughout this section I am endebted to Roy Armes's very full account of this period in the Italian cinema. For the most interesting and varied reaction in Britain to *Paisa* see *Penguin Film Review*, issue 9 (1949).

9. Roy Armes, op. cit., p. 94.

10. Vernon Jarratt, *The Italian Cinema*, p. 80.

11. The title implies, Angelina the Peoples' Representative. "L'Onorevole" is the title given to the equivalent of a member of Parliament or of Congress.

12. The Russians made their own compilation film, *Liberated France* (1945; Sergei Yutchevitch).

13. *Films Beget Films*, p. 71.

14. As part of the "rehabilitation" of French production, in October 1966 the French government set up a Centre Nationale de Cinématographie under the control of the Ministry of Youth, Arts and Letters. This stopped well short of nationalization (in contrast, for example, to presocialist Czechoslovakia), but aimed at coordinating all branches of the industry, supervising finance (many of the existant companies had been under German economic control), arranging for loans to new producers, and establishing a training school for young filmmakers, IDHEC. Production resources were virtually unscathed, and in 1946 ninety-four features were produced. In 1947 some five thousand theaters were in operation. Production costs, however, were esti-

mated as ten times up on 1939 figures, and production was also severely threatened. with the influx of American films, for which the French public were hungry. (See *DNL*, Oct. 1947.)

15. Another documentary of some interest was a joint French-Norwegian production, *The Battle for Heavy Water* (1947, *La Bataille du l'Eau Lourde*, or *Operation Swallow*), supervised by Jean Dreville and directed by Titus Vibe Muller. This reenacted the operation carried out by a party of Norwegian patriots dropped by parachute. The raid led to the destruction of a heavy-water plant in the Telemark Mountains necessary to German development of an atom bomb. The expedition involved a feat of mountaineering undertaken in winter conditions. The cast was made up in most cases of survivors from the actual operation, which took place in the winter of 1943–44, and involved not only putting the large plant out of action, but subsequently sinking a ferry in which it was intended to transport the equipment salvaged to Germany together with a stock of heavy water. *The Red Earth* (*De Røde Enge*, 1945; Lau Lauritzen, Jnr) was another Scandinavian story in the documentary style, showing activities of the Danish Resistance.

16. See *DNL*, January 1949, p. 7; Manvell and Fraenkel, *The German Cinema*, pp. 110–11.

17. American cold-war films began with such productions as *The Iron Curtain* (1948; William Wellman), *The Red Menace, I Married a Communist*, and *The Red Danube* (1949, George Sidney).

18. Writing in *DNL* mid-1946 (No. 53), Jiri Weiss, the Czech filmmaker who had spent the war years in Britain, described the Czech resources after liberation: "Victory found not only Czechoslovakia's production units intact, but also a leadership ready to take over. The German orgy of centralisation, forcing the Czechs to form a so-called 'Film Centre' . . . proved a boon to those who desired not only a centralised but also a nationalised film industry. . . . The Germans left behind a hugely expanded plant. . . . The only solution would be complete nationalisation. . . . In a nationalised film industry can there be freedom for the artist to say whatever he likes in whatever way he wishes? In Czechoslovakia there has been, so far, more freedom for the artist than in the formerly privately owned companies. Today all questions of film policy are decided by a special 'artistic board' which is composed of various elements with various political opinions, so that dictatorial decisions are out of question. The prevailing trend is to produce pictures of high artistic quality and good entertainment value together with a certain proportion of propaganda films—about a fourth of the total output. Party politics are banned, and an eye is kept on the box office, for the industry has to keep itself alive by its own income" [p. 38].

19. See Richard Storry, *A History of Modern Japan*, p. 237.

20. With the departure of the Japanese, the postwar situation in China resulted in a rival output of films from the Left and the Right during the period up to 1949. The most popular films came from the Left group, especially the films of the Kun Lun studios in Shanghai, notably *Crows and Sparrows* (1949). Other films of the period included Fu Shen's film of overcrowding in Shanghai, *Under a Shanghai Roof*, and King Shan's film set in Manchuria at the time of the Japanese invasion, *On the Sangri River*, which used a cast largely made up of nonprofessionals. Filmmaking resumed under Party auspices in 1950 following the foundation of the Chinese Peoples' Republic in October 1949.

Chapter 6
Retrospect: 1950–70

1. Television compilation series dealing with the Second World War include "Vic-

tory at Sea" (Henry Salomon for NBC), "The Twisted Cross" (Henry Salomon for NBC), relevant issues in "The Twentieth Century" (Isaac Kleinerman, with Burton Benjamin for CBS), "War in the Air" (John Elliot for the BBC), and "The Lost Peace" (Tony Essex for the BBC). The Churchill story was told in a series produced by the American Broadcasting Company, "The Valiant Years." In West Germany itself a number of television series on the Third Reich have appeared, including fourteen fifty-minute compilations from Nazi films, "The Third Reich," and "An Epoch on Trial" (*"Eine Epoche vor Gericht"*).

2. The script by Jean Cayrol is published in translation in Robert Hughes's *Film: Book 2*.

3. According to Jay Leyda, *Films Beget Films*, p. 93, the Swedish company responsible for Leiser's *Mein Kampf* has produced a sequel without him, *Mein Kampf–Part II–War Criminals*, shown in the United States with the title *Secrets of the Nazi Criminals*.

4. Alec Guinness's interpretation in the Anglo-Italian co-production, *Hitler—the Last Ten Days*, directed by Ennio De Concini, could well be the best performance so far, though it gives little impression of Hitler's personality as the former leader. See reference later in chapter.

5. See *Straub*, by Richard Roud, p. 40. The script of *Not Reconciled* is given complete in translation in Roud's book.

6. A unique experiment is the film by Kevin Brownlow and Andrew Mollo, *It Happened Here*, a remarkably successful attempt to reconstruct how Britain might have fared (and behaved) had the Nazis invaded successfully in 1940. Broadly speaking, the Germans are allowed to be subtle enough to let the British develop their own allied brand of fascism under right-wing puppet leaders, representing this as both nationalistic and patriotic, so that they can be prepared to fight alongside Germany against the Russians. A pastiche German-Nazi newsreel incorporated into the film is outstandingly well imitated. See Kevin Brownlow, *How It Happened Here*.

7. See *The Sunday Times*, July 4 1971, p. 9.

Selected Bibliography

Anderson, Joseph L., and Richie, Donald. *The Japanese Film*. New York: Grove Press, 1960.

Armes, Roy. *The Cinema of Alain Resnais*. London: Tantivy Press, 1968.

————. *French Cinema since 1946*. Vols. 1 and 2. Rev. ed. London: Tantivy Press, 1970.

————. *Patterns of Realism: A Study of Italian Neo-Realist Cinema*. London: Tantivy Press, 1971.

Balcon, Michael. *A Lifetime of Films*. London: Hutchinson, 1969.

Balcon, Michael, Lindgren, Ernest, Hardy, Forsyth, and Manvell, Roger. *Twenty Years of British Film*. London: Falcon Press, 1947.

Baxter, John. *John Ford*. London: Tantivy Press, 1972.

Bluem, A. William. Documentary in American Television. New York: Hastings House, 1965.

Bogdanovich, Peter. *John Ford*. London: Studio Vista, 1967.

British Film Institute. *Monthly Film Bulletin: Sight and Sound*.

Brownlow, Kevin. *How It Happened Here*. London: Secker and Warburg, 1968.

Bucher, Felix. *Germany*. Screen Series. London: Tantivy Press, 1970.

Capra, Frank. *The Name Above the Title*. New York: Macmillan, 1971.

Cowie, Peter, ed. *A Concise History of the Cinema*. London: Tantivy Press, 1971.

Dickinson, Thorold, and De La Roche, Catherine. *Soviet Cinema*. London: Falcon Press, 1948.

Durgnat, Raymond. *A Mirror for England*. London: Faber and Faber, 1970.

Film Centre. *Documentary News Letter*. London.

Furhammar, Leif, and Isaksson, Folke. *Politics and Film*. London: Studio Vista, 1971.

Gassner, John, and Nichols, Dudley. *Best Film Plays of 1943–44*. New York: Crown, 1945.

————. *Twenty Best Film Plays*. New York: Crown, 1943.

Gifford, Denis. *British Cinema*. London: Tantivy Press, 1968.

Gough-Yates, Kevin. *Michael Powell*. London: British Film Institute, 1971.

Gow, Gordon. *Hollywood in the Fifties*. London: Tantivy Press, 1971.

Grierson, John. *Grierson on Documentary*. Edited by Forsyth Hardy. London: Faber and Faber, 1956.

Griffith, Richard. *Frank Capra*. London: British Film Institute, c. 1950.

———. "The Use of Film in the US Armed Services," in *Documentary Film*, rev. ed., by Paul Rotha, 1952.

Guarner, Jose Luis. *Roberto Rossellini*. London: Studio Vista, 1970.

Halliwell, Leslie. *The Filmgoer's Companion*. London: MacGibbon and Kee, 1970.

Hibbin, Nina. *Eastern Europe*. Screen Series. London: Tantivy Press, 1969.

Higham, Charles, and Greenberg, Joel. *Hollywood in the Forties*. London: Tantivy Press, 1968.

Hull, David Stewart. *Film in the Third Reich*. Los Angeles: University of California Press, 1969.

Jacobs, Lewis, ed. *The Documentary Tradition*. New York: Hopkinson and Blake, 1971.

———. "World War II and the American Film," *Cinema Journal* (Winter 1967–68).

Jarratt, Vernon. *Italian Cinema*. London: Falcon Press, 1951.

Karmen, Roman. "Soviet Documentary," in *Experiment in the Film*, edited by Roger Manvell. London: Grey Walls Press, 1949.

Knight, Eric, and Rotha, Paul. *World of Plenty*. London: Nicolson and Watson, 1945.

Kracauer, Siegfried. *From Caligari to Hitler*. London: Dobson, 1947.

Larson, Cedric. "Domestic Movies of the O.W.I." In *Hollywood Quarterly*, Vol. III, No. 4, 1947–48. Los Angeles: University of California Press.

Leyda, Jay. *Films Beget Films*. London: Allen and Unwin, 1964.

———. *Kino*. London: Allen and Unwin, 1960.

Lo, T. Y. *The Underground Motion Picture Industry*. Reprinted from the *Journal of the Society of Motion Picture Engineers* (December 1942).

Lovell, Alan, and Hillier, Jim. *Studies in Documentary*. London: Secker and Warburg, 1972.

Lovell, Alan, and McArthur, Colin. *War on the Screen*. London: British Film Institute Study Unit.

MacCann, Richard Dyer. The People's Films. New York, Hastings House, 1973.

Manvell, Roger. *Experiment in the Film*. London: Grey Walls Press, 1949.

———. *New Cinema in Britain*. London: Studio Vista, 1968.

———. *New Cinema in Europe*. London: Studio Vista, 1966.

———. *New Cinema in the USA*. London: Studio Vista, 1968.

Manvell, Roger, and Fraenkel, Heinrich. *The German Cinema*. London: Dent, 1971.

———. *The Incomparable Crime*. London: Heinemann, 1967.

Movie Lot to Beachhead. The Editors of Look. New York: Doubleday, Doran, 1945.

Nemeskurty, Istvan. *Word and Image: History of the Hungarian Cinema*. Budapest: Korvina Press, 1968.

Noble, Peter. *Anthony Asquith*. London: British Film Institute, c. 1951.

———. *British Film Yearbook*, from 1949. London: Skelton Robonson, 1950.

Noel-Smith, Geoffrey. *Visconti*. London: Secker and Warburg, 1967.

Oakley, Charles. *Where We Came In*. London: Allen and Unwin, 1964.

Pickard, Roy. *A Companion to the Movies*. London: Lutterworth Press, 1972.

Political and Economic Planning (PEP). *The Arts Enquiry: The Factual Film*. London: Oxford University Press, 1947.

Polonia Publishing House. *Contemporary Polish Cinema*. Warsaw: 1962.

Rotha, Paul. *Documentary Film*. Rev. ed. London: Faber and Faber, 1952.

———. *The Film Till Now*. Rev. ed. London: Vision Press, 1970.

———. *Portrait of a Flying Yorkshireman: Letters from Eric Knight*. London: Chapman and Hall, 1952.

Sadoul, Georges. *French Film*. London: The Falcon Press, 1953.

Svensson, Arne. *Japan*. Screen Series. London: Tantivy Press, 1971.

Swallow, Norman. *Factual Television*. London: Focal Press, 1966.

Tabori, Paul. *Alexander Korda*. London: Oldbourne, 1959.

Truffaut, François. *Hitchcock*. London: Secker and Warburg, 1968.

Wells, H. G. *Things to Come*. London: Cresset Press, 1935.

Ward, John. *Alain Resnais*. London: Secker and Warburg, 1968.

Wood, Robin. *Hitchcock's Films*. London: Tantivy Press, 1965.

Writers' Congress. The Proceedings of the Conference held in October 1943 under the sponsorship of the Hollywood Writers' Mobilization and the University of California. University of California Press, 1944.

Zeman, Z. A. B. *Nazi Propaganda*. London: Oxford University Press, 1964.

Index of Films

(Figures in italics indicate illustration)

Index of Names